Beyond Accommodation

Beyond Accommodation

Creating an Inclusive Workplace for
Disabled Library Workers

Jessica Schomberg
Wendy Highby

Library Juice Press
Sacramento, CA

Published in 2020 by Library Juice Press.

Library Juice Press
PO Box 188784
Sacramento, CA 95818

http://litwinbooks.com/

This book is printed on acid-free paper.

Library of Congress Cataloging-in-Publication Data

Names: Schomberg, Jessica J., 1975- author. | Highby, Wendy, author.
Title: Beyond accommodation : creating an inclusive workplace for disabled
    library workers / Jessica Schomberg, Wendy Highby.
Description: Sacramento, CA : Library Juice Press, 2020. | Includes
    bibliographical references and index. | Summary: "Examines issues faced
    by disabled library workers, through the lens of critical disability
    theory"-- Provided by publisher.
Identifiers: LCCN 2020012645 | ISBN 9781634000864 (paperback ; acid-free
    paper)
Subjects: LCSH: Library employees with disabilities--United States. |
    Diversity in the workplace--United States. | Sociology of
    disability--United States.
Classification: LCC Z682.4.L46 S36 2020 | DDC 027.6/63--dc23
LC record available at https://lccn.loc.gov/2020012645

Contents

Acknowledgements

Wendy Highby

First, my thanks go to Rory Litwin for providing the fora in which progressive ideas of librarianship flourish. Thanks also for matching me with my co-author Jessica. And thank you to Jessica, a most patient and nurturing writing partner. I thank our interviewees for generously sharing their experiences and insight. I thank my colleagues and administrators at the University of Northern Colorado (UNC) for granting me a summer sabbatical, an officially-sanctioned, sacred time and space in which to create this book. I thank my supervisor and my dean for their positive, unwavering support. I thank my co-workers for their collegiality and daily acts of kindness (more energizing and influential than I realized until I was incommunicado during my reclusive summer). I thank the student researchers at UNC, especially those whom I've gotten to know as mentees. The courageous path they forge toward our uncertain future gives me hope. My gratitude for the love of my husband, family, and friends can only be expressed in poems, not prose, which I will now have some free time to write! I thank comedian and fellow INFP Stephen Colbert for his fearless improv and humor. I am fortunate to have these alternative medical practitioners in my life: acupuncturist Melissa, massage therapist April, physical therapist Jutta, and qi gong coach Tom. Each is an extraordinary healer who has walked side by side with me in my struggle with Parkinson's. I thank Kelly for the eye-opening, soul-enlightening implicit bias training. I thank my housemate for her perceptiveness and open heart. I thank my new niece for her faith that opened the door to forgiveness. I thank Julie for being the kind of friend at whom I can lob a meringue pie. I thank the universe for everything I've learned so far, and for everything that I'm about to find out. If you want to come along, I think I'll just keep walking, till I see what's around that next corner…

Jessica Schomberg

Thanks to my family who raised me to think that having diabetes was a totally normal thing that I didn't have to apologize for. I've learned over the years how rare and precious that is. Thanks to my friend Jessica Olin for letting me write a guest blogpost about having invisible disabilities at work. That opened the door for everything that has happened since then. Thanks also to my friend Jen Hanson for using her magical pharmacist skills to help me understand my options when it comes to antidepressants and contraindications. That helped me stay in the game. Thanks to Dr. Amelia Gibson, to Dr. Karen Nicholson and Maura Seale, and to Shanna Hollich and Lisa Hinchliffe for supporting me in earlier projects and helping me gain confidence in my own knowledge. Thanks to my coworkers Heidi Southworth and Mark McCullough for being my cheer squad during the writing of this book, and to Barb Bergman for providing practical support during various medical dramas over the years. Thanks to my union's disability caucus for keeping me hopeful. Other friends who've provided the sort of community I value more than I can express include Stephanie Sendaula, Becky Franklin, Ruth Tillman, Catherine Oliver, and so many more. I'm making myself stop here or this list would go on for literal pages. Also, many thanks to Wendy for proposing this book idea! It's been a delight.

Introduction

Let's Start with Pizza

Some people think pineapple on pizza is delicious, and some think it is disgusting. These differences in perception are accepted as benign. Now imagine a workplace which offers mandatory monthly pizza lunches, and all pizzas contain pineapple. This workplace doesn't allow workers to opt out of the lunches, doesn't allow employees to bring their own food, and doesn't respect requests for other food options. At this point, those benign differences are penalized, and anyone who doesn't like pineapple is discriminated against.

The social model of disability grounds much of this book. If you understand this pizza analogy, you understand the basics of that theory. We all have performance differences; those differences become disabilities when people are excluded or otherwise punished because of them.

Wendy and Jessica were motivated to write this book by shared goals and shared constraints. We both love working in libraries. We both have disabilities. We both have experienced difficulty balancing workplace expectations with our bodies' needs. We both have felt isolated because these experiences aren't talked about much. Even though there are laws and workplace policies that are supposed to protect our rights, there is still a feeling of un-safety in talking about being a disabled worker. For us, this means that trying to build a community of disabled library workers is a risk. But we want our experiences to be acknowledged, and we want others like us to feel valued as full humans—so we view it as a necessary risk. We hope disabled library workers reading this book feel like your experiences are recognized here. We hope nondisabled library workers gain a better understanding of what disability means and why disabled people may not respond to situations in the same ways that you do.

For both of us, fatigue from living with chronic illness is a constant challenge. To successfully write this text required regular communication and peer support. One manifestation of how peer support was entwined in our writing process was that we regularly acknowledged the value of taking a tag team approach, with one person picking up a little more when the other couldn't, in a continuous back-and-forth. We are both disabled librarians and librarian-researchers of disability, and as such can take a liminal stance in writing this book.[1] In other words, we are both part of the system we're examining and able to take a critical approach to it.

Jessica grew up in a family in which diabetes was normal and accepted, and the teachers at their elementary school were supportive. It wasn't until their teens, when they were first discriminated against in the workplace, that they started to think of diabetes as a disability. On the other hand, they are white and have been normatively sized most of their life, so they didn't have to deal with stereotype threat when talking about their diagnosis (stereotype threat is the fear of confirming stereotypes about one's identity group).[2] Their identity has been shaped by these experiences since childhood, so they didn't go through the same challenges during the self-acceptance process that people with adult-onset disabilities experience.

Wendy was diagnosed with Parkinson's disease in 2004, in her mid-forties, and until the last five years or so, her medications controlled her symptoms so well that to the casual observer she could pass as nondisabled. She feels she has only recently subsumed disability into her identity.[3] As an extraordinarily statuesque woman (six feet two and one-half inches tall), she is no stranger to stares, so any self-consciousness she feels about

---

1   Ramah McKay, "Critical Convergences: Social Science Research as Global Health Technology?" *MAT* (May 14, 2019), http://www.medanthrotheory.org/read/11308/critical-convergences.

2   Joshua Aronson, Diana Burgess, Sean M. Phelan, and Lindsay Juarez, "Unhealthy Interactions: The Role of Stereotype Threat in Health Disparities," *American Journal of Public Health* 103, no. 1 (2013): 50–56, https://www.ncbi.nlm.nih.gov/pmc/articles/PMC3518353/; Rebecca M. Puhl, Sean M. Phelan, Joseph Nadglowski, and Theodore K. Kyle, "Overcoming Weight Bias in the Management of Patients with Diabetes and Obesity," *Clinical Diabetes* 34, no. 1 (2016): 44–50, https://clinical.diabetesjournals.org/content/34/1/44.

3   It has been a very gradual process, beginning with her attendance at the National Parkinson Foundation 5th Annual Young Onset Parkinson Network Conference in 2007 in Chicago, where she heard a stirring speech by Andrew Imparato (at the time the president of the American Association of People with Disabilities).

people observing her Parkinsonian movements seems a natural extension of her reaction to the attention her height has always garnered. Sadly, Wendy is no stranger to stigma, as she grew up the younger sibling of a sister with severe mental illness (now deceased); once a sufferer of survivor's guilt, she is now a practitioner of self-compassion.[4]

While Wendy and Jessica have had different experiences in some ways, we also recognize that to provide a more inclusive portrait of disabled workers' lives we needed to get out there and ask people questions. So that we could include perspectives beyond what can be found in research articles, we conducted interviews with disabled library workers in various parts of the United States. All interviewees were assigned pseudonyms. We intentionally tried to hear the voices of those whose experiences are different from ours, so we recruited participants working at public, academic, and special libraries, ranging from new graduates still looking for their first professional position to people who've retired from the field. We also included perspectives from people who are cis and transgender and who have various sexual orientations. Some of our participants are white, some Black, one is a non-binary person of color whose racial/ethnic identity we're not going to share because librarianship is so white we're afraid just saying that much will identify them. Most interviewees are women and from either middle- or working-class backgrounds. All have a graduate degree in library studies. While our interviews were exclusively with library workers with the MLS degree, we want to prioritize the idea that we are all workers; we occasionally use the word librarian in the text, but our intent is to be inclusive of all workers employed in libraries.

While we consciously tried to include a variety of perspectives in this book, we know more work needs to be done. We hope this book inspires more people to share their stories, in whatever way is safe for them. As feminist disability philosopher Susan Wendell notes in her hugely influential book, *The Rejected Body*, referencing the seminal work of Black feminist scholar Patricia Hill Collins,[5] we can't understand the fullness of disabled peoples' experiences by adding them together in "disabled plus women" or "disabled plus Black" summations. Instead, we need to hear the stories of disabled people who live at those intersections and more. And

---

4   On a lighter note, Wendy would like to go on record that she prefers a gluten-free crust on her pizza!

5   Patricia Hill Collins, "The Social Construction of Black Feminist Thought," *Signs* 14, no. 4 (1989): 745–73.

we need to be attentive to both the commonalities and the differences in their perspectives.[6]

We've also tried to take a trauma-aware approach in writing this book. That is why you will see content warnings before some sections, to let readers prepare to read about things that we know are difficult for a lot of people. This includes warnings before sections discussing specific types of violence as well as warnings about ableist slurs. For people in dominant groups, slurs may seem like just words. But for those of us who've had those words used against us to coerce behavior, cause shame, or as justification for abuse, they can trigger feelings of imminent danger. Our goal is to enrich your lives, not to add to your trauma.

What's in This Book

This book covers disability from a variety of angles. We include references ranging from dense academic texts on disability policy to podcasts run by disability advocates. We include stories from our own lives to emphasize certain points. Also, as we mentioned above, we entwine excerpts from interviews throughout the text to let the voices of additional disabled library workers shine through.

We start by providing an overview of disability frameworks, because being able to recognize the difference between the social model and the medical model will help you understand much of the rest of the book. In that chapter, we also provide demographic information about people with disabilities. Those of us who identify as disabled are likely to already be aware of how common disability is, but our experience leads us to think that this will be very new information to many nondisabled people reading this book. Chapter 1 will also provide groundwork to help you understand why disability advocates often talk in terms of barriers: physical barriers, legislative barriers, funding barriers, and more. One type of barrier that is discussed throughout the book is cultural: as disability researchers Harlan and Robert note, "organizations create an environment for work that reflects and reproduces the culture of the larger society."[7] We can't address

---

6   Susan Wendell, *The Rejected Body: Feminist Philosophical Reflections on Disability* (New York: Routledge, 1996), 72–73.

7   Sharon L. Harlan and Pamela M. Robert, "The Social Construction of Disability in Organizations: Why Employers Resist Reasonable Accommodation," *Work and Occupations* 25, no. 4 (1998): 397–435.

workplace barriers without making sure the conversation is broad enough to include discussion of the larger culture in which we live.

Chapter 2 is where we go into more detail about these cultural barriers, and how they are maintained by inequitable power structures. As many disability, diversity, and sociology researchers have noted over the years, cultural expectations—including workplace and professional cultural expectations—are defined by those in power. These expectations will privilege the qualities that people in power also see in themselves. At the same time, they are likely to denigrate the qualities of those with less power, as a way of justifying that inequity. In the workplace, this impacts decisions about hiring, promotions, salaries, work assignments, and task management in ways that become routine and unquestioned.[8] In this chapter, we talk about how you are operating from different power positions when you're engaged in self-advocacy versus advocacy for others, the power of disability stereotypes in bureaucratic decision-making, and why it's important that workplaces intentionally incorporate the perspectives of disabled people. We also talk about the difference between retrofitting and planning for diversity, as well as the risks inherent in self-disclosure.

The nexus of the individual worker and the library organization is the topic of chapter 3. Is it possible to healthfully balance the demands of the body for attention with the demands of the organization for one's energy (patrons and co-workers and to-do lists)? These personal health issues are political and these political issues are personal. Onerous work conditions and lack of work-life balance harm people with disabilities and nondisabled colleagues alike. This chapter talks about how we can recognize the power dynamics that exist in our workplaces, and how to build collaborative power to teach old organizations new tricks. To improve workplace culture, people in those workplaces need to let down their defenses and recognize the impacts of cultural norms that exclude; there are more inclusive ways of operating. In chapter 3, we discuss how to create inclusive, flexible workplaces that recognize the inherent humanity of workers (and acknowledge the need to prioritize the health of the body) through options ranging from peer support programs to working toward union protections.

We look for strength in vulnerability in chapter 4. We expose stigma, stereotypes, and bias. We acknowledge that demonstrating vulnerability can be a risky strategy. But the richness that our lived experience adds to any conversation about workplace culture makes it a risk worth

---

8   Harlan and Robert, 402.

considering. We discuss the vulnerability and courage involved in making the decision to disclose one's disability in the workplace. And we suggest that the creation of a psychologically safe workplace is possible with the accretion of many actions emanating from the grassroots.

Chapter 5 is focused on accommodations. While the purpose of this book is to take the conversation beyond accommodations, we think it is important to let you know more about how this process works. Therefore, we provide information about what accommodations are, how they are implemented, the risks of seeking them, and the benefits of their gain.

In chapter 6, we hope to help you understand other options that may be available to you if the accommodations process doesn't meet your needs. Here, we start by acknowledging the lack of diversity in library work. The library profession is very monocultural, and because of the power inequities inherent in a monoculture, those of us who hold marginalized identities may need to go outside of the workplace to get support. We may also need to build our power from within, through unions or other groups that advocate for disability rights and workers' rights. We highlight some existing organizations and also encourage you to look for opportunities for peer support.

Library work is care work, and that is the focus of chapter 7. While this work is vital for societies and individuals, the expectations around care provide their own set of challenges. Among those challenges are vocational awe, saviorism, and fatigue. But we also talk about how valuing care lets us rethink the workplace norms which prioritize production over people and leads us to look for ways of challenging the status quo to build more inclusive, welcoming workplace cultures for ourselves and each other.

We round out the book with two chapters in which we each share our own experiences as library workers with different types of disabilities. These chapters are exercises in deliberate, radical vulnerability. We want to share parts of ourselves and our lives with you in the hope that, for those with disabilities, you will feel less alone. And for those without disabilities, or whose disabilities are very different from ours, we hope this exercise helps you understand library work in a different way. For readers who prefer memoirs to analytical texts with lots of citations, this is our reward to you for making it to the end.

In solidarity,
Jessica and Wendy

Chapter 1

Laying the Theoretical Groundwork

Starting with Workplace Discrimination

Jessica just saw someone post on Twitter about how her workplace provides Skittles in the first aid kit, so they're available if she has a hypoglycemic episode and needs sugar.[1] It makes them think back to their first library job.

Jessica's first job in libraries was as a student page in a public library. Jessica started in 1992, two years after the Americans with Disabilities Act (ADA) was passed. They already had insulin-dependent diabetes at that time. One day after their shift, while they were waiting for a ride home, they asked the librarian who was supervising their work that day if she had any food or candy that they could eat because their blood sugar was low and they didn't have anything with them. As an adult, they are much better about trying to always have glucose with them for these situations. At the time this happened they were a teen, and still had a lot to learn about being prepared. They do think it would have been reasonable for a supervisor to ask that they have an emergency plan in place, and at their best, workplace accommodations can support this.

In this case, that supervisor couldn't help them. So Jessica just waited for their ride, who got there before anything more serious occurred. When Jessica showed up for their next shift, they learned from their regular supervisor that the librarian had tried to have them fired because of their diabetes. They're not sure what would have happened had this event occurred more than a week earlier. The ADA wouldn't explicitly protect people in

---

1   Kate McMahon, "Today my new work team put skittles in the first aid box," Twitter, June 11, 2019, 2:01 p.m., https://twitter.com/KateMcMahon__/status/1138521648963948544.

Jessica's situation until the ADA Amendments Act of 2008,[2] and even now it's hard to win this kind of battle. But they do know that one reason they weren't fired is that the library director had been diagnosed with type 2 diabetes a week before this incident. He wasn't going to fire someone for having a similar health condition to his, and Jessica's supervisor just passed along what had transpired without sharing her perspective on events.

This established how Jessica defined work life. It taught them that they can't trust coworkers for support when their humanity—having fluctuating blood sugars—makes them unable to function at perfect levels. While they felt the unfairness in their gut, it wasn't until they learned the word ableism and theories of disability a few decades later that they developed the ability to look at this situation from a broader perspective. Now compare the silence and stigmatization of the surreptitious firing request they experienced with the example of the Skittles workplace. We know where we would rather work.

Disability as Identity and Lived Experience

We, the authors, both have disabilities. This is part of our identity and part of our lived reality. This has informed our practice as librarians and informed how we have written this book. We want to present a text that is useful to both disabled and nondisabled people. We want to present a text that centers the experiences of disabled library workers. We want to present a text that recognizes that disabled library workers exist. Borrowing language from the Libraries We Here[3] group, which intentionally recognizes the experiences of library workers of color: We are here, we are aware, we are capable, and we are being actively excluded by our profession in ways large and small.

Think about the last professional conference you attended. Was transportation to that conference easy to arrange? Was movement within that conference setting easy to accomplish? Was water freely available? Were food options inclusive of a variety of dietary needs? Did the conference setting have bathrooms that were fully accessible and plentiful for all attendees? Were there low-sensory or sterile places where people had the opportunity to take a break or administer medication? Did the chairs provided fit all the bodies present? Were there options for people who couldn't

---

2   Americans with Disabilities Act Amendments Act of 2008. Public Law 110–325. 110th Congress (September 25, 2008), https://www.eeoc.gov/laws/statutes/adaaa.cfm.

3   Libraries We Here (blog), https://librarieswehere.wordpress.com/.

be present? Did every speaker at that conference use a microphone? Were transcripts of presentations provided during or after the session for attendees? Did presenters use large fonts in their slides or provide their slides online with alt-text for images? Did fellow attendees ask invasive questions about someone's use of a cane or make rude remarks about someone's use of a scooter to get around?

All of these questions are prompted by real situations that the authors have experienced, witnessed or heard about from fellow disabled librarians. They reflect real inequities in just one aspect of professional work.

Demographics

It is hard to gather accurate statistics for the percentage of the global or U.S. population who have a disability or disabilities. This difficulty carries through to gathering accurate statistics for how many library workers have disability status. The American Library Association (ALA) Office of Research and Statistics gathers demographic information about members via surveys. While not all library workers in the U.S. belong to ALA, it is the best gauge we have. In 2014, 2.8% of members identified as having a disability; in 2017, 2.91% identified as having a disability.[4] Based on our personal observations, we suspect these numbers vastly underestimate the reality.

While disability is a universal condition, the actual definition and scope of what disability means varies by context, by culture, and—to an extent—by individual.[5] The World Health Organization (WHO) defines disability as "an umbrella term for impairments, activity limitations and participation restrictions [which are] neither simply a biological nor a social phenomenon."[6] Because of the stigma, discrimination, violence, abuse, and social inequalities that people with disabilities face, even though disability as a concept is fluid, WHO recognizes that the treatment of disabled people is a human rights issue.

---

4   Kathy Rosa and Kelsey Henke, "2017 ALA Demographic Study," ALA Office for Research and Statistics, http://www.ala.org/tools/sites/ala.org.tools/files/conten t/Draft%20of%20Member%20Demographics%20Survey%2001-11-2017.pdf .

5   Roddy Slorach, *A Very Capitalist Condition: A History and Politics of Disability* (London: Bookmarks Publications, 2016).

6   World Health Organization, *WHO Global Disability Action Plan, 2014–2021: Better Health for All People with Disability* (Geneva, Switzerland: World Health Organization, 2015), 1, http://apps.who.int/iris/bitstream/10665/199544/1/9789241509619_eng.pdf.

Global Statistics

At a global level, the World Health Organization estimates that about 15% of the population has a disability, and that most people with disabilities are from already marginalized communities: women, poor people, Indigenous people and people from ethnic minority groups, and older people.[7] This means that most people with disabilities are already at risk of experiencing discrimination, stigma, or violence because of other aspects of their identities. That mistreatment is compounded by disability status. In fact, poverty and sexual and racial violence have frequently been identified as *causes* of disability.[8]

While the WHO statistics are compiled from global data, the organization acknowledges that the 15% figure is just an estimate. Different countries and cultures use different definitions of disability, and often other forms of discrimination determine who gets labeled with a disability. In their *Global Disability Action Plan*, WHO notes that "children in ethnic minority groups were more likely than other children to screen positive for disability."[9] It is hard to know from this whether those children are more exposed to disabling conditions, or if ethnic stigma and ableist stigma work in tandem, resulting in the over-diagnosis of children from ethnic minority populations. This problem with data collection impacts WHO data as well as data collected within the United States, and the dilemma is not unique to the Global South. As Bowker and Star clearly noted in *Sorting Things Out*, medical classification systems work at the behest of dominant bureaucratic systems.[10] If, for example, governmental organizations are not directed to collect certain data, such as the impact of sickle cell

---

7 World Health Organization, *Who Global Disability Action Plan*, 2.

8 Jeanne Neath, "Social Causes of Impairment, Disability, and Abuse: A Feminist Perspective," *Journal of Disability Policy Studies* 8, no. 1–2 (1997): 195–230, https://doi.org/10.1177/104420739700800210; Rae Ellen Bichell, "Scientists Start to Tease out the Subtler Ways Racism Hurts Health," *NPR Health Shots* (November 11, 2017), https://www.npr.org/sections/health-shots/2017/11/11/562623815/scientists-start-to-tease-out-the-subtler-ways-racism-hurts-health; Rebecca Vallas and Fremstad, Shawn, "Disability is a Cause and Consequence of Poverty," Talk Poverty (September 19, 2014), https://talkpoverty.org/2014/09/19/disability-cause-consequence-poverty/.

9 World Health Organization, *WHO Global Disability Action Plan*, 36.

10 Geoffrey C. Bowker and Susan Leigh Star, *Sorting Things Out: Classification and Its Consequences*, (Cambridge, Mass.: MIT Press, 1999).

disease on the lives of people in the United States[11] or the number of Indigenous people with disabilities on reserves in Canada,[12] they won't. And as the WHO report notes, governments are better at recording mortality information than they are at recording information about the functional realities of living people with disabilities.

But Our Focus is Primarily on Experiences of People in the United States

Disabled people face many barriers that are the result of inadequate legislation and policies, discrimination, insufficient funding, and lack of consultation with disabled people by policy-makers. These barriers impede disabled people from accessing health care, education, employment, and social services.[13] This book highlights the work-related experiences of disabled library employees and then goes a step further, imagining how the work environment could be optimally supportive. Changes on the personal, organizational, and sociopolitical levels are proposed.

As Jessica's story at the beginning of this chapter illustrates, while the ADA was passed in 1990, it did not automatically guarantee workplace protections for people with disabilities. In fact, many researchers have observed that the labor participation rates of disabled people have actually decreased since that time.[14]

There are many reasons why "most people who meet official classifications of disability do not see themselves as disabled."[15] Part of it is a

---

11   Centers for Disease Control, "Sickle Cell Data Collection Program Report: Data to Action. Knowledge Gaps," September 7, 2018, https://www.cdc.gov/ncbddd/ hemoglobinopathies/data-reports/2018-summer/knowledge-gaps.html.

12   Mary Ann McColl, Alison James, William Boyce, and Sam Shortt, "Disability Policy Making: Evaluating the Evidence Base," in *Critical Disability Theory: Essays in Philosophy, Politics, Policy and Law*, ed. Dianne Pothier and Richard Devlin (Vancouver: UBC Press, 2006), 29.

13   Richard Devlin and Dianne Pothier, "Introduction," in *Critical Disability Theory: Essays in Philosophy, Politics, Policy, and Law*, ed. Dianne Pothier and Richard Devlin (Vancouver: UBC Press, 2006), 1.

14   Paul B. Gold, Spalatin N. Oire, Ellen S. Fabian, and Nancy J. Wewiorski, "Negotiating Reasonable Workplace Accommodations: Perspectives of Employers, Employees with Disabilities, and Rehabilitation Service Providers," *Journal of Vocational Rehabilitation* 37, no. 1 (2012): 25–37; Slorach, *A Very Capitalist Condition*, 250.

15   Slorach, 252.

worldview that disability only includes those with physical impairments such as using a wheelchair or being blind. Or that only people who have disabled parking placards or who receive government subsidies are really disabled. Part of it is that the experience of being discriminated against and the need for social assistance places people in an emotional and ontological quandary. Those who have jobs, higher levels of qualifications, and higher incomes are less likely to think of themselves as disabled. Those most likely to think of themselves as disabled don't have jobs, don't have the qualifications to get jobs, and have low income status. Also, those with impairments since birth are more likely to identify as disabled than those who acquire impairments during the aging process.

Related to this, when considering the power relations at the intersections of racial and gender identity, we see that white men are more likely to be in roles that are valued and highly compensated, while men of color and women[16] are more likely to be assigned work that requires skills which are less valued by organizations.[17] Within libraries, we can see these discrepancies: while 81% of ALA members are women,[18] only 63% of research library directors are women, and they earn consistently less than their male peers.[19] With these factors in play, we can recognize that people from already-marginalized groups may be unwilling to take the risk of identifying as disabled,[20] and at the same time understand that people from dominant groups may not want to risk losing their social dominance by admitting to having a stigmatized identity.

Now let's consider age. WHO observes that because impairments increase with age, the rate of disability is higher among older populations. But it is unclear what "older" means in this context. Returning to the ALA demographic information, we learn that about 20% of ALA members are

---

16   The statistics we found when doing our research do not account for people who do not have binary genders or who aren't cisgender. We think it's reasonable to assume that people whose gender identities aren't counted by researchers also hold marginalized identities.

17   Harlan and Robert, "The Social Construction of Disability in Organizations," 397–435.

18   Rosa and Henke, "2017 ALA Demographic Study."

19   Shaneka Morris, "ARL Annual Salary Survey, 2015–2016" (Washington, D.C., Association of Research Libraries, 2016).

20   Imani Barbarin, "On Being Black and 'Disabled but Not Really'," *Rewire.News* (July 26, 2019), https://rewire.news/article/2019/07/26/on-being-black-and-disabled-but-not-really/.

between the ages of 35–44, another 20% are between the ages of 45–54, and yet another 20% are between the ages of 55–64. After age 65, the membership numbers decline steadily.[21] So does *old* mean after what we consider retirement age? If so, it doesn't seem that the increase in disability status among older adults should be the main focus of discussions about library workers with disabilities. But as disabilities increase as we get older, it is an aspect to consider, especially for people who put off retirement for financial or other reasons.

Considering another aspect to who counts as disabled, diagnoses for behavioral disorders and mental illness are on the rise while diagnosed physical impairments are decreasing. In Roddy Slorach's book about the history and politics of disability, he notes that WHO predicts the most commonly diagnosed disability by 2020 will be depression.[22] But in a world where people with psychiatric disabilities were denied the right to vote in Canada until as recently as 1991,[23] are libraries equipped to create fully inclusive, nonhostile work environments for workers with mental illness?[24] Based on the stories we encountered while doing our literature search and in conducting interviews, we suspect that the answer is a resounding "no."[25]

While demographic information can provide a useful snapshot, that information needs a context for interpretation. There are multiple frameworks one can use to provide that context. In the next section, we will discuss several theoretical frameworks that are commonly used in North America.

Disability Theory

Why does theory matter? The statistics provided above make the case that disability is a human rights issue. Theory matters because it can help us

---

21   Rosa and Henke, "2017 ALA Demographic Study."

22   Slorach, *A Very Capitalist Condition*, 253.

23   Marcia H. Rioux and Fraser Valentine, "Does Theory Matter? Exploring the Nexus between Disability, Human Rights, and Public Policy," in *Critical Disability Theory: Essays in Philosophy, Politics, Policy and Law*, ed. Dianne Pothier and Richard Devlin (Vancouver: University of British Columbia Press, 2006), 55.

24   Pamela M. Robert and Sharon L. Harlan, "Mechanisms of Disability Discrimination in Large Bureaucratic Organizations: Ascriptive Inequalities in the Workplace," *The Sociological Quarterly* 47, no. 4 (2006): 599–630.

25   J. J. Pionke, "The Impact of Disbelief: On Being a Library Employee with a Disability," *Library Trends* 67, no. 3 (2019): 423–35.

examine our thinking and assumptions. This in turn allows us to better understand the world we live in and how it works. It helps us to move from our particular situation to a general concept. We are then able to recognize what is systemic and what happens systematically. As mentioned in Jessica's story at the beginning of this chapter, theoretical models can help us look at problems more broadly and clarify why something might feel unfair as well as what to do next. Ideally, using theoretical analysis helps us examine the power dynamics at work in a given context in order to pursue substantive equity. Less ideally, the theoretical models or worldviews we operate under can lead us to rationalize and perpetuate inequities.[26] Theory, as with any tool, can be used or misused. Our goal with this book is to use theory to work for expanded human rights.

The first time Jessica encountered the concept of the medical model of disabilities was from reading one of Netanel Ganin's blog posts on the Library of Congress Classification scheme specifically related to disability.[27] After reading the blog post, Jessica realized their thinking had been limited by the narrowness of the medical model of disability. From there, they discovered the social model of disability, and then critical disability theory. They can say without exaggeration that this series of discoveries changed their life. It expanded how they engage in research, how they relate to coworkers and friends, and how they think about themself. They are more able to recognize the lie within ideals of perfectionism, and more able to appreciate the complex humanity of people around them.

Below we present theoretical models that academics and writers use to describe patterns of thinking and behavior.[28] These were developed by scholars and disability activists based on observing how people speak and act. Many activists whose work falls in the social model might not be familiar with the name but have discovered this pattern of thinking thanks to their own experiences with disability and/or talking with other disabled people. Interviews presented in later chapters include stories of disabled library workers who may or may not explicitly identify themselves as following a particular theoretical model in thinking about their lives.

---

26 Rioux and Valentine, "Does Theory Matter?" 49.

27 Netanel Ganin, "Disability in the Library of Congress Classification Scheme, Part 2," *I Never Metadata I Didn't Like* (blog), August 16, 2015, https://inevermetadataididntlike.wordpress.com/2015/08/16/disability-in-the-library-of-congress-classification-scheme-part-2/.

28 An earlier version of this content appeared in Jessica Schomberg and Shanna Hollich, "Introduction," *Library Trends* [special issue: Disabled Adults in Libraries] 67, no. 3 (2019): 415–22, https://cornerstone.lib.mnsu.edu/lib_services_fac_pubs/170/.

Modeling Disability

Content warning This section includes discussion of eugenics and the
violence of the historical enslavement of African people
in the United States.

There are many possible approaches one can take to examine disabilities
and disability theory. Generally speaking, within this book we make use of
the idea that disablement occurs when there is a gap between environmental demands and personal capabilities. In a workplace setting in particular, this gap can be exacerbated by "inflexible working hours, architectural
barriers, social prejudice and disincentives from employment that exist in
disability insurance programs."[29] Examples of these kinds of gaps include
mandating overhead fluorescent lighting that doesn't account for people
with photosensitivity conditions, requiring that people work in high tem-
peratures without providing options for those with temperature-sensitive
conditions, requiring all potential hires to be able to lift fifty pounds even
for positions that primarily involve desk work, and demanding that all
workers be physically present in the building during set hours even if they
could accomplish their work via telecommuting.

Later in this book we will discuss ways to either close these gaps
or build bridges across them. But first we will discuss the worldviews that
people hold about disabilities, so we can get a clearer picture of what is happening and why. Theory helps to raise our consciousness, so that we recognize the roots of our mindset and behavior.

So, where did this particular type of workplace discrimination orig-
inate? Several researchers put the blame on a mixture of capitalism and the
Industrial Revolution. Prior to industrialization and wage labor, families had
more capacity to care for and make use of "partly productive relatives," but in
the world of mechanized factory labor, "employers began to demand workers
who had intact, interchangeable bodies."[30] At the same time, enslaved workers were exploited in ways that were highly profitable for slaveholders. "Thinking about human beings as interchangeable commodities for sale, or abstract
units of labor power, would lead merchants and planters to see human capital

---

29   Lois M. Verbrugge and Alan M. Jette, "The Disablement Process," *Social Science &
Medicine* 38, no. 1 (1994): 8.

30   Sarah F. Rose, *No Right to Be Idle: The Invention of Disability, 1840s–1930s* (Chapel
Hill: The University of North Carolina Press, 2017), 2.

in much the same way that they saw animals."[31] While white workers did not experience the same level of violence and control as enslaved Africans did, this profit-focused mindset brought about harm on a wide scale.

The combination of colonization and the Industrial Revolution made Britain a global power of unprecedented dominance and also led to a mechanistic view of humans and human labor. While these ideas of course extended beyond Britain, Roddy Slorach researched industrialization and disability in that region specifically and identified how the ideal of controlling nature and mass education systems worked together to create the idea of disability as broad concept.[32] Other researchers also noted that industrialization led to the separation of work and home, to the segregation of disabled people from daily life, and also to "production quotas, rigid time schedules, new technologies, and standardization of tasks, developed in ways that only able-bodied people could perform cost effectively."[33]

In the early twentieth century, employers pushed disabled workers out of the workforce because the worldview of industrialization led them to assume that disabled people could not be "efficient, productive workers."[34] This industrialized, mechanistic model focuses on efficiency of the workplace and the supposed inefficiency of disabled workers. Within this worldview are two assumptions that we intend to challenge: 1) that disabled people cannot be efficient, productive workers and, a larger point, 2) that efficiency and production are the most important qualities of a worker. We contend that a healthy workplace recognizes the importance of fluidity and allows for a more contextual, non-mechanistic view of human workers. In later chapters we question dominant workplace models in more detail.

This efficiency-obsessed discrimination, combined with eugenic movements based on a sense of (white) racial superiority and a view of physical and mental impairments as evidence of social decline, led to mass murders of disabled people who were viewed as an economic burden.[35]

---

31 Caitlin Rosenthal, *Accounting for Slavery: Masters and Management* (Cambridge: Harvard University Press, 2018), 58.

32 Slorach, *A Very Capitalist Condition.*

33 Harlan and Robert, "The Social Construction of Disability in Organizations," 401.

34 Rose, *No Right to Be Idle,* 111.

35 Mark P. Mostert, "Useless Eaters: Disability as Genocidal Marker in Nazi Germany," *The Journal of Special Education* 36, no. 3 (2002): 157–70; David Mitchell and Sharon Snyder, "The Eugenic Atlantic: Race, Disability, and the Making of an International Eugenic Science, 1800–1945," *Disability & Society* 18, no. 7 (2003): 843–64.

While some might suggest this is not work-related, we think this historical backdrop is part of the lived experience and cultural trauma that informs how disabled people survive.

Over the past few hundred years, disability models have undergone transformations in response to social and technological changes. The development of the concept of disability in the United States was inherently tied to the development of the concept of race as a way of justifying chattel slavery. For example, drapetomania was a so-called mental disorder with which enslaved Africans were diagnosed if they tried to run away. This diagnosis did not prevent them from receiving punishment for escape attempts—in fact the so-called treatment was whipping—but it did allow slaveholders to justify to themselves that slavery supposedly benefited enslaved people.[36]

Another cultural change was due to medical improvements beginning in the twentieth century. Because of this, many conditions that were terminal in earlier times have been transmuted into chronic health conditions.[37] At present, most common chronic health conditions are nonfatal; instead, people live with these impairments for years. These conditions range from arthritis and chronic back conditions to hay fever and migraines. They also accumulate over time.[38] The point at which these conditions become disabilities is blurry and contextual. As a result of these factors, in areas where health care is readily accessible, the idea of disability is more fluid today than it was in the past. An individual can pass in and out of disability at multiple points throughout their life, and there are some conditions, such as the chronic conditions just mentioned, that we may now consider disabilities that were not previously considered as such.

Over time, various models conceptualizing disability have been developed. While these models are presented here in the chronological order in which they were advanced, later models have not completely replaced earlier models. Some may predominate in certain contexts or regions, but you might encounter any of these models at work today. In order to clarify how powerful these theories are, we will use Wendy's Parkinson's disease as an example of a particular case.

---

36   Carlota Ocampo, "Drapetomania," in *Encyclopedia of Multicultural Psychology*, ed. Yolanda Kaye Jackson (Thousand Oaks, CA: SAGE Publications, 2006), 159.

37   John Christopher Feudtner, *Bittersweet: Diabetes, Insulin, and the Transformation of Illness* (Chapel Hill: University of North Carolina Press, 2003).

38   Verbrugge and Jette, "The Disablement Process," 1.

Moral Model

Content warning The quotations in this section includes ableist slurs.

The moral model was a pre-twentieth century view of disabled people as inferior and pitiful, their disability the result of sin or a sign they were in need of charity. People with disabilities were typically described in dehumanizing language.[39] This model continued into the twentieth century for people managing chronic health conditions and helped to form the medical model.[40]

Barely over a century old, the 1913 edition of the *Catholic Encyclopedia* entry on "Irregularity" sheds light on the moral model. One thing to note about these references is that while disabled people are described in demeaning language, Catholics were also outspoken against the eugenic policies for which many liberal Protestant leaders advocated.[41] Even within this one model, there is a lot of complexity.

Disabilities among those seeking to receive or maintain positions within the Church are described in a sub-entry, "Bodily Defects," as follows:

> These constitute an impediment to Sacred orders, either because they render a person unfit for the ministry or because his deformity would make him an object of horror and derision. The following are, therefore, irregular: mutilated persons, those having an artificial limb or who are unable to use their hand or thumb or index finger; the blind and those whose vision is too dim to allow them to read the Missal. Some authors, e. g. Noldin, think that, owing to the present ingenious construction of artificial limbs, this defect is no longer an irregularity, as it has ceased to be a deformity. The absence of an eye, even the left eye, may not constitute an impediment if the person can read the Mass without deformity. In case of doubt the bishop is judge, and, when the defect exists, he makes his

---

39 Dana S. Dunn and Erin E. Andrews, "Person-First and Identity-First Language: Developing Psychologists' Cultural Competence Using Disability Language" *American Psychologist* 70, no. 3 (2015): 255–64.

40 Feudtner, *Bittersweet*, 26–27.

41 Melissa J. Wilde and Sabrina Danielsen, "Fewer and Better Children: Race, Class, Religion, and Birth Control Reform in America," *American Journal of Sociology* 119, no. 6 (2014): 1710–60.

declaration to Rome, but in practice the Sacred Congregation generally inclines to the severer view. Total deafness, dumbness, and stammering to such an extent as to make it impossible to pronounce complete words are likewise impediments. Paralytics, the lame who cannot properly perform the ceremonies, those who cannot drink wine without vomiting, lepers, those afflicted with the falling sickness, and in general all whose deformity is very notable are irregular.[42]

In another sub-entry, "Defect of Reason," the list is short: "this irregularity includes the insane, energumens, and simpletons."[43] The entry explains that irregularity means "not according to rule." It explains why disabled priests would be unemployable in the hierarchy:

> A canonical impediment directly impeding the reception of tonsure and Holy orders or preventing the exercise of orders already received. It is called a canonical impediment because introduced by ecclesiastical law, for the canons prescribe certain requisites for the licit reception of orders, e.g. moral probity, proper age, legitimate birth, knowledge proportionate to each order, integrity of body, mind, will, and faith. A defect in these qualities prescribed by church regulations is rightly called an irregularity. The direct effect of an irregularity is twofold: first, it prohibits the reception of orders and, second, prevents an order received from being licitly used. Indirectly it impedes one who has become irregular from obtaining an ecclesiastical benefice.[44]

As evidenced in the way the Catholic Church officially responded to would-be workers in their organization, disability status was viewed as a moral impediment similar to other forms of illegitimacy. At the same time that it categorized disabled people as irregular, it also encourages self-flagellant thinking

---

42 Charles George Herbermann and Knights of Columbus, *The Catholic Encyclopedia: An International Work of Reference on the Constitution, Doctrine, and History of the Catholic Church*, Special Edition, under the Auspices of the Knights of Columbus Catholic Truth Committee (New York: Encyclopedia Press, 1913), 173.

43 Herbermann, *The Catholic Encyclopedia*, 173.

44 Herbermann, 170.

among those living with disability. This moralistic view is unbounded by religious affiliation. The fundamentalist Christian can pray for the hastening of the rapture to end all suffering; the Buddhist can chalk illness up to the universality of suffering (dukkha) caused by craving something different than what currently exists (attachment); the Protestant eugenicist can argue that removing disabled people from the general population is a moral good; the humanist may descend into existentialism and misanthropy. Many communities built around unquestioned moralism offer only blame and shame, asceticism and self-sacrifice, and do not lead believers to strategic, systemic change. However, there are alternative mindsets within moral communities, such as Liberation Theology.[45] We will include discussion of how the moral model manifests in library work in chapter 7.

Medical Model

The medical model focuses on individual impairments, sometimes referring to the impairment without acknowledging the person. This is still common in medical shorthand and is hugely depersonalizing.[46] In this model, individual disability is treated as the source of disadvantage, and responded to at the individual level as well. The response mechanisms are often medical treatment or government welfare systems.[47] The gap between ability and performance, in this model, is attributed to a deficit in the individual. This allows policymakers to justify continuing exclusionary practices at a societal level.[48]

On a personal level, the medical model manifests in a fixation on pathology and symptom alleviation. As Wendy shares, she is her disease and her disease is her; she focuses on fixing her condition, getting her next fix of dopamine-enhancing medication, and knowing about the latest surgery or drug. Her diagnosis is determinative. The medical model is a steel trap, wherein attention, hope, and energy are diverted toward cure, symptoms,

---

45 Scot Danforth, "Liberation Theology of Disability and the Option for the Poor," *Disability Studies Quarterly* 25, no. 3 (2005).

46 Dunn and Andrews, "Person-First and Identity-First Language," 255–64.

47 David Wasserman, Adrienne Asch, Jeffrey Blustein, and Daniel Putnam, "Disability: Health, Well-Being, and Personal Relationships," The Stanford Encyclopedia of Philosophy (Winter 2016 Edition), ed. Edward N. Zalta, https://plato.stanford.edu /archives/win2016/entries/disability-health.

48 Rioux and Valentine, "Does Theory Matter?" 56.

or the lack thereof. Potentially, being trapped in this model might mean the narrowing of expectations toward definitive diagnosis, total and complete cure, or activation of disability insurance or adjudication of disability status as ultimate outcomes. The negative prognostication within the medical model sets the stage for the need for a more positive, restorative approach, such as the rehabilitation model.

Rehabilitation Model

Content warning This section includes references to disableist slurs that were widely used in the past.

In the rehabilitation model, disability is a problem, but individuals can learn to cope using strategies or aids. The focus of this model is on recovery and adjusting the personalities of disabled people to the existing environment, rather than to ask for changes such as better wages. As the rehabilitation model was also closely tied to legislative action, it is worth noting that policymakers' racialized and gendered assumptions often barred men of color and women from gaining equal access to compensation and rehabilitation programs, and life outside of institutions.[49]

Rehabilitation seeks to restore former capabilities and integrate the disabled person back into society as it is, not to change that society. Rehabilitation services burgeoned in the U.S. following World War II and the influx of injured veterans. At that time, the goal of rehabilitation was to restore "the handicapped person to the fullest physical, mental, social, vocational, and economic usefulness of which they are capable."[50] It has also been described as a creative process aiming to define, develop, and utilize the assets of the disabled individual.[51] Rehabilitation may be seen as a concentration of individual and community resources to restore competitive ability, independence, economic self-sufficiency, and adjustment to work and social life.[52]

---

49   Rose, *No Right to Be Idle*, 204–05.

50   Wilbur I. Hoff, "Psycho-Social Considerations of Patient Care in Rehabilitation Programs," *Health Education Journal* 25, no. 1 (1966): 35.

51   Jennifer Harris and Alan Roulstone, *Disability, Policy and Professional Practice* (London: SAGE Publications Ltd, 2011), 20–22.

52   David L. Sills, *International Encyclopedia of the Social Sciences* (New York, N.Y.: Macmillan, 1968), 350–55.

Note that, as mentioned above, the person with disabilities must make the adjustment to work and social life. This model also conceives of rehabilitation as a creative process and emphasizes the individual's assets, which is a strength-based, positive message. But amidst such optimism, is there room for constructive criticism? There is no mention of social construction or the need for reciprocity. Can society also adjust to the disabled population? Can it collectively build part of the bridge?

Wendy experienced this model when she has been treated by physical therapists. Various exercise programs (boxing, tai chi, dancing the tango) and specific training (e.g., Big and Loud therapy) have been found to decrease tremors. Several people have suggested the use of voice recognition technology for typing when tremors make it difficult to do with finger motions. These programs and aids prove helpful, but do not address the entire context of one's life as the social model does.

Social Model

The social model of disability encourages us to separate the concepts of impairment and disability.[53] Impairments are the biological limitations we live with and range from a temporarily broken arm to chronic depression to degenerative illnesses. Disability in the social model is more of a political term related to discrimination faced by people with impairments.

The social model was a direct reaction to the earlier models and was developed by disability activists. In this model, disability is neutral, not a problem needing a cure or a representation of moral failure. The focus of the social model is on social barriers. This model led to person-first language, which advocates believed would help preserve their humanity and promote individuality. Person-first language follows the pattern of saying *person* before indicating which condition travels with them, such as *person with diabetes, person with autism*. The social model identifies the social or built environment as the cause of disablement. As such, the proper response to disabling conditions is to fix the environment via medical, legal,

---

53 Note that this division, and the term impairment, have been criticized by some as being ableist in itself, in how they frame the idea that there is a corporeal ideal and someone with an impairment is a defective other. See Shelly Tremain, "On the Subject of Impairment," in *Disability/Postmodernity: Embodying Disability Theory*, ed. Mairian Corker and Tom Shakespeare (New York: Continuum Press, 2002), 32–47.

and policy changes.[54] This model also articulates a difference between specific physical impairments (e.g., a broken arm) and socially-constructed disability (lack of power-access doors).

One variation of the social model is called the minority model, in which disabled people are treated as a marginalized population in need of civil rights protection against discrimination.[55] The focus is on disability as "a distinct, diverse cultural and sociopolitical experience and identity."[56] Because of this, the social model does not prioritize curing the impairment or modifying the individual to fit their environment. This variation of the social model critiques ableism as a barrier and supports identity-first language as a tool for political advocacy. Identity-first language follows a pattern of foregrounding a person's disability to acknowledge its formative role in their identity, such as *disabled person* or *autistic person*. This way of boldly proclaiming one's disability "is also linked to disability culture, which promotes connection, camaraderie, and shared purpose among the diverse range of people with disabilities; it entails pride."[57]

In 2007 Wendy attended the 5th Annual Young-Onset Parkinson Network Conference in Chicago. She had been diagnosed in 2004, but could often fly under the radar and pass as non-Parkinsonian because the early stage symptoms were mild. After this phase of denial, passing, and coming out, she was ready to embrace her identity as disabled and having Parkinson's disease. Participation in the conference helped her to find solidarity with others who also struggled with the same symptoms. Her experiences as a feminist in the 1970s and 1980s had primed her to see discrimination and denial of rights through a socio-political and culture lens. She realized that disability is socially constructed. But even with that consciousness, she struggled to express herself assertively. She has found that it takes years to undo and heal the harm caused by the social norms and conditioning that encourage self-effacement. Only relatively recently has she become an activist, and she continues to learn what it means to be an advocate for herself and others.

---

54 Geoffrey Reaume, "Understanding Critical Disability Studies," *Canadian Medical Association Journal* 186, no. 16 (2014): 1248.

55 Wasserman, Asch, Blustein, and Putnam, "Disability."

56 Dunn and Andrews, "Person-First and Identity-First Language," 258.

57 Dunn and Andrews, 259.

Critical Models

> If it were just a matter of making existing society more ac-
> commodating, then legislation such as the [ADA should]
> diminish disability oppression. However...unemployment,
> poverty, homelessness and life expectancy...have barely
> moved, and in some cases have actually worsened...studies
> show that an even greater number of people experience vari-
> ous forms of impairment and actually meet the official clas-
> sification of disability, without ever being officially counted
> in the relevant census data.[58]

Critical disability studies[59] and the related DisCrit[60] (disability critical race studies) question the assumptions that those who deviate from standards of ability necessarily want to achieve those standards. These models further assert that disabled people's lived experiences provide insights necessary to effectively critique power relationships, language choices, and worldviews that disenfranchise disabled people. These critical models examine how disability intersects with other marginalized identities, particularly racial identities but also gender and class identities and sexual orientations. This is important because people with these identities experience material and judicial impacts that demand "a social, political and intellectual re-evalu-ation of explanatory paradigms used to understand the lived experience of disabled people."[61]

Critical theory critiques the existing rules; the status quo does not suffice. Critical theory calls for liberation from the normative rules. People who are marginalized by their identities, all those who are what the moral model called "irregular" and do not conform, can become allies and (self-)

---

58 Keith Rosenthal, "Bringing Marxism to Discussions of Disability," *SocialistWorker. Org*, (May 9, 2017), https://socialistworker.org/2017/05/09/bringing-marxism-to-discussions-of-disability.

59 Reaume, "Understanding Critical Disability Studies," 1248–49.

60 Subini A. Annamma, David J. Connor, and Beth A. Ferri, "Introduction: A Truncated Genealogy of DisCrit," in DisCrit: Disability Studies and Critical Race Theory in Education, ed. David J. Connor, Beth A. Ferri, and Subini A. Annamma (New York: Teachers College Press, 2016), 1–8.

61 Helen Meekosha and Russell Shuttleworth, "What's So 'Critical' about Critical Disability Studies?" *Australian Journal of Human Rights* 15, no. 1 (2009): 49.

advocates by applying critical theory in everyday life. An example of the critical model in action is the work that feminist Robin Morgan has been doing with the Parkinson's Foundation to address the gender gap in service provision and the exclusion of women from research studies.[62]

Accommodations Theory

The theory behind accommodations as articulated in legislation such as the Americans with Disability Act[63] comes directly from the worldview of the medical/rehabilitation model. It views disability as an individual deficit that requires individual treatment. The disabled individual is contrasted with a normative nondisabled person, and efforts to bridge the gap are determined in part by need, as documented by a medical professional, and what the costs are. These costs, whether they be financial or social, cannot put an "undue burden" on the employer, facility, or transportation service in the process.[64] In this model, in which cost-benefit equations drive decision-making and the purported accessibility goal is improving access to a "competitive, individualist market," true inclusion of disabled people is fundamentally impossible.[65] As disability theorists Devlin and Pothier point out, this method of valuation "can only condemn [some disabled people] to a presumptive inferior status."[66]

As librarians, many of us work in the government and non-profit sectors and in the knowledge economy, where the benefits we provide may be difficult to measure directly. To some extent this may protect us from the brutality of the competitive, individualist market. However, it does not protect us from being put in an inferior position, of exercising caution by not demanding accommodations that might be deemed burdensome to our employer.

---

62 Parkinson's Disease Foundation, "Parkinson's Disease Foundation Mobilizes Community to Address Unmet Needs of Women with Parkinson's," (September 16, 2015), https://www.parkinson.org/about-us/Press-Room/Press-Releases/women-with-pd; Robin Morgan, "The Personal is Political is Revolution," *Robin Morgan* (blog), July 3, 2019, www.robinmorgan.net/blog/tag/parkinsons-disease/.

63 Americans with Disabilities Act of 1990, Public Law 101–336, 108th Congress, 2nd session (July 26, 1990).

64 Rioux and Valentine, "Does Theory Matter?" 50–51.

65 Rioux and Valentine, 54.

66 Devlin and Pothier, "Introduction," 18.

If Wendy's job performance were quantified, the raw data would show a decline in productivity because of the increase in the amount of time off due to the increasing inefficacy of her drug regimen. Wendy compensates for this by working longer hours, taking work home, and working on the weekend. Per the Job Accommodation Network, the lowering of production standards is not required by the ADA, but an employer can lower a production standard "if they wish."[67] Regardless of external pressures, Wendy has found that she can be her own worst task-master; she has internalized the perfectionistic production standards of tenure-track academic librarianship. She makes a concerted effort to be self-compassionate and strive for a healthy work-life balance.

Make Room for Skittles

We've spent many pages talking about disability theories because we need to understand where we are in order to find the path to where we want to be. The way we think about disability influences the way we talk about disability and the decisions we make about library services. Think about how you treat people, whether you accuse them of faking because you assume they're too young to be disabled, or you do not use the microphone when giving presentations because you assume everyone is fully hearing. Think about how you design built environments, whether you're intentional in making sure people with various physical needs can use the facilities by providing dimmable lights, adjustable-height tables, and power doors for both public and staff access. Think about the policies you create and how you enforce them, whether you're creating a workplace of silence and shame, or making room for Skittles.

In the next few chapters, we'll use our lived experiences and discussions we've had with other library workers with disabilities to inform our examination of library workplaces. In chapter 2, we'll spend time talking about discrimination and how it impacts us, and the personal strength we've found by engaging in self-advocacy and deliberate disclosure.

---

67   Job Accommodation Network, "Employees' Practical Guide to Requesting and Negotiating Reasonable Accommodations under the Americans with Disabilities Act (ADA)", 6, https://askjan.org/publications/individuals/employee-guide.cfm.

Chapter 2

Fighting Stigma, Building Power

A Disabling Focus on Control

Content warning Includes discussion of childhood trauma related to diabetes care.

Jessica was eating watermelon for breakfast one summer morning when they learned they had type 1 diabetes. Their first question was, "Can I still eat my watermelon?" and they were satisfied when the answer was "Yes." Nine-year-olds have a delightful sense of immediacy.

The official diagnosis came a few hours later at the hospital, but their mother already knew. Their grandfather had had diabetes for years, so their mother recognized the symptoms. Jessica's mother had obtained some urine testing sticks to do an at-home test before going to the hospital. Jessica quickly learned how to give injections to an orange and that they could drink sugar-free Kool-Aid instead of the kind with sugar, so they didn't find the diagnosis all that concerning. Looking back, the only memorable part was how much better they felt after starting insulin.

Shortly after that, they attended their first diabetes camp—a week-long Outward Bound type of experience, where they spent time with other diabetic kids. It was intended to be an empowering experience during which participants met people like them. Jessica learned how to save money by cutting blood glucose testing strips in half from their college-aged counselor—this was in the days when dye solutions were used to test blood glucose levels, before electrochemical strips were developed. They also learned that having the same medical condition didn't mean they would automatically be friends with everyone, but that's just a normal part of life.

Unfortunately for Jessica, this camp also invited in a motivational speaker of the Scared Straight variety. They vividly remember this bitter, angry young man who had lost both a limb and his sight, which was attributed to his lack of control over his diabetes. It was a strong mix of the medical and moral models of disability, in terms of presenting the situation as his moral failure and his medical failure. He wanted us all to learn from his mistakes. What Jessica learned was that they would likely have amputations and go blind before dying very young. Jessica's calm, practical approach to diabetes care disappeared forever in that moment.

There were three major problems with what was shared that day. First, the speaker blamed his diabetes complications on himself, which completely ignores whatever social support he wasn't getting from those around him. We don't make poor self-care decisions in a vacuum. It also completely ignores how the medical tools available at the time were less than ideal.

Second, presenting amputation and blindness as being almost as bad as dying is ableist in itself. Many people with those conditions live rich lives, and more would be able to if we were more supportive as a society.

Third, the diabetes camp organizers invited him in to speak to young children knowing what he was going to say, with the intent of terrifying them. Jessica remains horrified by this. Traumatizing children to gain compliance is repugnant.

Following this event, every time their blood sugar was out of range, Jessica became convinced they were going to go blind and die, and it would be their own fault. Add puberty to this, a time in which managing blood sugars is extra challenging because of growth hormones,[1] and you can probably imagine how quickly they developed a defeatist attitude about their own chances of survival. Basically, they gave up.

After several years of this and a doctor who fought with their insurance company tirelessly to get them onto a different treatment regimen, finally they were able to take a more mindful approach to managing diabetes. In this case, instead of giving up control, they tried to hold onto it as tightly as possible. And no matter how many doctors praised Jessica for their attentiveness and motivation, all they could see were their mistakes.

---

1 "Blood Sugar & Other Hormones," *Diabetes Education Online*, Diabetes Teaching Center at the University of California-San Francisco, 2019, https://dtc.ucsf.edu/types-of-diabetes/type1/understanding-type-1-diabetes/how-the-body-processes-sugar/blood-sugar-other-hormones/.

Too much control, too little control, an endless focus on control. These pressures are mentally and emotionally draining, and lead to the development of maladaptive behavior. Therapy and disability theory helped Jessica recognize that the ideal of control is an illusion. Unfortunately, that illusion still drives how society views disability.

Information and Power

Content warning This section includes discussion of ableist slurs.

Power, in the sense we're using it in this book, comes from what academics might call a constructivist approach. Power is built and maintained by people, and is highly contextual. For Jessica, power has always had an embodied component—it's how you stand, the tightness of your chest, where your eyes go in a conversation, whether you get external acknowledgement or feel invisible—and the flip side, whether you're hypervisible or feel like you blend in.

Now consider this definition in the context of Rebecca, a former librarian and current professional disability advocate, as she shares her awareness of power dynamics in advocacy work:

Wendy What do you think is the difference between advocating for yourself and advocating for others? Is there a crucial difference in that? What do you feel about that?

Rebecca I think it can be a lot easier to advocate for other people.

Wendy And why is that?

Rebecca Because you can ... your situation isn't specifically on the line. You can often speak more powerfully.

Does information equal power? No. Just knowing is not enough. Some librarians may emphasize information and in so doing de-emphasize action. In a work context, developing bureaucratic structures that are designed to enhance diversity and inclusion is crucial. Those doing this work need to be actively engaged in critical analysis and deliberate coalition-building. At the interpersonal level, recognizing, admitting to, and working to undo bias is key. In this chapter, we use a mix of the social model of disability and critical disability theory to argue that the language we use to organize and manage information is a mechanism of power that impacts library work and library workers.

Librarians are both workers and part of a professional class. We can critique the dominant class or align ourselves to it. Some of the primary ways we do this is through our choice of rhetoric, the policies and practices we empower, and the ideologies we support. This all manifests in how we organize our work. When we use the language of commodities, as when we talk about "selling" an idea, we are utilizing the ideology of neoliberalism. This rhetorical choice seems like a common-sense idea, because we have already internalized neoliberal ideas. The impact of internalizing those ideas is that, instead of using force to maintain power, dominant groups use language to guide our thinking and encourage us to consent to being controlled without our even realizing it.[2] Think of Jessica's experience with the diabetes camp speaker. Internalizing the idea that any bad health day is the result of our own errors means we don't ask our society to provide better care.

Despite being a field that espouses the value of lifelong learning, librarianship contributes to maintaining the status quo via workplace anti-intellectualism. This often takes the form of not supporting professional development or research activities. This limits workers' ability to contextualize and develop theories about the world. It also limits workers' ability to question the so-called common-sense assumptions which are based on a monocultural status quo.[3] These "ideologies and the power relations which underlie them have a deep and pervasive influence upon discourse interpretation and production."[4]

One of these status quo assumptions is that language is a neutral medium of communication. This is grounded in the ideology of classic liberalism, which views each party engaged in negotiation as a substantive equal.[5] This is problematic because it doesn't acknowledge power differentials. Let's say, for example, you express anger at your supervisor for not

2   Norman Fairclough, *Language and Power* (London: Longman, 1989), 101–27.

3   Jessica Schomberg and Kirsti Cole, "Hush…: The Dangers of Silence in Academic Libraries," *In the Library with the Lead Pipe*, April 17, 2017, http://www.inthelibraryw iththeleadpipe.org/2017/hush-the-dangers-of-silence-in-academic-libraries/.

4   Fairclough, *Language and Power*, 151.

5   Ravi A. Malhotra, "Justice as Fairness," in *Critical Disability Theory: Essays in Philosophy, Politics, Policy, and Law*, ed. Dianne Pothier and Richard Devlin (Vancouver, BC: UBC Press, 2006), 74.

providing accommodations you are guaranteed by law. If you can be reprimanded for your tone while the content of your speech is ignored, you are not in an equal power relationship.[6] Related to that, when a supervisor uses labels such as "stupid" or "lazy" to critique someone's work, they are reproducing stereotypes about people with intellectual disabilities.[7] Saying "This is dumb," when dumb equates to worthless has the effect of saying that the entire category of people labeled in this way are unemployable.[8] And the racist ways in which people are labeled with intellectual disabilities expands that harm.[9] Knowing how this type of stigma operates is essential for understanding how disability operates, and how power impacts people with disabilities. And to do that, we need to take an analytical approach that highlights political power and organizational structures over individual intentions.[10]

When examining how the U.S. court system has historically used ableist stereotypes in decision-making, we see how relying on status quo ideologies can lead to an institutional denial of civil rights. As mentioned in chapter 1, the history of disability status is tied into the development of factory work during the Industrial Revolution. The model of an ideal worker was developed, and it is against this model that other workers are compared. The vision of this idealized worker does not allow for the possibility that the ideal worker is disabled. The court system has historically relied on similar stereotypes to determine that disabled people don't have full human rights.[11]

At the same time, if your disability doesn't match the court's stereotypes about what disability means, you also don't have access to civil rights

---

6   For more on anger as the emotion of injustice and institutional tone-policing of that anger, see Alison Bailey, "On Anger, Silence, and Epistemic Injustice," *Royal Institute of Philosophy Supplement* 84 (2018): 93–115.

7   Eb, "#EbMetaThread On Ableist Slurs," Twitter, October 6, 2017, https://twitter.com/i/moments/915075910746898432.

8   Karen Soldatic and Helen Meekosha, "The Place of Disgust: Disability, Class and Gender in Spaces of Workfare," *Societies* 2, no. 3 (2012): 142.

9   Chris Borthwick, "Racism, IQ and Down's Syndrome," *Disability & Society* 11, no. 3 (1996): 403–10.

10   Devlin and Pothier, "Introduction," 7.

11   Martha Craven Nussbaum, *Frontiers of Justice: Disability, Nationality, Species Membership* (Cambridge, MA: The Belknap Press, 2006), 96–154.

protections provided by the Americans with Disabilities Act. Think of stereotypes about disability as an all-or-nothing condition: either you're disabled or you're not. Now let's consider the case of an airplane pilot whose vision met flight requirements when she wore corrective lenses. Her potential employer would not hire her because, without corrective lenses, she did not meet vision requirements. She sued for the right to accommodation: specifically, the accommodation of wearing corrective lenses. In this case, the U.S. Supreme Court determined that did not count as disabled in terms of receiving the ADA protections, because corrective lenses allowed her to see well enough to perform job functions. She was too disabled to be employed in her chosen profession, but not disabled enough to be protected by the law.[12]

Nothing About Us Without Us

One theme that comes up repeatedly when reading about the failure of international charities in the Global South is that Western agencies make decisions based on their own cultural norms and with a sense of paternalism, rather than listening to local experts. Those agencies then blame local cultures for failures, instead of changing their approach.[13] We want to encourage you to avoid this mistake by listening to those in your community, including the disabled people in your community. Listen to disabled people, trust disabled people, involve and incorporate disabled people into your work processes. This helps us, both as employees and as library users, and will also help you to be successful.

One problem we have seen is the relative lack of disabled people involved in making library decisions. These decisions range from ensuring that libraries anticipate and plan for their resources and services to be available for disabled people, which is a global rarity,[14] to ensuring that emergency planning decisions are made in consultation with disabled people.[15]

---

12   Carolyn Tyjewski, "Ghosts in the Machine: Civil Rights Laws and the Hybrid 'Invisible Other,'" *in Critical Disability Theory: Essays in Philosophy, Politics, Policy, and Law*, edited by Dianne Pothier and Richard Devlin (Vancouver, BC: UBC Press, 2006), 107.

13   Slorach, *A Very Capitalist Condition*, 140.

14   Birgitta Irvall, Gyda Skat Nielsen, and International Federation of Library Associations and Institutions, *Access to Libraries for Persons with Disabilities: Checklist*. IFLA Professional Reports, no. 89 (The Hague: IFLA, 2005).

15   World Health Organization, *WHO Global Disability Action Plan*, 6.

In terms of library workers specifically, we are still operating under an industrial model in which workers-as-people have little institutional value. "The actual value of labour power is determined by what is deemed socially necessary to keep workers alive and fit to work. This has little to do with the specific needs of workers."[16] Until that ideology is supplanted by one that is more humane, administrative units will need to deliberately and intentionally consult with disabled workers about their needs, because we don't yet have good mental models from which to draw.

Disability is a fluid experience that requires an intersectional approach. For example, adding an all-gender restroom that isn't accessible to wheelchair users means that in a functional way, you're not actually providing access to people of all genders.[17] To design for disability, organizations need to plan ahead instead of putting themselves in the position of only defensively reacting to demands for inclusion. As we'll discuss in the next section, "retrofitting fails to address the structural inequalities that created the need for such accommodations in the first place."[18]

Retrofitting

Sam, a librarian with chronic illness, shares how the rules don't always protect employees:

> Libraries prioritizing "efficiency" grinds people down. The institution needs to change. There's a supervisor where I work—we're unionized—he knows our contract inside and out, and can use his power to punish people in ways that don't violate the contract. For example, if someone has a vacation scheduled and cancels at the last minute, he'll deliberately schedule them to work at a branch all the way across town from where they usually work. It's so petty but it's not breaking any rules. That kind of thing just needs to stop.

---

16   Slorach, *A Very Capitalist Condition*, 76.

17   Christine M. Moeller, "Disability, Identity, and Professionalism: Precarity in Librarianship," *Library Trends* 67, no. 3 (2019): 458.

18   Moeller, "Disability, Identity, and Professionalism," 459.

Disabled people who require medical assistance, personal support, equipment, or travel resources cost more to employ than those who don't. They may require adjustments to the workplace or to work processes that nondisabled people don't require. All of these things cut into profits. From the perspective of valuing profits over people, hiring disabled people doesn't make sense. It's harder to "maximise exploitation"[19] when you can't treat employees as interchangeable.

In neoliberalism, the consequences of one's choices are one's own responsibility, but societal inequities aren't society's responsibility. This has led to writing affirmative action and accommodations policies to enhance individual autonomy.[20] This has also led to writing equal employment (EEO) laws using a model of workplace neutrality. Workplace neutrality assumes that applying the same rules to everyone will have equal effects, without taking into consideration organizational culture or social-level disadvantages.[21] Workplaces that view disability as negative create environments that encourage workers to dis-identify with disability. People with disabilities in those environments are pressured to overcome or pass as nondisabled in order to have a positive sense of self. At an institutional level, those workplaces are designed for an ideal nondisabled worker, and instead of planning for disability, retrofitting is the only option. At the same time that disabled workers are pressured to present themselves as nondisabled, they are also responsible for getting documentation from medical authorities to prove their lived experiences. Even with documentation, disclosure and accommodation negotiations in these environments are often lengthy and contentious.

We don't want to criticize workers with disabilities who've internalized this ableist approach. Unfortunately, the individualistic approach to disabilities leads to silence and isolation, and we're often not provided with models of how to embrace disability identity. Also, this ableist approach is often considered a professional norm in which "able-bodiedness and able-mindedness, as well as other forms of social and communicative

---

19   Slorach, *A Very Capitalist Condition*, 77.

20   Theresa Man Ling Lee, "Multicultural Citizenship: The Case of the Disabled," in *Critical Disability Theory: Essays in Philosophy, Politics, Policy, and Law*, ed. Dianne Pothier and Richard Devlin (Vancouver, BC: UBC Press, 2006), 95.

21   Harlan and Robert, "The Social Construction of Disability in Organizations," 398.

hyperability" are mandated.[22] Take the example of recent discussions about resilience in library work. This resilience model does not include or value the perspectives of disabled or other marginalized people. Instead, resilience mandates place the responsibility of solving structural inequities on the individuals experiencing them, which has the result of creating further marginalization.[23]

In addition to prioritizing liberal ideas of individualism (in which there is an ideal individual in mind), retrofitting processes are also often based on austerity spending models. As mentioned above, valuing profits over people is considered a rational choice. Stereotypes of disability as an individual problem combined with "economic rationalism" mean that governments and other institutions are reluctant to spend money or create policy that truly supports the human rights of disabled people.[24]

The reality is that despite laws such as the ADA, which purportedly protects the workplace rights of disabled people, there are widespread barriers to employment. Many workplaces have inflexible work schedules and are not actually accessible to people with mobility impairments. Can a gender nonconforming wheelchair user comfortably and safely use a restroom in your library? Can they use public transportation to get to your library? The answer to these questions is often "no," and these things effectively exclude many disabled people from the job market.

Even if a worker with disabilities is hired, in the few studies on the topic within libraries, library managers and workers have expressed stigmatizing views about disabled workers and reluctance to provide flexible working hours or make similar accommodations. This is often due to narrow, uninformed ideas about what disability is.[25] This is also due to a belief that accommodations provide unfair advantages to disabled people, in part because disabled people are viewed as less skilled and less worthy than their nondisabled peers. Providing accommodations that allow disabled workers

---

22   Jay Timothy Dolmage, *Academic Ableism: Disability and Higher Education* (Ann Arbor: University of Michigan Press, 2017), 53.

23   Moeller, "Disability, Identity, and Professionalism," 460.

24   Rioux and Valentine, "Does Theory Matter?" 48.

25   Joanne Oud, "Systemic Workplace Barriers for Academic Librarians with Disabilities," *College & Research Libraries* 80, no. 2 (2019): 169–94.

to be successful in the workplace challenges the idea that the nondisabled are inherently superior.[26]

Employers also have incentives to dispense accommodations in a way that maintains the status quo. There are public relations and monetary benefits to hiring a disabled person who looks like and can network with managers and community leaders—in other words, a white middle-class person skilled at negotiating the line between hypervisible and invisible in ways that make other white middle-class people comfortable.[27]

If an accommodation seems like it could be useful to other employees, employers are more likely to deny it for fear of signaling that workplace change is possible. They do this because they are afraid that other employees might ask for other things to change and they don't want to give more control to employees. It is also arguably legal for them to do this because the ADA does not require employers to provide accommodations that are "disruptive to the performance of other employees, or [that impact] the facility's ability to conduct business as usual."[28] Because of this, requesting individual accommodations to the physical environment, such as furniture or access to assistive technology, is more likely to be approved. Requested changes to the social environment of the workplace are more likely to be denied. This includes requests to modify work schedules and job functions or provide personal assistance such as an interpreter.[29]

Disabled workers often engage in rhetorical strategies to demonstrate and argue for their rights as part of their daily work.[30] If their rights and attempts at self-advocacy aren't respected, the Americans with Disabilities Act and its amendment are designed so that workers who are discriminated against must endure the cost and stress of securing legal representation to sue for their rights.[31]

We have heard many people express the idea that the ADA can and will protect disabled workers from this kind of discrimination. However,

---

26   Harlan and Robert, "The Social Construction of Disability in Organizations," 422.

27   Harlan and Robert, 423–24.

28   Harlan and Robert, 404.

29   Harlan and Robert, 420.

30   Annika Konrad, "Reimagining Work: Normative Commonplaces and Their Effects on Accessibility in Workplaces," *Business and Professional Communication Quarterly* 81, no. 1 (2018): 123–41.

31   Pionke, "The Impact of Disbelief," 423–35.

employers and coworkers can use resistance strategies that are hard to legally prove as discrimination. These strategies are not always conscious behaviors, and when they are, they are often done in compliance with perceived signals from those at higher levels. These perceived signals include silence: if administrators do not clearly demonstrate support for disabled workers, the default position signaled by their silence is resistance.[32] Resistance strategies include a reluctance to recognize disabilities. If a condition seems too serious, employers can refuse to provide accommodations; if a condition doesn't seem serious enough, employers can avoid providing accommodations.[33] Supervisors are also more likely to deny an accommodation request that might inconvenience them, and that denial may be either overt or covert. A covert denial is hard to argue with. A blatant denial may lead employees to seek support from someone else in the organization, which often results in retaliation and being labeled a troublemaker.[34]

Employers can also exploit the difference in knowledge of the law and legal resources when negotiating what counts as a reasonable accommodation.[35] Unfortunately for disabled people, U.S. court decisions are reached with the expectation that employees have the same negotiation power that employers have, and that employers have the same disability knowledge as their disabled employees.[36] Possibly because of this, "disabled faculty also lose their ADA cases at the summary-judgement stage, at the rate of 93 percent."[37]

Gene, a recent graduate with physical disabilities, shares her experience of searching for positions:

> I think that in my experience libraries like to present themselves as very inclusive spaces, and that includes being inclusive towards people with disabilities, but I also feel like they fall short of that ideal in terms of hiring people with disabilities and also their physical spaces that they provide, as well

---

32 Harlan and Robert, "The Social Construction of Disability in Organizations," 409.

33 Pionke, "The Impact of Disbelief," 423–35.

34 Harlan and Robert, "The Social Construction of Disability in Organizations," 420.

35 Pionke, "The Impact of Disbelief," 423–35.

36 Pionke, 423–35.

37 Moeller, "Disability, Identity, and Professionalism," 466.

as some services that they provide to people with disabilities....And some job ads will then also mention that there
are accommodations available, but many do not. And I often
feel like that statements such as the physical requirements are
kind of exclusionary toward people with disabilities. I'm sure
that once you got into the interview process or into the job
that obviously you're allowed to have accommodations, but
the phrasing from the get-go by a lot of libraries is not inclusive toward people with disabilities.

Planning for diversity and prioritizing disability justice means involving
a team of people to come up with creative ideas and solutions.[38] Creative
solutions won't come from a static model of decision-making, but require
contextual approaches to everyday problems. There is no single dominant
model or design approach that provides this.

Disclosure

In the disclosure process, those requesting accommodations are often required to provide access to medical documentation that describes their
specific condition and the specific solution (modification need) to their
problem. If a disabled person doesn't have the expensive, sometimes very
difficult to receive documentation needed, they are not allowed to play. If
they can provide the required documentation, and the authorizing bodies
accept it, they are then expected to perform in the same way as a nondisabled person. Medical privacy, disclosure risks, and the unpredictable nature of many disabilities are not considerations. The employee is required
to identify predictable solutions, yet the institution, because it approaches
each disabled employee as an individual aberration, provides accommodations in an unclear and inconsistent way, meeting only minimal compliance requirements. This process is designed to ensure individual compliance and minimize risk to the institution.[39]

---

38 Dana Bishop-Root, Dustin Gibson, and Bekezela Mguni, "Collecting [a] Home for
Disability Justice in the Library," *Disability Visibility Project* (blog), February 24, 2019,
https://disabilityvisibilityproject.com/2019/02/24/collecting-a-home-for-disability
-justice-in-the-library/.

39 Moeller, "Disability, Identity, and Professionalism," 463.

Because of this, individuals in need of accommodations often engage in risk management before and while disclosing their condition to their employer. Disclosure is risky. It can lead to loss of privacy, discriminatory treatment from supervisors and peers, and potential loss of employment and subsequent loss of health care. Also, as suggested above, different accommodation requests have different chances of success. Those with mental illness are at high risk of receiving stigmatizing treatment.[40] Those with learning disabilities and chronic illness are at high risk for being disbelieved and labeled as illegitimate. Because of this, disabled people engage in different strategies to minimize their risk. These strategies include passing as nondisabled, selectively disclosing less stigmatized conditions to get some needed accommodations and not sharing other conditions, or sharing in only a generic way with minimal detail. Some also pay for their own accommodation needs because it's easier and less risky than going through the employer.[41]

In a small qualitative study comparing employer and cancer survivor perceptions of stigma, employers said that they believed cancer stigma was unlikely.[42] Meanwhile, in a larger-scale study, nearly half of employers admitted that a current cancer diagnosis would make them unlikely to hire a job candidate.[43] So what is the truth? If employers know that this sort of discrimination is illegal and immoral, it seems to us that they will be unlikely to openly acknowledge it. If that is the case, they are unlikely to admit to other workplace discrimination charges, such as claims of harassment and hostility from coworkers, unmet accommodation needs, nonvoluntary reassignment of duties or demotion, and denial of promotion requests.[44]

---

40 Erin Burns and Kristin E. C. Green, "Academic Librarians' Experiences and Perceptions on Mental Illness Stigma and the Workplace," *College & Research Libraries* 80, no. 5 (2019): 638–57.

41 Moeller, "Disability, Identity, and Professionalism," 465.

42 Mary Stergiou-Kita, Cheryl Pritlove, and Bonnie Kirsh, "The 'Big C'-Stigma, Cancer, and Workplace Discrimination," *Journal of Cancer Survivorship: Research and Practice* 10, no. 6 (2016): 1035–50.

43 Michael Feuerstein, Amanda K. Gehrke, Brian T. McMahon, and Megan C. McMahon, "Challenges Persist Under Americans with Disabilities Act Amendments Act: How Can Oncology Providers Help?" *Journal of Oncology Practice* 13, no. 6 (2017): e543–e551.

44 Joanne Oud, "Academic Librarians with Disabilities: Job Perceptions and Factors Influencing Positive Workplace Experiences," *Partnership: The Canadian Journal of Library and Information Practice and Research* 13, no. 1 (2018): 1–30.

For library workers with mental illness, "the invisible character of madness [means not being] perceived as 'authentically' or 'truly' disabled and therefore [not] entitled to access accommodations."[45] For those with other marginalized identities, who are already more critically scrutinized and discriminated against, the risks of this disbelief are compounded.

Class is also a factor. Those in higher-status positions can often make informal accommodations on their own or with their supervisor's approval. Those in lower-status positions, where their job assignments allow less autonomy and flexibility, often don't have the option of informal accommodations.[46] This leaves them with the risky option of disclosing or else trying to pass as nondisabled by "coming to work sick, in pain, or without adequate sleep over a long period."[47] Again, having other marginalized identities also compounds the risks. White men are more likely to have higher-status positions than anyone else and are less likely to have the type of chronic illness that increases the risk of disclosure.[48]

White people are also more likely to be believed and receive supervisory support during the accommodations process than Black people with disabilities, because of racial stereotyping of Black people as dishonest.[49] Grace, a Black librarian with a congenital musculoskeletal disorder and an inner ear disorder, shares her experience of being disbelieved:

> I'm often open about my disability and often the only person of color in the room. This puts an extra spotlight on you. It's a problem when I'm hired because they want to check off the racial group, but they don't want to check off the disability box. Also, it took a long time to get my...diagnosis. Getting on a ladder with vertigo isn't a good idea, but my supervisor in a former position would demand it because they couldn't see the vertigo and I didn't have a diagnosis at that point. So, they just thought I was being lazy and didn't want to work.

---

45   Merrick Daniel Pilling, "Invisible Identity in the Workplace: Intersectional Madness and Processes of Disclosure at Work," *Disability Studies Quarterly* 33, no. 1 (2013), http://dsq-sds.org/article/view/3424/3204.

46   Harlan and Robert, "The Social Construction of Disability in Organizations," 413.

47   Harlan and Robert, 415.

48   Harlan and Robert, 414.

49   Harlan and Robert, 414.

Where I worked before diagnosis there was a policy, but supervisors made it an issue because they didn't believe me. I even had doctors write notes ahead of time because of that. Even when I was using a cane, supervisors wouldn't believe that I couldn't walk up a ladder or deliver mail. So, I had to find another job.

(Self-) Advocacy

Workplaces are often set up with normative bodies in mind, and normative expectations of work performance influence decision-making and communication. These normative ideas are cultural constructions. They inform the assumptions employers make about disabled workers in a negative way. These include assumptions that workers who need accommodations aren't pulling their weight, that they're less skilled or capable, that they're less knowledgeable—essentially that they are lesser in all ways.[50] By acknowledging and challenging these ableist constructions, disabled workers can help workplaces reimagine what work and working bodies are like.

In an interview with disability activist Alice Wong, Noor Pervez shares his story of identifying as a self-advocate: "I know what the rules are. I understand what you want me to do. But if they're a violation of my rights or what makes me feel safe, then I'm going to push back. And I feel like that's not the entirety of what self-advocacy is, obviously, but it's definitely a cornerstone. It's knowing where your boundaries are and being willing to kind of push back and find where you fit."[51] Self-advocacy involves speaking up about things that are important to you and speaking out against mistreatment and injustice. As Finn Gardiner reminds us in that same interview, to engage in productive advocacy work in a sustained way, it also really helps to have a community to support you and lift up your voice. Instead of trying to pass by accommodating yourself to your environment, self-advocacy skills help disabled people realize you have the right to expect that your environment accommodates your needs.[52]

---

50   Soldatic and Meekosha, "The Place of Disgust," 139–56.

51   Noor Pervez and Finn Gardiner (Self-Advocacy), Interview with Alice Wong, *Disability Visibility Project*, podcast audio, July 14, 2019, https://disabilityvisibilityproject.com /2019/07/14/ep-55-self-advocacy/.

52   Devlin & Pothier, "Introduction," 16.

Self-advocacy also facilitates successful employment. In a systematic review of research on the effectiveness of different types of workplace accommodations, Nevala et al. found evidence that educating workers about workplace accommodations helps disabled workers gain the confidence to ask for needed accommodations and to be active participants during the process.[53] These skills carry over to helping workers know when they need to take action themselves and when they need to focus their attention on asking for what they need.

In discussing the impact of telework options for people with complex communication disabilities, McNaughton et al. identified self-advocacy skills as beneficial.[54] Disabled workers who engage in self-advocacy identified these skills as developing over time thanks to positive influence from their families, schools, and workplaces.

The dominant worldview about disability is that it is the fault of disabled people and their families. This attitude leaves all the work of survival up to the disabled person and their family without requiring any adjustment of the structure, system, and status quo.[55] A different approach is provided by the social model of disability, which points out the social barriers that prevent disabled people from being active participants in society. And in turn, according to this model, removing those social barriers can free disabled people from their disablement. The critical disability model builds on this by acknowledging that impairments may still be there and should still be accommodated. Both of these approaches, the social model and the critical model, allow and encourage disabled people to be proud of and advocate for themselves.

Disclosure and self-advocacy decisions can be risky. Health care professionals and disabled people have identified strategies for making these decisions. These strategies include: deciding how much information to share in the workplace about your disabilities ahead of time, having discussions between the disabled person and the employer about

---

53 Nina Nevala, Irmeli Pehkonen, Inka Koskela, Johanna Ruusuvuori, and Heidi Anttila, "Workplace Accommodation Among Persons with Disabilities: A Systematic Review of Its Effectiveness and Barriers or Facilitators," *Journal of Occupational Rehabilitation* 25, no. 2 (2015): 432–48.

54 David McNaughton, Tracy Rackensperger, Dana Dorn, and Natasha Wilson, "'Home Is at Work and Work Is at Home': Telework and Individuals Who Use Augmentative and Alternative Communication," *Work* 48, no. 1 (2014): 117–26.

55 Slorach, *A Very Capitalist Condition*, 143.

communication and privacy preferences before any information is shared, and trying to anticipate how supportive the workplace is likely to be based on past reactions to similar situations.[56]

Barbara, a Black librarian with mental illness, shares how her self-advocacy and self-perception have changed over time:

Barbara So, I'm dealing with that self-esteem issue, because my smarts has always been the thing that entertained me. I love being alone. I'm smart. Alone time is great. Now it's just like, "Okay. What was that thing I used to do? Oh, think!" So, I've had to talk with my supervisor about that. It's just things have slowed down a bit, but it'll get done, and my supervisor's really sympathetic. She has some knowledge of this from her own life, working with previous people, so it's not new ground for her, so does my associate dean.

Jessica That's helpful.

Barbara I think it's shocking because most people, even them, they think bipolar, they think struggling, and not somebody with four degrees, who has bipolar, who is "functional." It's really odd for them, but I always have to remind them, "I have atypical bipolar, so what y'all see as functional—"

Jessica Is a warning sign.

Barbara Yeah. High producing. I've had people use it against me before. It's like, "When are you going to be hypomanic again?" Wait a minute. That's not something you want because that has a down side of it. You're going to be scraping me off of the floor.

Jessica That certainly would add to the risks of disclosure.

Barbara Yeah, it's like, "Why do I want to tell you, if you're going to use that against me? What happens when I'm not hypomanic? What happens when I baseline? Are you going to think I'm slacking?"

---

56 Nevala, Pehkonen, Koskela, Ruusuvuori, and Anttila, "Workplace Accommodation Among Persons with Disabilities," 432–48.

Because baseline looks like just normal folks working. It's not a powerhouse. That's what I got called in college, "She's a powerhouse." What people didn't know was that powerhouse kind of status was hypomania.

Jessica   So, it has a cost that other people don't see.

Barbara   Yeah. Yeah, the downside is, however high your hypomania goes, is how low your depression goes.

Less Control, More Support

People matter. We want to build library cultures that recognize the inherent worth of all people and the richness that comes with diversity. We have discussed how power inequities, discrimination, and the risks of disclosure make workplaces hostile and inaccessible for disabled workers. We have also discussed the risks and opportunities that inform self-advocacy and self-disclosure decisions. We strongly believe that collective action and exploration is the path to follow to get to a better place. This collaboration enables us to leverage our power and focus on disability as a social issue rather than an individual one. It also encourages us to be less rigid, less focused on compliance and control. By softening our approach to our own disabilities and to each other, we open our hearts and minds, engage the imagination, and accomplish great things. In the next chapter, we'll talk more about how to take this approach to library workplaces.

Chapter 3

The Library as Organization

A Change of Position

Wendy has an unspoken pact with many of her co-workers. They pretend not to notice the severity of her Parkinson's symptoms, and she doesn't tell them how much she is suffering. Her Parkinson's is so personal, really, that she views it as only her cross to bear. Yet it is also so public, her tremors bold and brash as she thrashes right out there for anyone to see. Her supervisor didn't ask her today how much time her symptoms stole from tasks of librarianship, and Wendy doesn't tell her that she spent the greater part of an hour mindfully listening to music (The Who's *Tommy*: "see me, feel me, touch me, heal me"), trying not to go out of her mind as the tremors refused to abate. After an hour passed and it became apparent that the medicine was not going to kick in properly, her muscular exhaustion peaked. She abandoned the Excel spreadsheet she'd been painstakingly filling with data, descended to the yoga mat, and torqued on the floor for twenty minutes or so, unable to fully relax or find a comfortable position.

About a year ago, she brought in the exercise mat and a neck pillow for these really tough times when she cannot hold herself comfortably upright. Lying on a mat is okay in a gymnasium, but in a library office it violates norms. Allowing this unusual change of body position is one of the ways her organization demonstrates flexibility toward her disability. Even though this doesn't happen every day, she worries about the lapse in time. If she spends some of it on the floor thinking about her disability and work, does that count as productive, even if it's "unbillable"? Is her disability merely an inconvenience, or is it an impediment, and ultimately grounds for her dismissal? But she is still adept at helping students... Did a student seeking a walk-in research consultation wander by, see her prostrate, shaking, and veer away? Should she throw in the towel and file for disability insurance, and can she live on the reduced amount of income? Younger, more able-bodied workers must be waiting in the wings. These worries and self-defeating thoughts thread through her internal monologue and sap her already ebbing energy.

The Pressure to Produce and the Passion to Perform

Yet paradoxically, the Parkinsonian sensations that enervate her body seem to infuse her with too much energy, causing a sensation of pressure that feels deceptively external. Can she stand the tightness in her jaw and neck? How many more minutes will the tractor beam hold her down? Every day there are tense negotiations between body and mind. She wants to move but her body won't always obey. Will she make it to work by 10 a.m.? Will she make it to the faculty meeting on time? Will she be able to sit still and not distract her colleagues? She'll be out tomorrow morning, by the way, and "thank you for answering that student's question while I was at my doctor's appointment last Wednesday." Maybe it is time to opt for the surgical implantation of electrodes that would stimulate her brain. But what about the risks? Every day is a neurochemical crap shoot. Will a good night's sleep result in a good day? Will insomnia make this a bad day?

As they sit together in front of a computer screen, she asks the student with whom she has a research consultation to "drive"—that is, to use the mouse and keyboard to click on the various databases, etc., because her tremors are so intense she cannot. She apologizes for the distracting movement. The student demurs, saying Wendy should not apologize; the student has an uncle with Parkinson's and she understands. Wendy tells her "I am sorry to hear that." She and the student search diligently and find pertinent information—the consultation ends well. Wendy loves her job. She wants to keep working as a librarian for as long as she is able.

Gonna Try with a Little Help from My Friends

Wendy feels fortunate that her disease has progressed slowly. Her productive hours vastly outnumber the fallow ones. The cascade of symptoms is often mercifully fleeting. But not always. And her bugaboo is unpredictability. Applying both flexibility and divination, she says, "I'll have to play it by ear, wait and see how I'm feeling, it all depends on my symptoms"— this is her new mantra and it doesn't mesh well with a busy academic library calendar bursting with back-to-back appointments, meetings, and instructional sessions. She is heartened that the issue of disability is being addressed in the library literature and is bolstered by the words of Joanne Oud who says "if we are serious about equity and inclusion in our profession, we need a better understanding of the barriers faced by librarians with disabilities and a commitment to minimize them."[1] Yet, simultaneously, she is embarrassed. She works with a fine group of people who daily show her kindness, but they have their own concerns. Is it really her colleagues' responsibility to understand the challenges she is facing and to know what could minimize her pain? Isn't this her personal problem?

It is both personal and also intensely public and political, because we are all so interdependent. When pressed, we have to admit that we know the social safety net is frayed and the current trend is toward austerity. Some of our fellow citizens have conveniently-timed opinions about health care, deeming it a right if they happen to be ill and in need, and deeming it a privilege when they are well and feeling invincible. We are sensitive social animals, regardless of whether we have recognizable disabilities on public display, or if our disabilities are hidden, or if we only admit to having quirks and eccentricities. And we all face barriers and challenges simply because of our humanity and our uniqueness.

The personal is political because we are connected, partnered because of our common work. The personal is political because you do have the power to help, and thank you for asking. Just holding Wendy's tremoring hand for a moment really helps, as does chatting for a moment, thank you so much. (And parenthetically, while she has your undivided attention, may she tell you her opinions about the social safety net, single-payer health insurance, and the regulation of pesticides?)[2] The bottom line is: we

---

1   Joanne Oud, "Disability and Equity: Librarians with Disabilities Face Barriers to Accessibility and Inclusion," *American Libraries* 50, no. 1/2 (January 2, 2019): 73, https://americanlibrariesmagazine.org/2019/01/02/disability-and-equity/.

2   These parenthetical conversation topics are not randomly chosen non sequiturs; they are socio-politically contextualizing, logical, and apt points of discussion for people with degenerative illnesses and projected futures of needing increased levels of care. Some disabling health problems, such as Parkinson's disease, are suspected to have environmental causes. Research indicates that a likely contributing factor is exposure to chemicals such as pesticides. See: Bret Stetka, "Parkinson's Disease and Pesticides: What's the Connection?" *Scientific American* (April 8, 2014), https://www.scientificamerican.com/article/parkinsons-disease-and-pesticides-whats-the-connection/ and E. Ray Dorsey, Todd Sherer, Michael S. Okun, and Bastiaan R.Bloem, "The Emerging Evidence of the Parkinson Pandemic," *Journal of Parkinson's Disease* 8, no. 1 (2018): S3–S8, https://content.iospress.com/articles/journal-of-parkinsons-disease/jpd181474.

all need each other. And we all need clean air and clean water. And furthermore, it is our contention that we all have the right to adequate health care and disability coverage so that people with disabilities have a modicum of economic security. The elimination of the fears engendered by economic insecurity would go a long way toward improving the quality of life for people with disabilities, as well as for people who are abled. In fact, as a baseline, we recommend starting with the United Nations Convention on the Rights of Persons with Disabilities and building up from there.[3]

Quid Pro Quo: Do I Owe My Soul to the Company Store?

We employees with disabilities present a corporate problem to be solved. Our disabilities are corporeal in that they manifest in our bodies, they are embodied. Our bodies or our behaviors are non-standard, non-conforming, sometimes unpredictable. We often serve as the canaries in the corporate coalmine, early reactors indicating that something is out of balance. As employees of organizations, institutions, and corporations, we give ourselves to those entities for many hours a week. Our identities, willpower, and natural inclinations are sublimated and subsumed;[4] the well-being of our bodies is lent to and consumed by the corporate entity for the attainment of its goals. Is the exchange conducive to individual creativity, autonomy, and health? If not, how can we change this employment transaction to a healthy and equitable exchange? This is part of the conundrum to be tackled in this chapter: while we are gainfully employed by a corporatized entity, how do we determine what is due to it? What do we owe to our own abled or disabled body and how do we maintain our physical and mental health and personal integrity while meaningfully contributing to the organizational good?

The other parts of the puzzle involve respectful communication and constructive critique. If we canaries in the corporate coalmine do not feel safe in openly communicating our needs without fear of reprisal, something is amiss. If people with disabilities do not feel safe enough

---

3   United Nations Human Rights Office of the High Commissioner, "Convention on the Rights of Persons with Disabilities, 1996–2019, Article 27, Work and Employment," https://www.ohchr.org/EN/HRBodies/CRPD/Pages/ConventionRightsPersonsWithDisabilities.aspx#27.

4   Mats Alvesson and Hugh Willmott, "Identity Regulation as Organizational Control: Producing the Appropriate Individual," *Journal of Management Studies* 39, no. 5 (2002): 619–44.

to participate in a creative collaboration with co-workers to brainstorm and propose solutions to overcome workplace barriers, something has gone awry. And if disabled employees are having these difficulties, it is likely that nondisabled employees are having communication and collaboration difficulties as well. Is this a workplace where we can learn from each other, teach one another, effectively collaborate with colleagues, and engage in direct and respectful confrontation as we advocate for differing ideas, and yet still stand with each other in solidarity when support is needed?

While an enlightened consciousness is preferable to ignorance, we warn of one pitfall: integrating knowledge of the implications of the social model can sometimes be overwhelming. The understanding of this power differential and its implications can make us feel comparatively powerless and even despondent, and also increase our level of fear. We recommend that you resist by not allowing the fear and despair of this social-level disparity to distract you from exercising your personal power. In almost any situation we have some leeway and can choose our actions and reactions to some extent. And if we combine our efforts in solidarity with others, the possibilities for the successful exercise of political power exponentially increase.

Talking Back to the Language and Reframing the Label

The personal becomes political when we realize we are not alone in a feeling or viewpoint about an issue. For example, if we live in a historically redlined neighborhood, chances are high that we are not the only ones in our neighborhood with asthma and concerns about the environmental consequences of pollutants in our air.[5] In that scenario, we are probably not the only ones at our library who need more paid sick leave days for our asthma than are allowed by the current workplace policy, and so on. This awareness of common cause is the beginning of the personal becoming political. For this potential to be fully realized, action must occur. We can exercise our power collectively as employees in the workplace and as activists in the political sphere.

---

5   Joseph P. Williams, "Air Pollution Rates Higher in Historically Redlined Neighborhoods," *US News & World Report* (May 24, 2019), https://www.usnews.com/news/healthiest-communities/articles/2019-05-24/asthma-air-pollution-rates-higher-in-historically-redlined-neighborhoods.

We can say that the personal is political because ableism is woven into our language. In the Oxford English Dictionary (OED), the definitions of "ability" and "power" are synonymous. "Ability" is the power to act; "power" is to be able to act. "Disabled" means to be deprived of ability by a limitation of movement, sensation, or activity. As you can see from further examining this gordian knot, the etymology of the word "disability" is intimately connected to the etymology of the word "power." The word "power" comes from the French and Latin, "posse" and "poeir," meaning to be able. The first meaning of "power" in the OED is "ability to act or affect something strongly; physical or mental strength; might; vigour, energy; effectiveness." The first meaning of "disability" is "lack of ability (to discharge any office or function); inability, incapacity; weakness." And how do these definitions relate to politics? While "politics" can refer to political or national strength, it also means "control or authority over others, social or political influence," and also "actions concerned with the acquisition or exercise of power, status, or authority."

In the linguistic sense, we have been written off as lesser beings. The change for which we advocate is simple and yet radical. We are advocating that we the disabled—the so-called powerless, those labeled by the language as not able to exert control or authority over others—embrace our identity, admit our vulnerability, and assert ourselves in all the arenas in which we have been excluded. For in vulnerability comes its own form of strength, a strength tied to compassion and love. We advocate not for authoritarian power-over, but for power emanating from within, collective power, solidarity, and social power.

Healthy Power Dynamics and Communications within Collaborative Groups

Building upon the discussion of power that began in the previous chapter, we will define and clarify the types of power for which we advocate. In the context of collaborative group interactions and dynamics, there are four types of power.[6]

Power-over is coercive power in a hierarchical context. It is the power to hire and fire, control resources, punish, and set work expectations. It

---

6　Starhawk, *The Empowerment Manual: A Guide for Collaborative Groups* (Gabriola Island, BC, Canada: New Society Publishers, 2011), 44–45.

is top-down, focused on dominance and control, and not concerned with relationship building.

Another type of power is power-from-within. This is the impulse to create. It can also be moral courage, the ability to stand up for a cause. It is our ability to act upon and change the world, even in small ways. One goal of writing this book is to help you develop your power-from-within by recognizing your value as a disabled library worker. We are exercising our power-from-within by sharing our stories and affirming our shared humanity.

Collective power is solidarity, the formation of community and the finding of commonality for the purpose of pursuing common goals. In writing this book, Wendy and Jessica are working together to accomplish more than each of us could have accomplished on our own. Collective power can also manifest as an individual citizen within a democracy or of a worker in a unionized or participatorily-managed workplace: the power of one vote for one person.

The final type of power is power-with, also called social power. This can be described by terms including influence, rank, status, authority. It can be earned or unearned. Unearned social power is privilege based on membership in dominant identity groups. Earned social power is acquired by taking on responsibility and following through. There are numerous ways to accomplish this, such as by upholding values, exercising good judgment, modeling self-care, and so forth. Earned social power builds connections within groups; it is inherently relational.[7]

Modeling self-care is a form of social power that is important to emphasize specifically for persons with disabilities and over-extended caregivers. This means that although they work hard for the organization or group, these socially powerful individuals also know the importance of breaks, naps, vacations, and of taking time for non-work aspects of life that feed the soul. This self-nurturing has a ripple effect and benefits the entire group. The self-nurturing member has more energy to bring to the group.

A new group has its work cut out. It takes time and concerted effort to connect in a meaningful way. In order to be successful, a group needs to learn to communicate constructively, establishing healthy patterns or norms, such as respectful attention, emotional and practical support,

---

7   Starhawk, *The Empowerment Manual*, 62.

constructive conflict and critique, and so on.[8] The overall frame and goal is not competitive. Instead, the object is to learn and grow, increasing capacity and deepening connections.[9]

Coalition Politics and Identity in a Collaborative Workplace: A Delicate Dance

As you read of our experiences and the experiences of our interviewees, we hope you will find a sense of shared identity and will even recognize the possibility of starting or joining a collaborative group to advocate for yourself and your co-workers and leverage the power of our growing numbers. Although we readily admit to our vulnerability, we refuse to accept the negativity attached to any ableist projections of weakness. We assert our human rights, wield our personal and political power, and fully employ our unique talents and abilities.

Political scientist Amber Knight philosophizes about human vulnerability, leaning on Alisdair MacIntyre's and Judith Butler's insights. She declares that our individualistic approaches to policy-making are self-defeating. Since everyone runs the risk of experiencing accident or illness, we should collaborate and pool resources to ensure that "all citizens have access to public spaces and services, some measure of health care coverage, and economic support in the event that steady employment is no longer possible."[10] Knight champions a shift from focusing on disability identity to "coalition politics, thereby removing the stigma of needing 'special' protections for currently disabled citizens, while making the case for the state to provide adequate social rights for all citizens."[11] An example of how coalition politics works to support disabled and nondisabled people is the design of universal health care proposals. We extend this sentiment to the workplace and contend that in working to address the challenge

---

8   Starhawk, 96–97.

9   *The Empowerment Manual* is replete with exercises for growing your group. Starhawk, 95–96.

10   Amber Knight, "Disability as Vulnerability: Redistributing Precariousness in Democratic Ways," *Journal of Politics* 76, no. 1 (2014): 15.

11   Disability is a particularly porous identity group, as people can join and leave this group over the course of their lives. It can also be difficult to organize around, both due to the isolation many disabled people experience and to social stigma. Knight, "Disability as Vulnerability," 1.

of integrating disabled workers into the workforce, organizations can improve the workplace environment for all workers.

Organizations operate on the synergy of the group, leveraging collective energy. They count on employees' loyalty and use the focus of group energy and the exponential power of combined efforts to accomplish their objectives. As an employee, one is often expected to sublimate the self within the group. In a vocational awe mindset, which we'll discuss more in chapter 7, part of professional growth expectations involves submerging one's identity into groups and contributing to the greater good. This greater good may be defined as serving the library or serving your patrons. We ask that you also value individual integrity and your own survival.

Look for ways to step back and work to harmonize corporate values with individual ones. This is a delicate dance and is the most difficult in authoritarian organizations. Arguably, this balancing act is easier to do when decision-making is decentralized and one has autonomy. It would also be more feasible in an organization that makes significant decisions via consensus. In both of the latter two scenarios, the workers have significant input, whereas in authoritarian workplaces, the workers must simply follow orders, without regard to whether or not they are in agreement with them.

We frame this discussion with the disability theories set forth in chapter 1, as that will present ideas in a common context. We'll start with organizations first, and then we'll circle back to the individual, weaving in our interviewees' lived experience as library workers who have disabilities. We'll also include references to cultural influences that affect how we view work and disability. It is our tenet that change has to happen on all levels and for everyone—the individual, the organization, the disabled worker, the adversary of the disabled worker, and the ally.

Organizations Can Learn and You Can Teach Them

Corporations and institutions are not people, but they are made up of people. And just as individual people have the capacity to learn new and more positive behaviors, so do groups of people in organizations.[12] In fact, legal scholars argue that corporate personhood (after 2010's *Citizens United* case) and recent civil rulings create a "new layer of corporate accountability" with

---

12 This academic idea that organizations can learn was popularized and mainstreamed by Peter M. Senge in the bestselling book *The Fifth Discipline: The Art & Practice of the Learning Organization* (New York: Doubleday, 1990).

regard to the corporate person's social responsibility.[13] As legal scholar Cheryl Wade notes, after the recent 2013 *Hobby Lobby* decision, even for-profit companies have legal protection to value their social responsibilities over shareholder profits. Now is the time to capitalize on this evolving status and to change our organizations and make them more responsive and responsible.

In order to do this, we need to know how our organization learns. Management scholars Wooten and James describe the organizational learning process as creating routines based on past experiences.[14] This process is often started in response to a problem that needs to be solved. Members of the organization seek out knowledge and strategies. These are the knowledge acquisition and information interpretation stages. Wooten and James caution that organizational learning also involves changes to behavior and ingrained assumptions. You can't just search for information or share information, you also need to use that information to change processes.

As library workers, we should feel right at home with the knowledge acquisition stage. The American Library Association's *Core Competencies of Librarianship* include this impressive range of expertise related to gathering, organizing, and administering information. In the "Foundations of the Profession" category, the Americans with Disabilities Act (ADA) is given as an example of one of the laws with which a librarian should be familiar:

> 1G. The legal framework within which libraries and information agencies operate. That framework includes laws relating to copyright, privacy, freedom of expression, equal rights (e.g., the Americans with Disabilities Act), and intellectual property.[15]

Administrative and management skills should also be transferable to management of persons with disabilities, and to the responsive and adaptive

---

13   Cheryl L. Wade, "Effective Compliance with Antidiscrimination Law: Corporate Purpose, Personhood, and Social Responsibility," *Washington and Lee Law Review* 74, no. 2 (2017): 1236, https://scholarlycommons.law.wlu.edu/ wlulr/vol74/iss2/22/.

14   Lynn Perry Wooten and Erika Hayes James, "Challenges of Organizational Learning: Perpetuation of Discrimination Against Employees with Disabilities," *Behavioral Sciences & the Law* 23, no. 1 (2005): 123–41.

15   American Library Association, "Core Competences of Librarianship," http://www .ala.org/educationcareers/sites/ala.org.educationcareers/files/content/careers/corecomp /corecompetences/finalcorecompstat09.pdf.

problem solving that effective organizational learning requires. These administrative skills include planning and budgeting; effective personnel practices and human resource development; assessment and evaluation of library services and their outcomes; development of partnerships, collaborations, networks, and other structures with all stakeholders and within communities served; and the methods for principled, transformational leadership. OCLC's *Competency Index for the Library Field* provides a list of similar competencies in greater detail. This index highlights two skills used in relation to the promotion of diversity. Within the section on personnel management, organizational leaders are expected to support and respect the needs of diverse staff within work processes, as well as recruit for diversity. Within the section on interpersonal relationship building, leaders are expected to pursue an understanding and embrace of individual and organizational diversity.[16]

There are a variety of guidelines about what library managers are expected to know and learn. Remember, though, that these information resources need to be brought back into library work in a functional way. Knowledge acquisition and administration need to work in tandem. It's not enough to learn about the ADA, for example; you also need to learn how to implement it. Ideally, this is not just a top-down, one-shot approach but an ongoing discourse across the organization. Activists and allies can foment this conversation, keeping it on the agenda as long as necessary to effect change.

Because Organizations Can Learn, Organizations Can Change

Two levels of organizational learning identified by management scholars are single-loop learning and double-loop learning. Single loop learning involves taking a discrete action for a discrete problem. In a disability context, this looks like making an accommodation for one person without taking a broader look at existing policies or practices. Consider, for example, having student workers open bathroom doors upon request rather than providing doors that wheelchair users can open on their own. In double loop learning, also called reflexive learning, those existing policies and practices are looked at whenever an accommodation request is made, or even before.[17] An example of this recently happened at Jessica's workplace.

---

16 OCLC, *Competency Index for the Library Field: Compiled by Web Junction*, 2009, https://www.webjunction.org/content/dam/WebJunction/Documents/webJunction/Competency%20Index%20for%20Library%20Field.pdf.

17 Wooten and James, "Challenges of Organizational Learning," 123–41.

After many years of requests for door-opening help from students, library staff eventually realized that what was truly needed was a bathroom that went beyond minimal legal requirements for accessibility to being actually accessible for wheelchair users. They used those insights to lobby for funds for several years, and eventually the library and university were able to raise the money needed to add two new single-stall bathrooms with appropriate hardware and maneuvering space for wheelchair users to be more independent. The organization was able to transition from single loop learning to double loop learning.

The double-loop, reflective type of learning is indicative of a deeper level of change. It does not stop at knowledge acquisition and short-term response. In addition, it conducts a systemic evaluation, exposes ignorance and bias, and roots out discriminatory practices. It then creates new practices that ensure diversity. These practices include taking a proactive stance by acknowledging the different needs of disabled employees and users, seeking out and listening to the expertise of disabled people, and making appropriate organizational modifications.[18]

This concept of organizational intelligence and malleability offers hope for the possibility of change. With this construct in our toolboxes, activists and allies for disabled workers can expect more from our organizations. Instead of being impenetrable and unchanging bureaucracies, they become potential allies with which to communicate, negotiate, and share power. But to engage in the double-loop reflective learning, rather than the single-loop process, workers need to have power and influence to modify policies and objectives, and a sanctioned avenue by which to constructively and openly challenge behavioral norms and values with regard to disability and employment.

Corporate Culture, Covert Behavior, and the Grassroots: Mind the Gap

When we negotiate with organizations, we need to be aware of their complexity and cognizant of our place in the hierarchy. Management scholars Schur, Kruse, and Blanck have developed a model identifying three levels of shared culture.[19]

---

18 Wooten and James, 136.

19 Lisa Schur, Douglas Kruse, and Peter Blanck, "Corporate Culture and the Employment of Persons with Disabilities Behavioral Sciences and the Law," *Behavioral Sciences & Law* 23, no. 1 (2005): 3–7.

The first level of shared culture consists of the unspoken and unconscious values and norms used by an organization to guide it in problem-solving and the integration of new ideas and experiences. Think of a moment in your workplace when you or a new employee encountered one of these unspoken rules by stumbling over it. The unspoken rule might be "don't schedule Catherine and Heathcliff to work the same reference shift because they are too disruptive when left alone." The unconscious value might be conflict-avoidance, as manifested by a supervisor's unwillingness to reprimand Catherine for slapping someone.

The second level contains the values expressed in the explicitly-stated strategies, goals, and mission statements that guide the entity's policies. At a broad level, this might include the American Library Association's Interpretations of the Library Bill of Rights. This document includes explicit language about, for example, not charging fees to access digital resources in publicly-funded libraries because those fees act as economic barriers. As of the time this is written, you will not see similar language about the accessibility of digital resources for people with sensory or mobility impairments. Looking at these statements provides insight into what initiatives organizational leaders will be most positively responsive towards.

The third level of shared culture includes the physical and social environment, such as the organization of physical space and the overt behavior of members.[20] One of the organizations Jessica used to work for had overt expectations about employees being physically present during specific hours to engage in computer-oriented work. That was a clear part of their expressed values. However, the same workplace also refused to invest in routine ergonomic supports for employees, the kind of supports that can keep employees working productively. This part of that organization's culture was not written in policy but was manifest in the physical resources provided and the overt refusals to do more.

This model of organizational culture offers explanation for the discrepancies we often notice between the content of the sermon and the actual practice of what is preached. Do the unconscious values and norms differ greatly from the stated policies? Does overt behavior differ from covert behavior?[21]

---

20 Schur, Kruse, Blanck, "Corporate Culture and the Employment of Persons with Disabilities," 5–6.

21 For a comprehensive list of thirteen actions to change the corporate culture, see Schur, Kruse, Blanck, "Corporate Culture and the Employment of Persons with Disabilities," 16–17.

Along with the three levels of corporate culture, it is helpful to know that workplace well-being researchers identify two ways in which organizations can be influenced to move in a healthier direction. In the first, work structures, past decisions, and institutional culture drive the direction of the organization and can maintain organizational health without much conscious effort. The second is a deliberate bottom-up process in which individuals and groups of individuals drive the organization in a new direction. If these influences are in sync, well-being could be enhanced by, for example, top-down promotion of thoughtfully selected wellness practices in conjunction with a grassroots effort from groups of individuals to enhance their well-being and that of their peers.[22] The synergistic potential for positive change exists.

Reviewing the social impacts of the Americans with Disabilities Act (ADA) upon corporate culture is illuminating. Corporate knowledge of the ADA is more often used as a ceiling rather than a floor.[23] As was mentioned in the previous section, providing the minimum that is legally required does not guarantee true accessibility. While "the ADA has made acting upon overtly prejudicial attitudes illegal, more implicit forms of discrimination continue to influence perceptions of employability."[24] Why did these avoidant and arguably cowardly approaches persist?

Why didn't more knowledge of the ADA and experience with accommodating workers result in pro-diversity attitudinal changes and significant advances for disabled workers? The organizational learning was likely of the single-loop kind; it stopped at knowledge acquisition and was situational and short-term. It was not the double-loop, reflective type of learning by which the organization learns from its employees and vice versa. This more productive pedagogy examines underlying norms and then takes action to make significant changes. The conflicting norms and values

---

22 Biggio Gianluca and Claudio G. Cortese, "Well-Being in the Workplace through Interaction between Individual Characteristics and Organizational Context," *International Journal of Qualitative Studies on Health and Well-being* 8, no. 1 (2013): 19823, DOI: 10.3402/qhw.v8i0.19823.

23 Robert Gould, Sarah Parker Harris, Kate Caldwell, Glenn Fujiura, Robin Jones, Patrick Ojok, and Katherine Perez Enriquez, "Beyond the Law: A Review of Knowledge, Attitudes, and Perceptions in ADA Employment Research," *Disability Studies Quarterly* 35, no. 3 (2015), http://dsq-sds.org/article/view/4935/4095.

24 Robert Gould, "Turning 25: A Systematic Review on the Social Impact of the Americans with Disabilities Act," PhD diss. University of Illinois at Chicago, 2016.

would have been resolved and policy and behavior evolved to be in sync. This deeper level of transformative learning is bi-directional, emanating from structural modifications and also from behavioral changes in people.

Free Speech and Fear of Hierarchy

Fear is an impediment to change. Workplace culture influences both disabled employees and their employers. People with disabilities are afraid to demand the civil rights provided to them by the ADA in part because we know that "fear of disrupting workplace culture also impacts employer decisions about the perceived reasonableness of accommodations and making hiring decisions."[25]

These unspoken and unconscious norms and values have power. They need to be brought to light, aired out, discussed and debated, and hopefully harmonized with explicitly stated diversity-friendly and disability-friendly policies. Librarians are well-suited to this work thanks to their range of skills, training as generalists, and flexibility to understand knowledge production in many subject areas. Researchers emphasize the importance of an interdisciplinary approach, drawing from experts ranging from corporate anthropologists to people with direct experience of living with disability. This diversity of perspective and lived experience provides creative and innovative solutions in ways that monocultural groups cannot.[26]

We have the skills and interdisciplinary mindset, but do we have the temerity? Are we too cautious, too nice, to the point of cowardice? Does a fear of disrupting workplace culture pervade our profession? At the ALA Midwinter 2019 President's Program, invited speaker Robin DiAngelo asked the audience, "How can you as professional librarians trained to do research not know what to do about racism?"[27] This question also applies to disability, as well as other axes of oppression. Perhaps a change in culture to encourage more democratic participation is in order.

The creation of more participatorily managed workplaces could be part of the strategy for furthering diversity goals. In his article touting

---

25   Gould, Harris, Caldwell, Fujiura, Jones, Ojok and Perez Enriquez, "Beyond the Law."

26   Schur, Kruse and Blanck, "Corporate Culture," 3–20.

27   Robin DiAngelo, "ALA President's Program," ALA Midwinter Conference (January 27, 2019), https://www.eventscribe.com/2019/ALA-Midwinter/fsPopup.asp?Mode=presInfo&PresentationID=479061. Recording available only to registered attendees.

workplace democracy, Stephen Carney gives examples of non-democratically and pro-democratically governed library workplaces and provides the philosophical and rhetorical justification for changing our organizational structures to a more egalitarian, non-hierarchal form: "In order to ensure that library employee intellectual freedom is protected and to foster a free speech situation, libraries and librarians should consider adopting organizational structures or practices that allow the worker to take an active, responsible, participatory, and equal role in the operation of the library workplace"[28]

This, again, requires that your organization go beyond the minimal requirements. The codified ALA library value of intellectual freedom does not explicitly protect the speech of library workers.[29] It would behoove us to begin lobbying for this protection. In the meantime, without national expectations protecting this value for library workers, regional library organizations and individual libraries need to step up to provide these protections.

With this type of governing system in place, workers can expect to communicate, negotiate, and share power with the corporate entity. Workers will have sanctioned avenues by which to challenge and change entrenched norms, values, policies, and procedures. Without these sanctioned democratically participatory pathways, fears of rocking the boat may hold sway and change will be more difficult and protracted.

Library administrators caution that implementing this new management style is not easy. Art Lichtenstein's critique of participatory management contends that training in participatory management processes is essential, as such processes are very time consuming, full participation is unlikely, staff resentment may rear its head, and it is no substitute for good leadership.[30] Because ineffective leaders can use participatory management to avoid personal responsibility, Lichenstein recommends applying the style selectively, only in certain situations. He recommends that the leader make it explicitly clear when the group has genuine decision-making responsibility and when they are simply being asked for information.

---

28   Stephen Michael Carney, "Democratic Communication and the Library as Workplace," *Journal of Information Ethics* 12, no. 2 (2003): 17–55.

29   Noriko Asato, "Librarians' Free Speech: The Challenge of Librarians' Own Intellectual Freedom to the American Library Association, 1946–2007," *Library Trends*, vol. 63 no. 1 (2014): 75–105.

30   Art A. Lichtenstein, "Participatory Management: A Critical Look," *Journal of Library Administration* 31, no. 1 (2000): 29–40.

The transformation to democratic, participatory management is likely a daunting change in most organizations. Most seem to revert to reliance on authoritarian or concentrated power in times of crisis, when it could be argued that collective wisdom is most needed. A more democratic style of leadership is worthy of pursuit, as it would support Stephen Michael Carney's conception of a democratically communicative workplace.[31] The transition will be an intensive project requiring significant staff education and training, application of organizing skills, and lots of political savvy.[32] While the prospect of eliminating authoritarian-style workplaces is appealing to progressive librarians, it is not a quickly achievable goal, so you may not want to choose that as your initial project. We recommend starting exactly where you are, and begin with small, achievable goals. Soon enough, you may wish to tackle the long-term goals on a tandem, parallel timeline. So, let's get going!

Modern Library Organizations: The Facts

For what type of organization do you work? According to the U.S. Department of Labor's Bureau of Labor Statistics, 138,200 librarians were employed in 2016, and the largest groups were in the following types of organizations: 34% in elementary and secondary schools (state, local, and private); 30% in local government entities; 19% in colleges, universities, and professional schools; and 5% in information agencies.[33]

---

31 Carney, "Democratic Communication," 17.

32 Idealists among our readers may be inspired by Professor Joe Kincheloe's ten principles of ethical work in a democratic society: 1) self-direction; 2) the job as a place of learning, a research laboratory; 3) work variety and freedom from repetitive burden; 4) workmate cooperation to overcome fractured social relations of the workplace; 5) individual work as a contribution to social welfare and serving the public good; 6) work as an expression of self; 7) work as a democratic expression free from the tyranny of authoritarian power; 8) workers are participants in the operation of an enterprise, enabling genuine workplace cooperation; 9) play as a virtue that must be incorporated into work because play is a path to freedom and fairness; and 10) better pay for workers (narrowing the growing disparity between managers and workers). See Kincheloe's book, *How Do We Tell the Workers? The Socioeconomic Foundations of Work and Vocational Education* (Boulder, CO: Westview Press, 1999), 64–70. Those readers who are interested in the spiritual dimensions of their work might want to refer to the "Spirituality of Work Questionnaire" in Matthew Fox' soul-searching book, *The Reinvention of Work: A New Vision of Livelihood for Our Time* (San Francisco: Harper Collins, 1994).

33 Bureau of Labor Statistics, U.S. Department of Labor, "Librarians," *Occupational Outlook Handbook*, https://www.bls.gov/ooh/education-training-and-library/librarians.htm.

Statistics indicate that disabled people are not well represented in the workforce, and Black and Asian disabled people are even less included than white disabled people. For those with post-secondary education, those numbers get slightly better. Overall, those disabled people who are employed are more likely to be engaged in office work than in management positions and are more likely to be employed only part-time.[34] Markel and Barkley advocate that organizations expand their social responsibility when employing people with disabilities. To do this, they propose asking if your organization has training in both the legal environment and in managing persons with disabilities; whether the organization's procedures are inclusive of people with disabilities and free from unfair discriminatory practices; what is a reasonable accommodation on the job and how might it impact the overall working environment and employee retention; and what are the costs?[35]

Rebecca, a former librarian and current professional disability advocate, shares her experience with a workplace designed to support disabled people and contrasts that with a warning she received at the beginning of her library career:

Rebecca People have different accommodations. One thing that [my supervisor] has implemented, is that we now have quarterly reviews, and no PTO [paid time off] limits. She just wants to make sure that we are meeting our goals.

Wendy I'm imagining that one advantage, since so many of you…maybe don't have the same disabilities, but you share having disabilities in common. But there's openness and honesty about…yeah, you just don't have to worry about covering or hiding, or …

Rebecca And I've never been able to cover, or hide. This may come up later, but when I was graduating from…where I got my MLS, I was advised by at least one HR person not to mention my CP [cerebral palsy].

---

34 Bureau of Labor Statistics, U.S. Department of Labor, "Persons with a Disability 2018, Current Population Survey (CPS)," presented at ODEP, (March 17, 2019), https://www .dol.gov/odep/pdf/DOL_ODEP_2018_Briefing_with_notes_ODEP.pdf.

35 Karen S. Markel and Lizabeth A. Barclay, "Addressing the Underemployment of Persons with Disabilities: Recommendations for Expanding Organizational Social Responsibility," *Employee Responsibilities and Rights Journal* 21, no. 4 (2009): 305–18.

Rebecca's work experience is full of dramatic contrasts, and thankfully has gotten better and more supportive at this point in her career. Initially advised to somehow cloak or ignore her cerebral palsy, she has moved from a hostile environment to one that is accommodating. Case studies and systematic reviews in the research literature provide sobering data[36] but are also replete with good news for disabled librarians and their allies. There are many changes that can be implemented to enhance the accessibility of the workplace for disabled workers and ensure their successful performance.

Evidence-Based Changes You Can Initiate Now to Transform Your Organization

Researchers across disciplines ranging from business management to rehabilitation recommend making positive changes by promoting initiatives to encourage organizational growth. They advise organizational leaders to strategically disseminate information and to decentralize processes to be more flexible,[37] with appropriate accommodations offered to all employees. To accomplish these initiatives, organizations need to offer relevant diversity training and be attentive to the psychoeducational needs of employees.[38] For more on this topic, see chapter 5.

As individual employees, some of these may seem beyond our control. Even if you are not in a participatorily-governed environment or situated at the top administrative level, you could work with peers to try to accomplish some of these initiatives. Information dissemination can occur on an informal basis, as one-to-one word of mouth at the least. The decentralization of evaluative processes,[39] detailed development of accommodation plans,[40] and design and implementation of training and education

---

36 For a description of the tenacious grip of the dominant paradigm of ableism, see Harlan and Robert, "The Social Construction of Disability in Organizations," 397–435.

37 Miriam K. Baumgartner, David J.G. Dwertmann, Stephen A. Boehm, and Heike Bruch, "Job Satisfaction of Employees with Disabilities: The Role of Perceived Structural Flexibility," *Human Resource Management* 54, no. 2 (2015): 323–43.

38 Lauren B. Gates, "Workplace Accommodation as a Social Process," *Journal of Occupational Rehabilitation* 10, no. 1 (2000): 95.

39 Baumgartner, Dwertmann, Boehm, and Bruch, "Job Satisfaction of Employees with Disabilities," 323–43.

40 Kim L. MacDonald-Wilson, Ellen S. Fabian, and Shengli Dong, "Best Practices in Developing Reasonable Accommodations in the Workplace: Findings Based on the Research Literature," *The Rehabilitation Professional* 16, no. 4 (2008): 221–32.

programs[41] could be accomplished by many librarians under the auspices of scholarly research or pilot projects. Any successful outcome has the potential to become exponentially influential because of the following research finding. Success breeds success. Exposure to working with people with disabilities has a potentially positive influence. Employers are more willing to provide accommodations if they have more experience working with disabled people: "Willingness to provide accommodation is influenced by previous experience with disability. The evidence shows that the more exposure that employers have/have had in the past to working with people with disabilities, the greater the willingness is to provide reasonable accommodations."[42]

In this case, familiarity breeds greater openness and acceptance. Fomenting change from the grassroots can be effective. So, regardless of the management structure of your library, you can begin to make your organization more diverse and disability friendly.

Workers of the World Unite: Library Work as Work

While putting together this section, we originally categorized things based on library types (academic, public, special, etc.), but after trying to articulate the differences in terms of work, we realized that work protections may provide more useful distinctions. Librarianship is often described as a profession, and as such is not well served by discussion of work conditions.[43] However, we firmly take the viewpoint that library work is work and library workers are workers. By focusing on work protections, we can think about how to create an environment that is better for workers instead of staying focused on the often-artificial distinctions between different library types. Library services have some unique elements that carry across library type, the primary one being helping our user populations navigate through available information to find and retrieve what they need.[44]

---

41 Gates, "Workplace Accommodation as a Social Process," 95.

42 Gould, Harris, Caldwell, Fujiura, Jones, Ojok and Perez Enriquez, "Beyond the Law."

43 Roma Harris, *Librarianship: Erosion of a Woman's Profession* (Norwood, NJ: Ablex, 1992), 18–20.

44 Many different people have articulated many different purposes that libraries serve. We would like to thank Flan Park, Tammy Troup, and Melissa Hubbard for helping us articulate this aspect, which we think is important for framing this discussion.

According to article 23, section 4 of the Universal Declaration of Human Rights, "Everyone has the right to form and join trade unions for the protection of [their] rights." While some states within the United States don't abide by this declaration and prohibit unionization, library workers have among the highest unionization rates in the United States.[45] Unionized library workers earn an average of thirty-one percent more per week than their nonunion counterparts, and are more likely to receive health coverage, sick leave, and other benefits that are especially important to people with disabilities.[46] Unfortunately, state laws allow some employers to restrict or prohibit collective bargaining. Wendy lives in such a state so it's not as safe for her to express her opinions publicly as it is for Jessica, who is part of a union that protects academic freedom. Wendy feels her membership in the American Association of University Professors (AAUP) provides some benefit, though it is not analogous to union membership.[47]

In those states where collective bargaining isn't allowed, at-will contracts dominate. Many of these at-will contracts contain arcane, demeaning language indicating that the employee works/serves at the pleasure of the contracting authority. At-will contracts mean that workers can be fired, demoted, or reassigned for any reason not protected by law. These reasons can include disagreeing with a supervisor or coworker, refusing to attend company functions, refusing to perform dangerous tasks, as well as many other examples of things that are not related to work or that are related to workers trying to protect their own well-being.[48] James Bowman observes that harming people without cause and not engaging with workers in a reciprocal relationship are ethical violations: "Since all power needs to be

---

45   Katherine de la Peña McCook, "Collective Bargaining is a Human Right: Union Review for 2011," *Progressive Librarian* 38/39 (2011): 69.

46   Carrie Smith, "Unions 101: What Library Unions Do—And Don't Do—For Library Workers," *American Libraries* (November/December 2018), https://americanlibraries magazine.org/2018/11/01/library-unions-101/.

47   American Association of University Professors, "Report: Accommodating Faculty Members Who Have Disabilities," (January 2012); Stephanie L. Kerschbaum, "Faculty Members, Accommodation, and Access in Higher Education," *Modern Language Association* (2013), https://profession.mla.org/faculty-members-accommodation-and-access-in-higher-education/; Stephanie A. Goodwin and Susanne Morgan, "Chronic Illness and the Academic Career: The Hidden Epidemic in Higher Education," *Academe* (May-June 2012), https://www.aaup.org/article/chronic-illness-and-academic-career#.XWrLkHtOm71.

48   Michael D. Yates, *Why Unions Matter*, 2nd ed. (New York: Monthly Review Press, 2009): 25–26.

restrained, such concerns should inspire public employers to unambiguously reject the at-will doctrine."[49]

Within educational settings, the system of academic tenure awards longevity. However, using higher education as an example, there is also a parallel system of adjunct professors and low-paid teaching assistants, which takes advantage of younger and entry-level workers. The AAUP, mentioned above, provides guidance and ideas for advocating for better conditions for contingent faculty.[50]

Jessica currently works in a tenured faculty position with collective bargaining protections. Jessica is also a representative on their local and regional caucus for faculty with disabilities. This has allowed them the opportunity to learn more about how human resources units, administrators, peers, and students treat disabled faculty. The reality is grim. As we mentioned in chapter 2, the limited legal protections provided by the ADA are not enough to overcome entrenched ableism on its own. That is why Jessica is working with other disabled faculty in their union to support peers and improve accommodations processes at a local level. One avenue for accomplishing this is to make these discussions part of the contract negotiation process. Unions can request certain information from employers, including reports about health care utilization, complaints from employees about health care plans, discrimination suits filed against the organization by employees, and job classifications broken down by demographic data.[51] This information can then be used to push administrators to do better.

However, unions are not magical solutions in themselves. Sam is a librarian with multiple marginalized identities. They are a nonbinary person of color with chronic health conditions. Even with union protections, they have noticed problems caused by inflexible benefits administrators:

> Supposedly there's employee counseling and supposedly you can request accommodations. In reality, it requires that you have money to see a doctor who can give you a diagnosis. When I was hired, I elected not to provide gender information

49 James S. Bowman and Jonathan P. West, "Lord Acton and Employment Doctrines: Absolute Power and the Spread of At-Will Employment," *Journal of Business Ethics* 74, no. 2 (2007): 119–30.

50 American Association of University Professors, "Issues: Contingent Faculty Positions," https://www.aaup.org/issues/contingency.

51 Yates, Why Unions Matter, 90–91.

to the insurance company, so they didn't process my paperwork and I was without health insurance, so I couldn't get a
doctor to sign off on the accommodation I needed…I took
the lack of health insurance issue to the union steward, who
took it to the office of civil rights. Because the library is part
of the city's insurance, the library HR decision not to process
my paperwork or tell me what was happening with my paperwork could impact all city employees.

Despite the limitations of unions, they are powerful avenues for negotiating workplace conditions and benefits that recognize workers as people,
not just as "factors of production." This may be of particular interest to
disabled workers.[52] These union-won rights vary by location and industry
but have included parental and family leave to take care of sick relatives, as
sometimes disabled people also have caretaking responsibilities. At Jessica's
place of work, these leave protections explicitly included caring for domes-
tic partners before marriage equality was legislated. The union-negotiated
rights may also include financial support for childcare or on-site childcare,
which can support the needs of disabled parents; alternative work schedules that can be negotiated without the need to go through a burdensome
ADA process; and safety protections including ergonomically appropriate
work stations, regular breaks, and appropriate lighting.[53]

This Must Be the Place: Transplanting Yourself to a Nurturing Environment

Despite all the complications of being a disabled librarian, if you had the
chance to do it over again, would you? Did you know if you wanted to spe-
cialize and work at a certain type of library? What was your first job in a
library? If being a librarian is indeed following your bliss, or is a close ap-
proximation, you are truly blessed. After four years of word processing and
thirteen years of being a paralegal, Wendy finally found the right profession; and after six more years of exploration, trying out bookmobile, public
library, archives, and community college environments, she settled into academic librarianship. She had located the right type of organization for her.

---

52 Yates, 163–66.

53 Professional and Specialized Services of the Occupational Health and Safety Branch,
    Ontario Ministry of Labour, *Health and Safety Guidelines: Rest Breaks for Video Display
    Terminal (VDT) Operators*, 1993, https://www.ccohs.ca/otherhsinfo/alerts/alert81.txt.

Jessica started working in libraries as a student page at a public library when they were in high school. As mentioned in chapter 2, they already had a disability before starting that job, and the drive to find employment which provides health care influences all their career decisions. They continued working at the same public library during college breaks and were encouraged by the cataloger to pursue graduate school in library studies. Jessica entered the field focused on the goal of being a cataloger in a public library, but the reality of job searching led them to briefly work for a special library and for a vendor before being hired in an academic library. They considered pursuing opportunities to be a library director, but soon realized that their body's needs and their potential employers' needs were not aligned. Thanks to that realization, they were able to redirect their focus to researching and talking about working with disabilities. Jessica integrated disability into their identity much earlier than Wendy, as they had dealt with diabetes since elementary school.

Wendy's identity formed in the second wave of feminism, as she came of age in the late 1970s. Wendy's ego strength includes an unhealthy dose of hubris as a hard-working, productive cog in the capitalist machine. Co-workers in her word processing pool in the early '80s used to say, "Slow down Wendy, you are making the rest of us look bad!" In retrospect, she thinks she really should have followed their lazy lead and taken a post-lunch siesta, as she feels the way she pushed her body has compromised her health.[54]

Wendy and Jessica had different experiences while searching for a fitting vocation because their disabilities arose at different times in their lives. Decisions about where and how to work are complicated by bodies and by society's treatment of those bodies, by pre-existing disability or diagnosis of disease, and by accidents. Thinking about your own career progression, how would changes to these factors have changed your vocational life? As Michele Lent Hirsch notes in her book on young women with chronic health issues, "Those who have a visible disability while trying to find work or keep their jobs have to navigate a system that wasn't built for them [and] being a young woman with a body that isn't doing the things people expect can jeopardize a job, a career, and a chance at a savings account."[55]

---

54 This manifested at the time as several chronic, low-grade conditions: sinusitis, dysthymia, dysmenorrhea, and ulnar compression.

55 Michele Lent Hirsch, *Invisible: How Young Women with Serious Health Issues Navigate Work, Relationships, and the Pressure to Seem Just Fine* (Boston: Beacon Press, 2018), 88–89.

Rocky, an openly gay man and sexual assault survivor, shares how mental health stigma impacts his employment prospects:

> I needed psych meds [when I was first diagnosed], so needed a job with coverage and the one job in my town that provided coverage was at a call center...I'm well paid in the field now but I'm always afraid of going back down the pay scale. It impacts my anxiety and all my anxiety is related to the workplace, this fear of losing the kind of income that pays for treatment. It's kind of ironic.
>
> I'm on the universal healthcare bandwagon. But even with that—when I was looking for a therapist, I noticed that a lot of the therapists where I live don't even accept insurance so universal healthcare would need to be accompanied by changes to healthcare access. There are so many people who've found workarounds to that market at this point. Also, mental illness on my medical chart doesn't impact my job prospects as a librarian but other fields are different. I know people who haven't sought treatment because having that on their medical chart would make them ineligible to have the career they want. The way we treat mental health in this way is ridiculous.

After looking back to why you chose library work, go beyond that memory. Why did you choose your current employer (or for those of you on the job market, how are you deciding where to look)? How did you know that you wanted to say "yes" to this particular offer of employment? Did things turn out as you anticipated?

Eventually, Wendy found a nurturing, welcoming environment. For the most part, Wendy has been able to flourish in her current position. If she tempers her idealism with the realism of comparison, she knows that she is very fortunate. Higher education is changing under pressure from various forces to the detriment of the liberal arts and humanities. She tries to find ways to deal with the pros and cons of becoming grant-funded, evidence-based, assessment-oriented, corporatized, and neoliberal. The county in which she is located has a humungous carbon footprint stemming from CAFO agriculture and a fracking free-for-all for fossil fuels, all the while denying the impact of these industries upon global warming and its economic externalities.[56] She feels that all of this together created the perfect storm and the ideal location for an environmental activist to attempt some collective consciousness-raising, and for a librarian to provide reliably curated information for risk assessment and participatory decision-making. Kismet led her to this place.

Shifting Frames: Using Improvisation for Political Gain

In chapter 1 of this book, we listed the theoretical models used to frame disability. These models are used by academics to analyze, but they can also come in handy for the disabled self-advocate. If you can figure out the frame that is being used by the other party (co-worker, client, administrator, counselor, medical professional, complete stranger, politician, and so on) with whom you are communicating, you can use the "yes—*and...*" tenet of theatrical improvisation to respond positively.

Improvisation requires that you be open and willing to try new things. Your focus isn't on controlling the dialog, but on maintaining the relationships you have with others in the moment. Your peers will present ideas and opportunities to you, and your credo is to say "yes" with a spirit of courage and optimism. With improvisation, you don't know where you will end up, so you get to practice being open to new possibilities as they appear.[57]

For example, if you notice that a co-worker is judging you morally, you normally might be angered and overwhelmed. In some situations, it might be wholly appropriate to tell the person that they are dead wrong. But if this approach feels to you that it might be counter-productive, the "yes—*and...*" approach provides an alternative to quietly sitting on your feelings and convictions. You are providing the conversant with another lens rather than spending the energy to counter their wrong-headed moral judgment of your situation. Think of it is simply providing them with more information, a very librarian-like thing to do!

---

56 For a description of the climate change denial that prevails in Weld County, Colorado see: Amanda Paulson, "Why Climate Change Divides Us," *The Christian Science Monitor* (October 12, 2016), https://www.csmonitor.com/USA/Politics/2016/1012/Why-climate-change-divides-us.

57 Cathy Belben, "YES Indeed! Improv and the Art of Library Science," *Library Media Connection* 29, no. 2 (2010): 16; Dohe, Kate and Erin Pappas, "The Many Flavors of Yes: Libraries, Collaboration, and Improv," *College & Research Libraries News* 78, no. 8 (2017), https://crln.acrl.org/index.php/crlnews/article/view/16750.

When younger, Wendy felt that this type of engagement was manipulative and unethical. Now she is convinced it is often the way to go. She was a purist who thought work relationships were sacrosanct. Now she sees that almost everything is political! And as such, it is an opportunity to raise consciousness. The possibility of broadening a narrow-minded person's views of disability is worth the effort. You must be the judge of the appropriate times and places for these conversations. If she had remained a purist, Wendy would have missed many opportunities, many teaching moments. Granted, a marginalized person has little extra energy for didactic interludes; on the other hand, you as a disabled person, or as the advocate for one, are the best person to represent that lived experience. If a person interprets everything through a rehabilitation lens, and once again recommends, for example, the latest gizmo for voice-recognition, thank them for the suggestion, compliment their technology savvy nature, and perhaps comment, "I'm glad that kind of technology is improving; but when will an automatic empathy pill be invented?"[58] Thus, you have not negated their rehab tech suggestion, but you have diverted and elevated their attention to another conceptual frame, you have broadened their view of disabilities.

Would You Like a Burger & Fries with Your Bibliography?

It will save you heartache if you assume that your current employer, be it a school, university, municipality, or corporate entity, has been McDonaldized.[59] To put this another way, assume that your employer is focused on increasing consumption, not on recognizing your humanity or that of others. Assume this unless you have been shown otherwise. And leap at the opportunity to find those pockets that have not become corporatized. Those are the friendships, connections, and sources with whom you can be scrupulously honest and forthright. And coming out about your disability is part of the path to liberation, if you feel safe to do so. The more people that you tell about your disability, the more people will have to think about the realities of disabled people.

---

58 Some stereotypes assert that non-neurotypical people are incapable of feeling empathy. We want to acknowledge here that expectations of how empathy is expressed can also be unfairly normative.

59 Karen P. Nicholson, "The McDonaldization of Academic Libraries and the Values of Transformational Change," *College & Research Libraries* 76, no. 3, (2015): 328–38, https://ir.lib.uwo.ca/cgi/viewcontent.cgi?article=1035&context=fimspub.

Often these McDonaldized environments focus on efficiency, predictability, and rules rather than on humanity.[60] This can cause many people to make accusations that disabled peers aren't proving their worth by working endlessly. Using a "yes—*and...*" response and an having an awareness of the worldview they're coming from can help you say, "Yeah, I heard he was spending a lot of time outside and he does seem to be happy for the first time in years, it would be nice if none of us had to spend all our days at work!" Their knee-jerk reaction of envy is a sign that people need to admit they abuse their bodies, work compulsively, and aren't caring for themselves. Statistics indicate that in recent years, average Americans work more than we did even thirty years ago. The average American now works 38.7 hours a week and 46.8 weeks out of the year,[61] and 54% of Americans had unused vacation time at the end of their work year.[62] Unfortunately, those long hours of work did not mean workers performed better or were happier. In general, many of us just work too much.

Using data from the latest American Time Use Survey, we can construct the time use of a composite worker. Her week contains 168 hours, and if she sleeps 8 hours a night, 112 hours remain. Of the remaining time, 44 hours are consumed by work (using the figure that full-time employed persons averaged 8.5 hours of work time on weekdays they worked), 5 hours are spent on the average commute, 15 hours are used for child care if there are young children in the home, 21 hours are devoted to housework, and 28 hours are reserved for leisure activities.[63]

The statistics regarding paid sick days in the US are equally sobering. Paid sick days are not mandated under federal law. While highly paid workers often have sick leave, most low-wage workers do not.[64] This gap

---

60   Nicholson, "The McDonaldization of Academic Libraries," 328.

61   Maurie Backman, "Here's How Many Hours the Average American Worked Per Year," *The Motley Fool* (December 17, 2017), https://www.fool.com/careers/2017/12/17/heres -how-many-hours-the-average-american-works-pe.aspx.

62   Project: Time Off, "The State of American Vacation 2017," https://www.ustravel.org /sites/default/files/media_root/document/2017_May%2023_Research_State%20of%20 American%20Vacation%202017.pdf.

63   Bureau of Labor Statistics, United States Department of Labor, "American Time Use Survey, 2018," June 19, 2019, https://www.bls.gov/news.release/pdf/atus.pdf.

64   Elise Gould and Jessica Scheider, "Work Sick or Lose Pay? The High Cost of Being Sick When You Don't Get Paid Sick Days," *Economic Policy Institute* (June 28, 2017), https://www.epi.org/files/pdf/130245.pdf.

in benefits harms our collective well-being. Health advocates find that this lack of paid sick days negatively affects public health.[65] Ours is a nation that consumes workers for the sake of efficiency, that expects sacrifice from its workers. Anyone with a disability, anyone with a body that is perceived as less than fully exploitable, less than "healthy" or "whole" when viewed through this hierarchical lens, is less desirable as an employee or as a cog in the corporate body. As disabled workers in a capitalist neo-liberal economy, it is easy to get mired in an unwinnable and unproductive interior monologue or exterior dialogue about productivity.[66]

A Bridge to the Business Realm: Hidden Talent

New narratives can be created, and bridges can be built across ideological divides. Part of that connection building is finding the optimal communication style to speak to our intended audience. The following list of positive actions are written in corporate lingo. If we bristle at the verbiage, we can take a deep breath, tune into our mindfulness, consider the consequences of being more flexible, and perhaps take the risk of doing things outside of our comfort zone. For example, we may agree with James Elmborg that we do not want the academic library commercialized or commodified. Consider that a person from the business world might find the concept of the academic library as a "third space," in the language of the academy, to be a foreign or esoteric confabulation.[67] There are advantages to broadening our horizons. If we do, we find this bright spot within corporate culture. In his book *Hidden Talent*, Mark Lengnick-Hall makes the "business case" for hiring people with disabilities,[68] and recommends actions ranging from partnering with community resources and schools to recruit people with

---

65   National Partnership for Women and Families, "Paid Sick Days Improve Public Health," (February 2019) [Fact Sheet], http://www.nationalpartnership.org/our-work/resources/workplace/paid-sick-days/paid-sick-days-improve-our-public-health.pdf.

66   Eline Jammaers, Patrizia Zanoni, and Stefan Hardonk, "Constructing Positive Identities in Ableist Workplaces: Disabled Employees Discursive Practices Engaging with the Discourse of Lower Productivity," *Human Relations* 69, no. 6 (2016): 1365–386, https://doi.org/10.1177/0018726715612901.

67   James K. Elmborg, "Libraries as the Spaces Between Us: Recognizing and Valuing the Third Place," *Reference & User Services Quarterly*, 50, no. 4 (2011): 338–50.

68   Mark L. Lengnick-Hall, ed., *Hidden Talent: How Leading Companies Hire, Retain, and Benefit from People with Disabilities* (Westport, CT: Praeger, 2007), 110–12.

disabilities to creating affinity groups, task forces, and information clearinghouses related to disability.

Keep the expansive, open-minded improvisational technique of "yes—*and…*" at the ready when you are dealing with an unfamiliar realm such as the business world. Many of the above suggestions are top-down, structural changes. But we can't let that stop us, even if we are positioned on a lower branch of the organizational chart, presumably with less power in the hierarchy. If our workplace has a democratic structure and avenues for participatory management, we are positioned well for political action. But if not, we have to be more creative and use informal networking, scholarly and service-related activities, and ad hoc groups to effect change. Being willing to communicate to a party that you consider to be adversarial does not mean you have compromised your principles. Keep an open mind about the possibility that all parties may change during this process. Schur, Kruse, and Blanck encourage employees with disabilities to form their own networks or caucuses within the company, providing information, support, and an institutional vehicle that can present the concerns of employees with disabilities to management.[69] They also mention unionization: working with unions to ensure that the provisions of collective bargaining agreements allow for accommodating workers and job applicants with disabilities. We recommend Schur's research and body of work as pivotal. The following finding was particularly heartening. In workplaces judged by employees to be fair and responsive, employees with and without disabilities reported comparable levels of job satisfaction, company loyalty, willingness to work hard, and turnover intention.[70]

Unfortunately, the flip side of this is that at the worksites judged by employees to have lower levels of company fairness and responsiveness, employees with disabilities expressed very low levels of job satisfaction, were unwilling to extend loyalty or work harder than they needed to, and were more likely to leave the organization. Schur and her co-authors found these results to be consistent with the theory that "workers with disabilities fare better in companies viewed as fair and responsive to the needs of all

---

69 Lisa Schur, Douglas Kruse, Peter David Blanck, *People with Disabilities: Sidelined or Mainstreamed?* (New York: Cambridge University Press, 2013), 85.

70 Lisa Schur, Douglas Kruse, Joseph Blasi, and Peter Blanck, "Is Disability Disabling in All Workplaces? Workplace Disparities and Corporate Culture," *Industrial Relations* 46, no. 3 (2009): 381–410.

employees."[71] Part of this is because in very rigid organizations, workplace accommodations are more likely to be viewed as special treatment, with all of the bureaucratic hassles and peer disapproval that comes with that.

Anything that we can do to improve our organization's climate and culture will have a positive influence on employees with disabilities. There is really no excuse for apathy.

Implementing This Research in Your Library: You Are the Creator of Now

The research indicates the need for change on multiple levels. Organizations need to be flexible and provide support networks. Workplace communication across organizational levels and between peers needs to reflect disability knowledge and positive attitudes about disability. Disabled individuals can pursue opportunities to develop self-advocacy skills to help them communicate their needs effectively if they feel safe and adequately supported in doing so.

Library leaders and workers can learn the skills needed to implement these changes. What is it that we might do to advocate for a more disability-friendly library workplace? What can we do to make our workplace more democratic, more responsive to all workers' individual, unique needs?

MIT's "Building Organizational Infrastructure for Diversity, Inclusion and Justice"

We can strive for more open, structurally flexible, responsive organizations. We can encourage democratic political processes in all spheres, including the workplace. We can promulgate and model best practices with regard to employment of disabled library workers. As an exemplar, we suggest you investigate this excitingly innovative and very specifically aspirational blueprint created by MIT Libraries' Collections Directorate. They convened a task force to identify ways that their archives, technical services, preservation, scholarly communication, and collections strategy staff could incorporate values of diversity, inclusion, and social justice on a daily basis in their work. They have published a report of the Collections Directorate Diversity, Inclusion, and Social Justice (DISJ) task force that includes a description of the social and economic contexts for academic libraries, a listing of professional values, and recommendations for operationalizing their values. The section "Building Organizational Infrastructure for Diversity, Inclusion,

---

71   Schur, Kruse, Blasi and Blanck, "Is Disability Disabling in All Workplaces?" 402.

and Social Justice" begins with the declaration that a cultural shift is being proposed and new organizational infrastructure is required.

The shift in culture would entail a purposeful reprioritization of their work. They ask for relevant professional development, including bias training. They request policy reviews with regard to hiring and other employment related processes and issues: "Systematically and regularly review and update all policies and procedures through the lens of diversity, inclusion, and social justice. This would include hiring, onboarding, workflows, decision trees, training, etc."[72] The MIT example is inspiring. We don't have to reinvent the wheel. MIT's libraries are a bellwether that is pointing the way for all of us, extolling the importance of inclusivity and social justice. Collectively librarians seem to be ready to hear it. Remember that none of us are alone. When we join with our colleagues on like-minded projects, this can quell our fears and increase our hopes.

The possibilities are limitless, and we have more power and influence than we realize. We each have encountered many challenges in the past but using the "yes—*and…*" tenets of improvisational speaking we can use "the now" to shape the future. The next time we are on a committee tasked to revise the mission, vision, and goals of our organization, we can lobby for the inclusion of diversity initiatives and disabled workers' rights. Whether in our roles as supervisor or supervisee, we can more honestly communicate about disability and performance expectations. Whether we are Library Friends, shelvers, or deans, we have personal power and energy and we can spend it in the area of advocacy if we so choose. The next time we are asked to be a member of a hiring committee, we can raise the question of recruitment of disabled candidates. We can educate ourselves about the ADA and disability rights. There is no lack of ideas, just the limits of the hours in a day and our personal energy level. We can advocate/lobby for more decentralization, more structural flexibility, more responsiveness of our organization to individual needs. We can make it our personal mission to move our organizations toward more democratic participation.

---

72   Michelle Baildon, Dana Hamlin, Czeslaw Jankowski, Rhonda Kauffman, Julia Lanigan, Michelle Miller, Jessica Venlet, Ann Marie Willer, "Creating a Social Justice Mindset: Diversity, Inclusion and Social Justice in the Collections Directorate of the MIT Libraries," Massachusetts Institute of Technology (2017), https://dspace.mit.edu/handle/1721.1/108771.

Chapter 4

Coming Out: Giving Voice to Our Vulnerability and Exercising Our Strength

The last chapter began with a story of Wendy's fear of communicating to co-workers in her library organization about the true, lived experience of her disability, the day-to-day struggle. The premise of this chapter expands upon that theme. It proposes that perhaps the most radical and healing thing we can do for ourselves, our workplace, and the planet is to communicate honestly about our vulnerability in carefully chosen moments and also at times of spontaneous improvisation.

This chapter explores the individual level of the nexus of disability and librarianship more deeply in the context of psychological and sociological theories. We discuss the nuanced decision-making process involved in the self-disclosure of disability and in creating effective employee training about disability. We advocate for the transformation of workplaces into safe, inclusive spaces within which it is safe to disclose disability. We confront bias and other problematic interpersonal reactions to disability. We argue that pedagogical and didactic possibilities present themselves in the library when we are open about our lived experience with disability. We create these teaching moments when we share our experiences mindfully in the appropriate context.

We address the powerful influence of free-market capitalism and the cultural mythology of rugged individualism upon our collective psyche, resulting in the impossible ideals of up-by-your-bootstraps independence, a mythology of upward mobility that pervades the socio-political unconscious. This chapter delves into subconscious and unconscious realities, the liminal and the subliminal. When we show compassion toward ourselves we maximize our efficacy as self-advocates.[1] Advocacy gives voice to our concerns and activates our capacity to exercise strength both individually and collectively.[2] We recommend the practices of mindfulness and an ethic of care.[3] We differentiate between structural forced vulnerability and vulnerability chosen by the individual, eschewing the former and condoning the latter. We call for the redirection and redistribution of projections of vulnerability. These projections should be directed away from people with disabilities and aimed at the projectors, to be integrated into their consciousness. As we mature, experience life, and develop deeper compassion, we become reflexively aware of our own fragility and strength. Our goal is *inter*dependence.[4]

Pay No Attention to the Shaking Woman Behind the Curtain (Disability as Distraction)

Wendy shares this story about how she explains her tremor and other Parkinson's symptoms when they occur in her library workplace:

---

1   Susan Stuntzner and Michael T. Hartley, "Balancing Self-Compassion with Self-Advocacy: A New Approach for Persons with Disabilities," *Annals of Psychotherapy and Integrative Health* (2015), https://self-compassion.org/wp-content/uploads/2015/08/Stuntzner_Hartley.pdf.

2   Steven M. Koch, Katy Beggs, Joy Bailey, and Jacqueline Remondet Wall, "Advocacy in the 21st Century: An Integrated Model for Self-Advocates, Parents, and Professionals," in *Disabilities: Insights from Across Fields and Around the World*, ed. Catherine A. Marshall (Westport, CT: Praeger, 2009), 245–65.

3   The ethic of care includes four pillars:1) all relationships are political; 2) public and private spheres are not distinct; 3) difference is respected; 4) the ethic is discursive, a critically open dialogue. The concepts of care ethic and vulnerability are the subjects of much debate, redefinition, and refinement in the literature. Ruth O'Brien, *Bodies in Revolt: Gender, Disability, and a Workplace Ethic of Care* (New York: Routledge, 2005).

4   "'Disability' is one of the 'risks' facing every individual in society and understanding that we are all physically vulnerable and interdependent at some point in our lives should be a central part of understanding the late modern condition…In this respect, therefore, since we are all vulnerable with regard to acquired disability, we are also vulnerable with regard to experience the 'disabling society.'" Angharad E. Beckett, *Citizenship and Vulnerability: Disability and Issues of Social and Political Engagement* (Basingstoke: Palgrave Macmillan, 2006), 3.

As much as I would like to pretend it does not, I know that at times, my disability affects everyone around me. (And at other times, it does not, I must remind my inner self-conscious teen.) It is up to me to discern when to address it and when to ignore it. Soon after my diagnosis in 2004, it was my personal decision to be open about my Parkinson's disease. I first revealed it to my supervisor and other administrators during a performance evaluation shortly after my diagnosis. I blurted it out, my revelation unplanned, and shared it with other colleagues soon thereafter. To library patrons (mostly university students and faculty) initially, I revealed it selectively. Now I disclose it as a matter of course, as my symptoms have escalated and are more pronounced, and my medication is less predictably effective. This is especially a concern when public speaking is involved. Initially, my symptoms were well-controlled if I scheduled my medication properly. Now, the tremor may emerge in the middle of a class, and I don't want students to be startled or to worry unnecessarily. So, I simply say at the beginning of the class that "I have Parkinson's disease and don't be concerned if you notice tremors. Hopefully my meds will kick in quickly and I apologize if the uncontrolled movement is distracting." I started incorporating this pre-emptive apology because of the comment I received on a teaching evaluation that my tremor was disconcerting to the student. At first it was difficult for me to react to that feedback constructively, but I grew to appreciate that the student was honest and open enough to share that response. Though I realize that students are ultimately responsible for their own reactions to my disability, I want to reassure them that they are not alone in finding my movement disorder distracting.

We Have the Power to Set the Tone (Pre-emptive Disclosure)

In the beginning, Wendy only discussed her disability when she deemed it necessary, when she felt it was visibly apparent and had the potential to disrupt a presentation or consultation. Some of us have visible disabilities, some have hidden disabilities, and some have disabilities that are apparent only in certain circumstances. Each person is unique, and one strategy for disclosure does not fit all. We would like to be able to control others' reactions, and we cannot. And while it is true that we cannot control others' reactions, in another sense we have control. We mean this in a very particular way. We set the tone for interactions when we play the role of presenter or consultant. If we convey acceptance, confidence, and ease during a library tour, program, research consultation, presentation, or instruction session, our audience will be more comfortable. A pre-emptive disclosure and discussion of one's disability will not automatically dispel all the weird, inappropriate, or negative reactions, but it will give us a good start on the right foot, because we are framing the event positively.

Connecting to Students in Research Consultations

Meaningful connections are forged in one-to-one interactions with library users during research consultations. Wendy finds that sharing her lived experience with Parkinson's disease enhances many of her conversations with library users:

> Sometimes my disability fits naturally into the conversation. I feel it enhances my role as a mentor and teacher. For example, a psychology student's research topic may touch upon a neurological problem similar to Parkinson's and I can commend their choice of topic. A political science student's research question may deal with universal health care policy and chronic conditions and I can briefly share relevant experience (careful to keep it appropriate and non-partisan). A sociology student seeks an internship in a non-profit agency and to be encouraging I can briefly share my positive experience with a non-profit Parkinson's organization. I share my experience and viewpoint judiciously, however, as sometimes, reflective listening is the most appropriate response.

Connecting in the Classroom: Engaged Teaching and Vulnerability Produce Knowledge

Professor Amber Knight describes how she incorporates disability disclosure in her classroom. She describes her vulnerability as an "ethos" that she chooses to "embrace" and that it is not easy to be so open.[5] It can be emotionally draining and make one an easier target for criticism. The teacher who chooses the vulnerability of disclosure must tolerate unpredictability and be willing to cede some classroom control. Knight models a stance that is authoritative and not authoritarian.

Though Knight teaches in the discipline of political science, her story should be of particular interest to library workers engaged in knowledge production and dissemination. She argues that when students and teachers share personal narratives and then link them to theories and other class materials, the result is knowledge production. In other words, academic theories come alive when they are tied to personal experience; students are engaged. Knight describes her discussion facilitation as the channeling of "lived experiences into knowledge production."[6] She feels this skill is worth the time and effort it takes to develop. Her student evaluations demonstrate the value of this practice. It supports reciprocal relationship building, allowing students and instructors to view each other as full humans. Knight credits bell hooks' teaching philosophy (expressed in hooks' *Teaching to Transgress* as her "commitment to engaged pedagogy") as seminal to her pedagogical approach.[7] This teaching style emphasizes our shared humanity. Another variation on this theme is librarian Jessie Loyer's discussion of building reciprocal relationships with students.[8] We can learn from these discussions how to deliberately seek pedagogical approaches that acknowledge our inter-relationships and our possibly divergent experiences within educational systems. In these models, we are not just pouring knowledge from one vessel into another.[9] This relational approach allows

5 Amber Knight, "Feminism, Disability and the Democratic Classroom," in *Negotiating Disability: Disclosure and Higher Education*, ed. Stephanie Kerschbaum (Ann Arbor: University of Michigan Press, 2017), 71.

6 Knight, 65–67.

7 bell hooks, *Teaching to Transgress: Education as the Practice of Freedom* (New York: Routledge, 1994).

8 Jessie Loyer, "Indigenous Information Literacy: nêhiyaw Kinship Enabling Self-Care in Research," in *The Politics of Theory and the Practice of Critical Librarianship*, ed. Maura Seale and Karen Nicholson (Sacramento: Library Juice Press, 2018), 145–58, https://mruir.mtroyal.ca/xmlui/handle/11205/361.

9 For discussion of the banking model of education see Paolo Freire, *Pedagogy of the Oppressed* (New York: Bloomsbury, 2000), 71–86.

for more vulnerability, more interdependence, and more support for student-driven learning.[10]

We can use Dr. Knight's example as inspiration for deliberately sharing our own disability identities. We can look for opportunities for this type of engaged, paradoxical pedagogy that openly embraces our identity as librarians with disabilities. We can embody wisdom, naïve wonder, wholeness, and fragmentation if we are willing to be vulnerable and strong in simultaneity. We can plan on being spontaneous and being surprised—we can improvise. As we said in chapter 3, "yes, *and...*"—think of what else might be possible!

Attempting to Connect to the Community: Vulnerability and Environmental Science

The above story explained that showing vulnerability can actually strengthen pedagogy. In what other situations might this be true? Wendy recounts an experience of self-disclosure of disability in her personal/political life that she risked in order to teach her region's politicians and policymakers about the environmental impacts of extracting and continuing to consume fossil fuels.

In her citizen activism with regard to fracking[11] in her community, Wendy has testified to Greeley City Council, Weld County Commissioners, and State of Colorado Oil & Gas Conservation Commission on health and safety issues. She always cited peer-reviewed research and expected that it would be convincing to some of the politicians and civil servants. But to her surprise, she encountered an interesting and disturbing phenomenon: those who stood to gain the most financially were in a state of denial about the environmental consequences of fracking and also wanted

---

10 bell hooks, *Teaching to Transgress: Education as the Practice of Freedom* (New York: Routledge, 1994), cited in Amber Knight, "Feminism, Disability and the Democratic Classroom," in *Negotiating Disability: Disclosure and Higher Education*, ed. Stephanie Kerschbaum (Ann Arbor: University of Michigan Press, 2017), 57–74.

11 Fracking is an oil and gas extractive technology involving horizontal drilling and the shattering of shale; it has significant environmental, health, and safety impacts: e.g., it removes water from the hydrologic cycle, emits methane (thus contributing to global warming), and emits dangerous volatile organic compounds (such as BTEX). John L. Adgate, Bernard D. Goldstein, and Lisa M. McKenzie, "Potential Public Health Hazards, Exposures, and Health Effects from Unconventional Gas Development," *Environmental Science & Technology* 48 (2014): 8307–20.

to site surface operations near schools. They would not consider the vulnerability of children, let alone adults, to the various hazards of fracking (air, water, soil, noise, threats to wildlife, etc.).[12] Their refusal to admit to environmental impacts and their feelings of invulnerability have significant short- and long-term consequences for the community and the surrounding ecosystem. Preparing for these public speaking opportunities, Wendy wracked her brain trying to think of convincing rhetorical strategies. It occurred to her that she could use her disability—her Parkinson's and what she contends is its likely causality, aerosolized spraying of cotton fields—as an analogous example to try to convince the audience of the community's vulnerability to harmful exposure to petroleum production's pollutants. She always emphasized the precautionary principle.[13] Alas, her argument was seldom convincing to the largely pro-fossil fuel and pro-oil and gas development block in her region.

In hindsight, she realizes that she learned so much from these experiences of vulnerability, coming out as a citizen activist with the disability of Parkinson's disease. In this time of environmental emergency due to global warming, it is critical that our citizens, politicians, civil servants, experts, and policymakers see our collective vulnerability as well as our strength. In this case they instead chose to believe that any environmental risk could be engineered out of existence.

Wendy analyzed why her strategy failed. Some in her audience were calloused by cynicism, others deluded by greed, and perhaps some had never learned the basics of ecological and environmental science. They seemed oblivious to our interconnectedness and comfortable in their denial.[14] Oth-

---

12　Adgate, Goldstein, and McKenzie, "Potential Public Health Hazards," 8307–20.

13　This seminal article's abstract defined the precautionary principle—"proposed as a new guideline in environmental decision making, has four central components: taking preventive action in the face of uncertainty; shifting the burden of proof to the proponents of an activity; exploring a wide range of alternatives to possibly harmful actions; and increasing public participation in decision making." David Kriebel, Joel Tickner, Paul Epstein, John Lemons, Richard Levins, Edward L. Loechler, Margaret Quinn, Ruthann Rudel, Ted Schettler, and Michael Stoto, "The Precautionary Principle in Environmental Science," *Environmental Health Perspectives* 109, no. 9 (2001): 871–76.

14　For a comparison of perceptions of climate change in Weld County and Larimer County, Colorado, see Amanda Paulson, "Why Climate Change Divides Us," *The Christian Science Monitor*, October 12, 2016, https://www.csmonitor.com/USA /Politics/2016/1012/Why-climate-change-divides-us.

ers were afraid of losing their livelihoods in fossil fuel-related industries.[15] People with disabilities can certainly relate to that fear of losing one's livelihood. Thinking through the situation compassionately, with an emphasis on building relationships and acknowledging vulnerability, helps us think of the humanity of those with whom we're in an adversarial relationship. From that viewpoint, we can see a new strategy—acknowledging our opponent's fears and offering job training and placement programs for those in the fossil fuel industries as part of public policy proposals to shift to renewable energy as soon as possible.

Wendy's story is a cautionary tale of miscommunication because of the inability to empathize with personal vulnerability to environmental hazards. The ability to empathize on an even greater, planetary scale is critical. It is essential that we as a society face the vulnerability of the planet Earth with regard to climate change. Policy expert Alex Ghenis at New Earth Disability, a non-governmental organization in Berkeley, California, suggests that people with disabilities are one of the most vulnerable groups to the effects of climate change.[16] We advocate that people with disabilities should be one of the most pro-actively consulted constituent groups in the political process regarding this issue.

What story comes to mind from your lived experience? Maybe you can think of an instance where being vulnerable in a work-related or other situation led to a successful outcome of some sort? Were you successful in redirecting and projecting nondisabled people's vulnerability and social dependency back at them? This deflection would correct the phenomenon noticed by Vic Finkelstein, that "the natural vulnerability of human beings has significantly shaped the development of all the machinery of modern life" and those qualities have been "deposited…into us as if this was unique to being disabled."[17] This correction is only the first step in confronting ableism and creating an inclusive workplace and world.

---

15 McCright finds that "identification with or trust in groups representing or defending the industrial capitalist system increases the likelihood of skepticism of the reality and human cause of climate change." Aaron M. McCright, "Anti-Reflexivity and Climate Change Skepticism in the US General Public," *Human Ecology Review* 22, no. 2 (2016): 77–107.

16 World Institute on Disability, "New Earth Disability (NED)," World Institute on Disability, September 25, 2018, https://wid.org/2018/09/25/ned/

17 Vic Finkelstein, "Emancipating Disability Studies," in *The Disability Reader: Social Science Perspectives*, ed. Tom Shakespeare (New York: Cassell, 1998), 29–30.

Quotidian Courage and Quite Ordinary Fatigue: Falling Off the Pedestal of Saintly Suffering

In the midst of these aspirational stories, we share a reality check: Some days, it is just too damned difficult to have a disability and there is nothing heroic about it—it is just hard! On those days we have no extra energy and oomph to educate anyone about the universality of vulnerability and interdependence.

On her good days, Wendy models acceptance and confidently performs in spite of mild to moderate symptoms. In contrast, on her worst day last semester, she had to reschedule a class at the last minute because her symptoms became suddenly, unexpectedly severe. The prospect of this happening more often causes her to seriously contemplate getting deep brain stimulation surgery to improve movement and minimize symptoms. On Wendy's bad days, she can't help but exhibit some impatience and chagrin. Those intermittently intense symptoms cause her to do a painfully awkward dance with her disability. While she believes she also displays a modicum of perseverance and courage, she feels obviously outfoxed by her brain's deficit of dopamine. The best way she can spin those days is to say that she is dispelling any stereotype of sainthood—and good riddance to that myth!

The Limbic Dragons: Disability Stereotypes and Implicit Bias

In the previous sections, we suggest that projections of vulnerability, dependency, and suffering sainthood be redirected back to the sender. This is easier said than done. The potential for prejudice persists and lurks like an untamed, fire-breathing dragon in our neural pathways. This internal monster exists to help us to persist. We humans have survived because we evolved with the ability to quickly process information. We are hardwired to notice irregularities and variations, and then to jump to conclusions. Our tendency is to interpret those differences as threats, thus enhancing our chances of survival. We all have the potential to behave like a fire-breathing dragon—we may say or do something monstrous, hurtful, or socially awkward, because we have concluded too quickly and wrongly. Our brain has a reptilian section that controls automatic functions such as reflexes and breathing; a neocortex in charge of thinking, attention, and abstract reasoning; and a prefrontal cortex controlling executive functions. But we also have the hyper-vigilant, emotionally centered limbic part which includes the amygdala. This part of the brain deals with the fight-flight-freeze response and scans for threats, so it is implicated in our formation of stereotypes and biases.[18]

When we stereotype, we generalize about a social group and categorize each member without considering individual differences. Similarly, implicit bias is a covert or unintentional preference for a particular group based on their social identity. These phenomena are powerful drivers of social interactions.[19] They are a type of heuristics. Heuristics are mental shortcuts that help us process lots of information very quickly. They evolved as a survival skill, enabling us to zero in on certain details and filtering out others. Unfortunately, we tend to exclude information that is contrary to what is already familiar and agreeable to us. These habitual, misguided ways of thinking become reinforced neural pathways and are difficult to change.[20] Then compound this conundrum with group behavior, including the additional layer of culture (shared values, morals, behaviors, customs, and worldviews held by a large group of people). The result is in-group behavior motivated by risk intuition which predisposes us to perceive as threatening those who are different from members of our group.[21]

Soon after she was diagnosed and began telling friends and co-workers about her Parkinson's disease, Wendy didn't know it consciously, but she had embarked on an observational study of behaviors influenced by the stereotypes and biases of ableism. Wendy was piqued, amused, bemused, and intrigued by the various reactions to her revelation of her disease. To cope with her feelings about these interactions (and following the orderly inclination of a librarian), Wendy started making a mental catalog of the responses she received upon revealing the nature of her disability to others. While she experienced many responses of kindness, and most reactions were benign, she also encountered some dragons.

The first dragon she encountered was the Woody Allen-esque Hypochondriac: this dragon identifies too much with you and your disabling condition. They might even go so far as to make an appointment with their physician for a checkup and to be tested for your condition, as if it were contagious.

---

18   Shakil Choudhury, *Deep Diversity: Overcoming Us vs. Them* (Toronto: Between the Lines, 2015), 35–37.

19   Choudhury, *Deep Diversity*, 49–50.

20   Choudhury, 52–54.

21   Choudhury, 77.

There was the dragon with the Knock-Wood and Kneel complex, expressed as "there but for the grace of God go I." This dragon compares their good health and non-disability favorably to your disabled condition; this serves as an indicator to them of their good fortune or perhaps a reward for their religiosity.

A cousin to the Knock-Wood and Kneel dragon, the Know-It-All, is distinguished by its scorching comments that minimize your experience, such as "everyone has something," and "God wouldn't give you more than you could handle."

Just when she thought it was safe to wander across the castle moat, Wendy met the Pity Partier. This maximizing monster exaggerates your illness or disability, and imagines you with one foot in the grave, subsisting on alms instead of disability insurance.

This amusing game helped to temporarily minimize the pain and somewhat diminish the power of others' projections. But it wasn't really all that amusing. Wendy felt burdened by the weight of the projections of fear, and upset by the pity, religiosity, and hypochondria. When she came upon psychologists Colella and Bruyere's list of eight "psychologically based theoretical reasons for biased treatment of people with disabilities," it was a very therapeutic discovery. Here was a well-researched, footnoted, dispassionately academic listing of the dragons that Wendy had been mentally cataloging.

Five of Wendy's cataloged mythical monsters matched up with five items on their list. Their "just world hypothesis" (the need to blame the disabled person so that belief can be maintained) matched her "Knock Wood and Kneel" pest; their "existential anxiety" (fear of their own development of a disability/illness) category matched her "Woody Allen-esque Hypochondriac." Their "norm to be kind" (exaggerated niceness) and "ambivalence response theory" (divergent reactions like pity, disgust, and nurturing) synched with her "Pity Partier." It was affirming to have her anecdotal experience confirmed by these researchers—that was the upside. But that was also the downside. To know these eight reasons was to perceive on some level the magnitude of the problem of bias. This realization was overwhelming; Wendy realizes there is so much to be confronted and changed. Colella and Bruyere list some of the stereotypes disabled people encounter:

> People hold negative stereotypes about people with disabilities that influence how they process and recall information about them. Stereotypes include helpless, benevolent, hypersensitive, inferior, depressed, distant, shy, unappealing,

unsociable, bitter, insecure, nonaggressive, unhappy, submissive, saintly, and less capable of competing. Specific stereotypes vary with type of disability.[22]

Given that this list of stereotypes is a well-documented, thoroughly researched list, and the result of a naturally hard-wired phenomenon, it is no wonder that the thought of disclosing one's disability can be daunting. Educating co-workers about these misconceptions could be exhausting and time intensive, ironically a full-time job in itself. Disabusing these dragons of their delusions and dowsing their inflammatory rhetoric could be a lifelong task. And does the responsibility for education about inclusion rest only on the disabled worker? Wendy wants to do more than mentally catalog the hurtful behavior. She's seen the dragons and she can describe their dastardly habits; now she wants to domesticate them, to significantly change their ways. She wants to ensure that all library workplaces are psychologically safe environments, ones in which disabled workers feel safe to disclose, ones in which disabled workers not only survive, but thrive.[23] Later in the chapter we will cite the research literature, but first we turn to the experiences of our interviewees, which are instructive.

When we ask one of our interviewees, Gene, if her attitude, her continuing "embrace" of her disability, has changed how people reacted to her, she responded by describing this interaction with a casual friend:

> They were talking to me about my disability and their mindset about disability was something along the lines of sympathy or pity, and there was also a little bit of religious perspective embedded in that. And that conversation really infuriated me because I realized that I am proud of the person that I am and I don't like being pitied by people. And also they…made it sound as though my disability was a flaw or something like that, and I didn't want people to view it that way because I don't feel like it's a flaw, I feel as though

---

22 Adrienne J. Colella and Susanne M. Bruyere, "Disability and Employment: New Directions for Industrial and Organizational Psychology," in *APA Handbook of Industrial and Organizational Psychology*, ed. Sheldon Zedeck (Washington, DC: American Psychological Association, 2011), 473–503.

23 Amy C. Edmondson, *The Fearless Organization: Creating Psychological Safety in the Workplace for Learning, Innovation, and Growth* (Hoboken, NJ: Wiley, 2019).

I was created that way that I'm supposed to be...after that conversation I realized that my disability was actually a positive for me, because it allows me to have empathy for other groups of people that are discriminated against.

Gene's reframing of her friend's judgment into a positive statement of the power of empathy is impressive. Gene changed what she could: herself and her attitude. When we decide to disclose our disability, or in situations when our disability is recognized, we need to be prepared for these responses. Then we can choose whether to deflect them, ignore them, react to them, educate about them, or correct them. But at some point, we may not have the energy to deal with them at all. And it should not be solely the responsibility of the individual; some of this education has to be undertaken on the organizational and societal levels, as we advocated in chapter 3. When we asked our interviewee Sam, a library worker with disabilities, what needs to change in their workplace in order to make it more inclusive, they brought up the importance of training:

Train employees about ableism and its relationship to library policies. That would reduce the number of little battles that I have to fight, to just get people up to speed on what ableism is and why it matters.

Sam expressed the importance of organization-wide education. Their comments acknowledge the drain on time and energy when education takes place on the individual level only. However, research shows that confronting biases and stereotypes is worth the time and energy, if you can muster it. Speaking up does make a difference. Researchers have discovered that people exhibit less bias in their behavior after they are challenged for such behavior.[24]

A Tool to Change the Odds: Targeted Norm Violations

While research shows that speaking up does make an impact, confronting people one at a time is not the only way. We can change more than one person at a time by violating the norms we consider harmful. Social

---

24 Alexander M. Czopp, Margo J. Monteith, and Aimee Y. Mark, "Standing Up for a Change: Reducing Bias through Interpersonal Confrontation," *Journal of Personality and Social Psychology* 90, no. 5 (2006): 784.

psychologist Dolly Chugh offers practical tips to tame this monster. She tells us how to coax it up from the unconscious, bring it out into the light, and extinguish its fire. She bases her self-help system on cultivating a "growth mindset" as opposed to a "fixed mindset." She defines "growth mindset" as a belief that we have the capacity to learn and improve with time, effort, and feedback. The growth mindset allows us to avoid the either/or thinking patterns in which the fixed mindset is entrenched.[25] She offers a system that can help us make quick decisions about how to react to biased behavior. She suggests we deploy the following decision tree. We can decide:

> WHOM to engage with (and whom not to); WHY are you engaging them (to change behavior or to change norms); HOW you engage (making your growth mindset visible to others); WHERE AND WHEN to engage (on the spot versus later, in public or in private); and WHAT you say (humanize or factualize).[26]

Chugh theorizes this rough breakdown of the human population: twenty percent of people will be resistant and drain your energy, another twenty percent will be enthused and supportive, and the middle sixty will be passive and silent. This milquetoast middle is your target group: they are susceptible to and influenced by social norms. This is where your attention can be focused and how you can be most optimally effective.[27] Thus, we don't even have to engage the dragon. We can consider it part of the resistant and energy-draining twenty percent. Instead, we should expend our energy upon communications with the convincible middle group members. While the numbers 20/60/20 are symbolic, not literal, they help us determine the scope of persuasive work we are willing to undertake. Educator Shakil Choudhury suggests that we unmask systemic discrimination by persistently asking four versions of the same question: what are the influences of emotions/bias/in-group positioning/power in this situation, group, or issue?[28]

---

25 Dolly Chugh, *The Person You Mean to Be: How Good People Fight Bias* (New York, NY: Harper Collins, 2018), 23–24.

26 Dolly Chugh, *The Person You Mean to Be*, 208.

27 P. Wesley Schultz, Jessica M. Nolan, Robert B. Cialdini, Noah J. Goldstein, and Vladas Griskevicius, "The Constructive, Destructive, and Reconstructive Power of Social Norms," *Psychological Science* 18, no. 5 (2007): 429–34.

28 Choudhury, *Deep Diversity*, 172.

Become Aware of Your Own Biases: "That Was a Good Mistake"

Mistakes are an important part of learning. To help people take the risks that can lead to meaningful learning, we need to praise them for trying regardless of the results. This helps us normalize mistakes as part of the learning process in a way that can help people avoid the intimidating, polarizing point of view that pits failure versus success.[29] Wendy shares this story of a powerful, game-changing professional development event at her workplace:

> A bias trainer visited our library and we did an exercise (essentially, a form of the Implicit Association Test)[30] in which we were presented with evocative photographs of diverse people in various situations, and we documented our gut reactions on post-it notes. The photograph that led me to expose my bias was of a man in grubby clothing accepting paper money from a nattily-dressed individual on an urban street corner. I had interpreted the exchange as a homeless person begging and receiving money from a wealthier passerby. During the discussion phase, I was presented with an alternative scenario. The grubby person was not homeless nor was he jobless. He was dressed in work-clothes that had become soiled during course of his workday, and he was giving money to the more neatly dressed individual [I can't recall the reason for the exchange, but it had nothing to do with poverty or homelessness]. This was incredibly enlightening. If I had judged so wrongly about this photograph, I knew that I could be wrong about a lot of other people and situations. The training was very cathartic and powerful for me because it burst through my veneer of propriety. I had biases! Yuck! But now I was aware of them, now we were getting somewhere—to the truth! What a good mistake I had made in revealing my bias to myself!

---

29 Dolly Chugh, *The Person You Mean to Be*, 136.

30 The Implicit Association Test is available free online at the Project Implicit website at https://implicit.harvard.edu. Here are the six key findings of Project Implicit: We all have implicit biases of which we are unaware; we differ in our levels of implicit bias; the biases predict behavior; group power can buffer or magnify bias; and minority groups internalize negative bias. Choudhury, *Deep Diversity*, 56–58.

In this training session, Wendy had discovered the "moral identity," the fact that we care about being a good person, as distinguished from whether we are in fact a good person.[31] When our energy is bound up in protecting this moral identity, we go to great lengths to protect this image. We employ our resources to preserve the binary of good versus bad and maintaining our standing in the former camp. Instead, it is a better use of our energy to admit that we are human, merely good-ish, and we need to continually work at becoming conscious of our bias and improving ourselves. This continual incremental practice is less taxing than clutching at the illusion that we are always good.[32] The more we work on ourselves, the more we can be helpful to others.

To prepare oneself for building a less biased, more inclusive world, social psychologist Dolly Chugh advises deploying the growth mindset. The growth mindset is an attitude that enables us to learn from our mistakes, and to experiment and innovate enough to make them. Chugh also recommends "using our ordinary privilege" to help others.[33] By this, she means that people with dominant group advantages need to get involved as advocates. For example, if you are part of the heterosexual group, it is likely that you can display pictures of your romantic partner at work without wondering if that is safe. Being part of that group also means that you can speak out for those who have minority sexual orientations with less risk. "Opt for willful awareness" is her third suggestion.[34] By this she encourages advocates to face the truth about exclusion and discrimination, instead of opting for willful ignorance. Finally, Chugh says that we can engage, meaning that we can take action, actually practicing what we preach, so that people with whom we work are truly included.

If a person with disabilities had co-workers with Chugh's growth mindset, the burden of teaching those co-workers about the realities of the quotidian experience of one's disabilities would be eased. If a person with disabilities had co-workers committed to using their privilege, being

---

31 Karl Aquino and Americus Reed, II, "The Self-Importance of Moral Identity," *Journal of Personality and Social Psychology* 83, no. 6 (2002): 1423; as cited in Dolly Chugh, *The Person You Mean to Be: How Good People Fight Bias* (New York, NY: Harper Collins, 2018).

32 Dolly Chugh and Mary C. Kern, "A Dynamic and Cyclical Model of Bounded Ethicality," *Research in Organizational Behavior* 36 (2106): 85–100.

33 Dolly Chugh, "Use Your Everyday Privilege to Help Others," *Harvard Business Review* (September 18, 2018), https://hbr.org/2018/09/use-your-everyday-privilege-to-help-others.

34 Dolly Chugh, *The Person You Mean to Be*, 19.

willfully aware, and engaging, a person with disabilities would feel safer to be vulnerable and reveal their disabilities. Researcher Amy Edmondson found that "the most important influence on psychological safety is one's manager." She recommends that leaders foster psychological safety by "acknowledging the limits of their current knowledge, displaying fallibility, highlighting failures as learning opportunities, and inviting participation."[35] If one is employed at a workplace in which psychological safety exists, then disclosure is not a terrifying prospect.

Why Disclosure Helps on So Many Levels

Why disclose? Psychologists at Rice University contend that disclosure of disability helps the person with disabilities for the following reasons: it furthers their personal well-being, creates the potential to have closer relationships with co-workers and supervisors, lowers stress by providing a sense of relief, and frees up cognitive resources that were devoted to secret maintenance and reallocates them to the tasks at hand. Other possible positive effects include decreased self-stigmatization, reduction of worry and concern, finding peers and family members who are supportive, and the promotion of a sense of personal power and control over one's life.[36]

Disclosure also helps others, in that accurate counts of people in categories and types of disabilities can be attained. And when disclosure is in a public forum, people are influenced in a positive way, becoming more accepting. Conditions become more relatable and less stigmatized. Organizations are helped by disclosure because it improves organizational policies and social norms. The more experience organizations have with disabled individuals, the more they are likely to continue those relationships in the present and future. And the earlier that individuals disclose, the more proactive organizations can be in their responses. Disclosure also has the potential to encourage organizations to implement universal design in the work environment. Disclosure helps globally, across our society, because it promotes a universal reduction of stigma.[37]

35 Amy Edmondson, "Psychological Safety and Learning Behavior in Work Teams," *Administrative Science Quarterly* 44, no. 2 (1999): 350–83.

36 Christine L. Nittrouer, Rachel C.E. Trump, Katharine Ridgway O'Brien, and Michelle Hebl, "Stand Up and Be Counted: In the Long Run, Disclosing Helps All," *Industrial and Organizational Psychology* 7, no. 2 (2014): 235–41.

37 Nittrouer, Trump, O'Brien and Hebl, "Stand Up and Be Counted," 235–41.

Jessica Violates Some Social Norms

Content warning references to gun violence.

Jessica came out to their coworkers about having mental illness in a work meeting. This wasn't an intentional act, but a reaction to their boss essentially blaming campus shootings on mentally ill people. This was said while he was leading a library leadership meeting. Quashing that ableistic rhetoric is hard, but if you can do it, it is important. Jessica pointed out that the vast majority of mentally ill people are nonviolent.[38] More mentally ill people have violence directed at them for their illness than the other way around.[39] Jessica didn't have enough time or composure to get into an analysis of how blaming mentally ill people for gun violence is a deliberate strategy to deflect responsibility away from slack gun regulations,[40] how it provides cover for the white supremacist and misogynistic men who engage in the vast majority of mass violence in the United States,[41] and how terroristic rampages, misogyny, and racism are not caused by mental illness—although those phenomena cause trauma that can lead to victims developing mental illness.[42]

Shortly after that meeting a coworker came up to Jessica to self-disclose privately and thanked Jessica for interrupting. Sometimes all we can do is interrupt the conversation, but even that little bit matters for the victims of ableist rhetoric. In this situation, Jessica was able to employ two strategies: they said something, and they broke the norm of not speaking truth to power during a meeting. If the boss leading the meeting was open to hearing the viewpoint, so much the better; but if not, Jessica influenced

---

38   "Mental illness and violence," *Harvard Mental Health Letter,* January 2011, https://www.health.harvard.edu/newsletter_article/mental-illness-and-violence.

39   Daven Morrison and Phillip Resnick, "Violence in the Workplace," *American Psychiatric Association Foundation Center for Workplace Mental Health,* 2012, http://www. workplacementalhealth.org/Mental-Health-Topics/Violence-in-the-Workplace.

40   Vivian Kane, "Trump Blames Mass Shootings on Mental Illness, 'the Media,' & Video Games," *The Mary Sue* August 5, 2019, https://www.themarysue.com/trump-blames-mass-shootings-on-everything-but-guns/.

41   Alison J. Marganski, "Making a Murderer: The Importance of Gender and Violence Against Women in Mass Murder Events," *Sociology Compass* 13, no. 9 (2019): e12730; Eric Madfis, "Triple Entitlement and Homicidal Anger: An Exploration of the Intersectional Identities of American Mass Murderers," *Men and Masculinities* 17, no. 1 (2014): 67–86.

42   Kwame McKenzie, "Racial Discrimination and Mental Health," *Psychiatry* 5, no. 11 (2006): 383–87.

a majority of the people (the "movable" symbolic sixty percent) in the room by breaking the norm and expressing a divergent opinion—they played to the crowd. Jessica advocated for themselves, spoke truth to power, and countered common misconceptions about mentally ill people. Thus, they bravely broke at least three social norms, making them visible and in the exponentially maximizing circumstance of doing this in front of a group.[43]

How Fragile We Are—Picking the Time and Place

Where are you in your identity formation as a person with disabilities?[44] Could you find the courage to spontaneously out yourself as Jessica did? Are you ready to disclose? You must determine the time to do so and to whom. The federally sponsored Job Accommodation Network offers helpful tips about disclosure, including suggestions about timing and selectivity of recipients.[45] The Michael J. Fox Foundation also offers advice about disclosure at the workplace.[46]

Remember that accommodation is a social process.[47] When the time comes to disclose at your workplace, to whom and how much about your disability will you reveal? You may reveal your disability to many: interviewers, supervisors, coworkers, clients, customers, patrons, students. Timing could be at application, when hired, during training, after a probationary period, when tenured, or perhaps only when you must, for the purpose of asking for accommodation. While irrational fears can be dismissed in the light of reason, socioeconomic realities can and should be explored

---

43   Choudhury, *Deep Diversity*, 85.

44   Anjali J. Forber-Pratt, Dominique A. Lyew, Carlyn Mueller, and Leah B. Samples, "Disability Identity Development: A Systematic Review of the Literature," *Rehabilitation Psychology* 62, no. 2, (2017): 198–207, https://doi.org/10.1037/rep0000134.

45   Job Accommodation Network, "Disability Disclosure," https://askjan.org/topics/Disability-Disclosure.cfm?csSearch=2430572_1.

46   Rachel Dolhun and Marti Fischer, "Sharing Your Parkinson's Diagnosis at Work: A Practical Guide," Michael J. Fox Foundation for Parkinson's Research (2017, May), https://files.michaeljfox.org/100915_MJFF_WORKPLACE.pdf; Rachel Dolhun and Marti Fischer, "Talking about Parkinson's at Work: A Practical Guide, Part 2: Managing Long-Term Professional Relationships," Michael J. Fox Foundation for Parkinson's Research (2017, May), https://files.michaeljfox.org/052617_MJFF_WORKPLACE_PT2.pdf.

47   For a description of a psychoeducational training that includes the supervisor, work group members, the people with disabilities, and the administrator who has authority to approve the accommodations, see Gates, "Workplace Accommodation as a Social Process," 85–98.

through financial inventory and remedies brainstormed with a certified financial planner or trusted rehab expert (see the socioeconomic section below). Is this a long-term disability, something you have dealt with your entire life, or you are newly diagnosed? Is your disability one that is prone to stigma? Have you gone through all the stages of denial, anger, bargaining, depression, acceptance? Where are you in your emotional process?

Wendy shares this story about the stigma of mental illness and its power in her psyche:

> I encourage you to pick your time to reveal. Be cautious, think it through (even though I didn't). I want to be especially cautionary about the stigma around mental illness. It is real, though not as universally pervasive as I imagined. As the sibling of a severely mentally ill sister (who is no longer living), I have direct experience of this. I can share that I internalized the stigma and it wasn't until my fifth decade that I could be open about having had a mentally ill family member. I can tell you that being open about it is much preferable to holding it as a secret. But I can also attest to the fact that the internalized stigma was a powerful force and it took years of soul searching, struggling with survivor's guilt, and some counseling to get to the point that I could be honest about this aspect of my life. I knew I was on the way to healing when, in my forties, I dreamed that my sister teasingly told me I "was not playing with a full deck." The fact that I feared inheriting mental illness for so many years (in the danger zone, teens and twenties), and instead came down with a neurological disorder, Parkinson's, is the ultimate irony. Now that I have experienced the vagaries of neurochemistry, I finally have the level of compassion for my sister that I wish I had when she was alive. I tell this story not to berate myself, but to help you, the reader, to understand and work diligently at recognizing your own biases and tendency to stigmatize or self-stigmatize when it comes to mental illness and families of mentally ill people.[48]

Sometimes, though, the stigma is so powerfully repressive that we feel we have no choice. Our interviewee Barbara frankly discussed the stigma she has encountered regarding her mental illness:

---

48   NAMI, the National Alliance on the Mentally Ill, is a good resource for family members: www.nami.org.

I think my mental illness and being African American has been hard…and working class; there's no one to really talk to because it's so shunned in our community. You don't have time to have a mental illness. You need to go to work. Black people don't get mental illnesses.

Barbara's lived experience demonstrates the power and pervasive hurtfulness of stigma when it intersects with poverty, race, and austerity. In such a precarious environment, the acknowledgement of emotional distress is a forbidden indulgence. Compassionate treatment is so out of reach economically and socially that it is considered an unimaginable luxury. Untreated mental illness is a significant problem. We contend that universal healthcare for all illnesses, including mental illness, should be a right and not a privilege, something affordable for all.

Precarity, Privilege, Production, and Socioeconomic Class

Financial precarity can be one of the most difficult issues with which to wrestle. When one's livelihood is threatened, the fear of poverty can be a constant low-grade terror, causing one to dread the future and resist the loss of control. Mindfulness training encourages us to live calmly in the present moment and not dwell upon the uncertain future. Yet it is difficult not to envision a financial debacle. This fear of financial precarity can be approached two ways. We can tackle this head on and "buy into the system" in a pragmatic manner by diagnosing our financial health, making a financial survival plan, and learning about the social safety net.[49] We can inventory our monetary assets, assess our social capital and get help from support groups, nonprofits, and foundations.[50] How are we positioned? Why isn't the middle class more comfortable? Why don't we feel safe?

---

49 Andrew I. Batavia and Richard Beaulaurier, "The Financial Vulnerability of People with Disabilities: Assessing Poverty Risks," *Journal of Sociology & Social Welfare* 28, no. 1 (2001): 139–62.

50 There are many financial planning resources available on the web. We've listed a few here that provide proactive planning resources for people with disabilities. Council for Disability Awareness, https://disabilitycanhappen.org/; National Disability Institute, https://www.nationaldisabilityinstitute.org/wp-content/uploads/2018/11/supplemental-guide-adult-instructor.pdf; Consumer Protection Financial Division of the U.S. Government: "Your Money, Your Goals: Focus on the Disability Community: A Companion Guide to Empower the Disability Community," https://files.consumerfinance.gov/f/documents/cfpb_ymyg_focus-on-people-with-disabilities.pdf.

Most library workers fall somewhere in the middle-class income range. The median librarian's wage of $59,050 and the library assistant's wage of $29,640 puts paraprofessional library workers in the lower middle class wage tier and professional librarians in the middle echelons of the middle class wage tier (if a household size of one).[51] This position in the wage hierarchy is then modified by inherited family wealth, or the lack thereof. Even though statistics show that upward mobility is largely mythological, library science professor Christine Pawley contends that this illusion motivates the middle class as well as the library profession. Middle class library workers gain monetary assets from their relationship to institutions, as well as skills, education, and organizational infrastructure. They also accumulate moral assets, the privilege "to determine the moral agenda, to decide what counts as good character and ethical behavior. A major preoccupation of the middle class is to retain and accumulate these assets and to pass them on to new recruits."[52]

If we recognize the brutality of unfettered free market capitalism, we can begin to fight this on another front—not by counting our coins but by modifying the market driven neoliberal capitalist system, making it more fair. However, Pawley cautions that "the class perspective is not cheering. Short of revolution, it fails to present solutions to problems of exploitation and inequality."[53] The Marxist viewpoint is adamantly unequivocal: "Because ability is defined in direct relation to one's capacity to enable the accumulation of capital and prejudicial attitudes are a byproduct of the social relations of production, it is clear that liberation from ableism is not possible within a capitalist economy."[54]

---

51   Bureau of Labor Statistics, United States Department of Labor, *Occupational Outlook Handbook*, "Librarians" https://www.bls.gov/ooh/education-training-and-library/librarians.htm; "Library Technicians and Assistants," https://www.bls.gov/ooh/education-training-and-library/library-technicians-and-assistants.htm; Richard Fry and Rakesh Kochhar, "Are You in the American Middle Class?" PEW Research Center, https://www.pewresearch.org/fact-tank/2018/09/06/are-you-in-the-american-middle-class/.

52   Christine Pawley, "Hegemony's Handmaid? The Library and Information Studies Curriculum from a Class Perspective," *Library Quarterly* 68, no. 2 (1998): 123–44.

53   Christine Pawley, "Hegemony's Handmaid," 138.

54   Laura Jaffee, "Marxism and Disability Studies," in *Encyclopedia of Educational Philosophy and Theory*, ed. M.A. Peters (Singapore: Springer Science, 2016).

As we work toward economic reforms, or plot to peacefully over-throw the system, we must live—and it is expensive to be disabled.[55] Many people with disabilities experience poverty. Federal statistics indicate that "more than 60 percent of people with disabilities ages 25–64 have no savings for unexpected expenses that they can turn to in a time of crisis."[56] All of the people we interviewed mentioned that access to health care had a huge influence on their employment decisions. Our interviewee, Barbara, frankly discussed her financial predicament:

> ...having disabilities is unaffordable, period, end of story, end of essay, end of dissertation, it is unaffordable. I live on a shoestring budget, and people are shocked, because I earn as much as my colleagues. "Why can't you buy a house?"..."Because the [amount of] money you spent on that trip to Europe went to my meds, went to my ten doctors."

Barbara's candid recounting of her discussions with colleagues reveals the need for education of all workers—nondisabled and those with disabilities—with regard to socioeconomic factors surrounding disability. The precarious financial circumstances experienced by many people with disabilities profoundly affects their decisions with regard to disability disclosure and asking for workplace accommodations. Is it fair to expect them to risk their livelihood when they lack personal savings, access to affordable housing, solvent retirement funds, single-payer health insurance, adequate disability insurance, or inherited wealth? The fear of poverty is a powerful motivator to overwork and keep one's head down.

Dialing It Down: Integrating Self-Compassion and the Capitalist Identity

In chapter 3, Wendy shared her story of her proclivity to work too hard. While she consciously tries to balance work and life, she derives ego strength

---

55 The comparable stress-related consequences for people of lower-class levels is staggering and ignored in our culture. See William Ming Liu, Theodore Pickett, Jr. and Allen E. Ivey, "White Middle-Class Privilege: Social Class Bias and Implications for Training and Practice," *Journal of Multicultural Counseling and Development* 35, no. 4 (2007): 194–206.

56 Consumer Protection Financial Division of the U.S. Government, "Your Money, Your Goals: Focus on People with Disabilities: A Companion Guide to Empower the Disability Community," March 2019, https://files.consumerfinance.gov/f/documents /cfpb_ymyg_focus-on-people-with-disabilities.pdf.

from the mythos of the hard-working superwoman: think super-heroes Lynda Carter of *Wonder Woman*, Jamie Sommers of *Bionic Woman*. The magnetic pull of the dominant culture's veneration of rugged individualism and independence can be mesmerizing. Dustin Galer studied the ethos of capitalism as it manifests in people with disabilities and articulated how we feel the same societal pressures to think of ourselves in the same individualistic, competitive ways as our nondisabled peers. Autonomy and independence are provided in exchange for something. Most of us are required to engage in paid work to get the money we need to stay alive. This inherently creates friction within disability communities between those who want to and can engage in the capitalist labor markets and those who want to create a shared identity in pursuit of civil rights.[57] The realities of our lives are much more nuanced, protracted, and unresolved than the cartoon experience of a bout with an evil villain and the triumphant conclusion enabled by a super-hero's sudden burst of strength. Behave like a super-hero (in other words, abuse your body with overwork), and your body will present a bill in the form of stress-related illness. We advocate for the primacy of the body's needs and a balance of life and work.

Engineering a Safe Workplace in Which to Disclose

Content warning Includes ableist slurs.

Fear of poverty is a strong motivating force for disabled people. Fear is also heavily involved in the disclosure-related decision-making processes of people with hidden disabilities. What factors are predominant in the decision to disclose? Research on disability disclosure indicates that that the supervisee's relationship with their supervisor is the most important factor facilitating disclosure. Disabled employees are more likely to disclose their disability if their relationship with their supervisor is positive. Additionally, the culture of the workplace and its commitment to including people with disabilities also influence disclosure decisions.[58]

---

57 Dustin Galer, "Disabled Capitalists: Exploring the Intersections of Disability and Identity Formation in the World of Work," *Disability Studies Quarterly* 32, no. 3 (2012), http://dsq-sds.org/article/view/3277/3122; Teodor Mladenov, "Performativity and the Disability Category: Solving the *Zero Theorem*," *Critical Sociology* (2018): 1–14.

58 Sarah von Schrader, Valerie Malzer, and Susanne Bruyère, "Perspectives on Disability Disclosure: The Importance of Employer Practices and Workplace Climate," *Employee Responsibilities and Rights Journal* 26, no. 4 (2014): 237.

Research reveals that facilitators and barriers to disability disclosure exist on several levels. At the individual level, knowledge of workplace rights and self-advocacy skills can encourage people to disclose. On the other hand, severity of disability, poor self-concept, and lack of advocacy skills can lead people not to disclose. At the organizational level, training and effective communication with employers can encourage people to disclose. Poor working conditions and lack of support, however, discourage people from disclosing. Finally, at the societal level, when the community demonstrates positive attitudes toward people with disabilities, disabled people feel safer. When stigma and discrimination are rampant, people are less likely to disclose.[59]

We can find insights into the sense of precarity that workers with mental disorders experience, due to high levels of stigma associated with mental illness, both from talking with them and by reviewing existing research. In a qualitative study, scholars Kate Toth and Carolyn Dewa interviewed thirteen workers diagnosed with mental disorders[60] about their decision-making process regarding whether to disclose their disorder at their workplace, a post-secondary educational institution in Canada. The researchers discovered that workers with mental health disabilities perceived the key problem was fear of stigma. Participants brought up their perception that mental health issues are more severely stereotyped and stigmatized than physical disabilities; they worried they would be treated differently if they disclosed. They were concerned that people would think they were incompetent, that it was their fault for not being able to fix themselves, or that they are faking it and/or trying to manipulate the system. Privacy and confidentiality were added concerns; they wanted to keep a boundary between their home and work lives and feared that confidentiality would not be honored if they disclosed.[61]

---

59 Sally Lindsay, Elaine Cagliostro and Gabriella Carafa, "A Systematic Review of Workplace Disclosure and Accommodation Requests among Youth and Young Adults with Disabilities," *Disability and Rehabilitation* 40, no. 25 (2018): 2971–86.

60 The researchers note in their discussion of study limitations that these workers were diagnosed with common mental disorders (e.g., anxiety and mood disorders) as contrasted with more severe mental disorders (e.g., schizophrenia). Kate E. Toth and Carolyn S. Dewa, "Employee Decision-making about Disclosure of a Mental Disorder at Work," *Journal of Occupational Rehabilitation* 24, no. 4 (2014): 744.

61 Toth and Dewa, "Employee Decision-making," 732–46.

A key finding of the study was that non-disclosure was the default position, until a triggering incident occurred and the person with the disorder was motivated to make a decision. Most participants made disclosure decisions spontaneously, in the moment. The participants' decision-making processes shared a common pattern. First, the triggering incident occurred. Second, the participant gathered information and the reasons to disclose fell into these categories: interpersonal (the desire to be altruistic and to share reciprocally), work-related (their disability was affecting work and sharing would facilitate better understanding of the situation), or personal (they desired to be more authentic and not carry the burden of keeping a secret). Third, the worker assessed conditions surrounding disclosure. They looked at interpersonal, work, and personal conditions. They judged whether the person to whom they would disclose was likely to be understanding and supportive; could they be trusted and would they be non-judgmental? Trust was the bottom line.[62] The way this decision-making is presented implies that it's a linear, one-time process. However, thinking back to Jessica's and Wendy's stories of times they self-disclosed and their reasons for doing so, we can see that disclosure can occur multiple times and in a variety of circumstances.

The creation of an environment of trust in which disabled workers are psychologically safe to disclose is no simple process. It needs to counter deep-seated, stigmatizing attitudes. Knowledge is not enough: "We need to go beyond simple education to provide concrete tools and strategies that managers can use to address challenges related to working with employees diagnosed with mental disorders."[63] Business and mental health researchers Toth and Dewa recommend implementing robust training programs and ongoing troubleshooting. Their recommendations inform the next few paragraphs.

We need to promote mental health in the workplace by proactively creating organizational conditions that enhance mental health. We need to be systematically vigilant in detecting mental health risks. Those mental health risks include an unsupportive work climate, a pattern of supervisory mishandling of sensitive situations, and poor enforcement of positive behavioral expectations.

Managers need to disseminate accurate information that confronts disability stereotypes. Specifically, managers need to affirm that employees

---

62 Toth and Dewa, 743–44.

63 Toth and Dewa, 744.

with disabilities are competent at their jobs, that their disability is not their fault, and that they are not faking.

Employees also need to be told that disabilities are real, whether they are physical or mental. It is hurtful to gossip about coworkers' mental illnesses, and related to that, slurs like "crazy" don't belong in the workplace. Employees also need guidance in knowing what kinds of responses are welcome, if a coworker with disabilities has consented to public disclosure. If employees understand the nuance of the body-mind perspective, they can see the folly and unfairness of assigning greater stigma to mental illness than to physical ailments or impairments, let alone assigning any stigma at all.[64]

Going back to Toth and Dewa's recommendations, supervisors need to recognize the power imbalance inherent in the supervisory role. They need to learn how to demonstrate openness, understanding, supportiveness, and trustworthiness. They also need to learn how to respond to behavioral changes and claims of harassment in a helpful way. Managers also need training to identify employees who may be in difficulty and assist them during times of absenteeism, performance problems, leaves of absence, and returns to work.

Toth and Dewa advocate that these tools and strategies be widely deployed because everyone in the organization needs awareness raising, education, and fear reduction in regard to mental illness in the workplace.[65] While these recommendations were taken from research focused on employees with mental illness, we think they are helpful in responding to a variety of different types of disability. Jessica, for example, has personally had all of the stereotypes mentioned above directed at them because of their diabetes.

To create a "fearless organization" means that "interpersonal fear is minimized so that team and organizational performance can be maximized in a knowledge intensive world."[66] This is not just the work of people in formal leadership roles, but also part of the interpersonal work of relationship building. To create an environment of psychological safety, "Sometimes, all you have to do is ask a good question. This is truly a great place to start. A good question is motivated by genuine curiosity or by a desire to give someone a voice. Questions cry out for answers. They create a vacuum that serves

---

64 Margaret Price, "The Bodymind Problem and the Possibilities of Pain," *Hypatia* 30, no. 1 (2015): 268–84.

65 Toth and Dewa, "Employee Decision-making about Disclosure," 744.

66 Edmondson, *The Fearless Organization*, xv.

as a voice opportunity for someone…A small safe zone is automatically created."[67] We library workers know this already, but it is helpful to have it confirmed by Edmondson, an expert on leadership, teams, and organizational learning. Haven't we all expressed this genuine curiosity? Don't we often give our library users a voice when we say the proverbial, "There are no dumb questions" in response to an insecure inquiry tentatively prefaced with the phrase, "This might be a dumb question, but…"?

Those in leadership do play important roles in this work. To create a culture of interdependence, reminding people that "the work is uncertain, challenging, or interdependent—helps paint reality in ways that emphasize that no one is supposed to have all the answers. This lowers the hurdle for speaking up. It reminds people that their input is welcome—because it's needed."[68] Again, this recommended behavior plays into library workers' strengths. We don't expect all the answers to come from one single source. We already know this from our library training and experience. Full implementation of an interdependent ethos is within our reach as it is already a viable part of our organizational culture. We understand the difference between being authoritative and authoritarian. Libraries are already hotbeds of pluralism. They can also become oases of psychological safety.

The following phrases make the workplace feel safer: "I don't know; I need help; I made a mistake; I'm sorry."[69] They increase safety because each expresses vulnerability. Anyone can engage in this practice, but people in formal leadership roles can serve as important models for this. You can let people know that it's ok to be human and make mistakes by acknowledging and apologizing for your own missteps. You are taking an interpersonal risk to lower interpersonal risk. Again, library workers can access this healthy humility. We are practiced at saying that we don't know the answer. And better yet, we are resourceful and persistent and will pursue the needed information or answer.

As we said at the beginning of this chapter, perhaps the most radical and healing thing we can do for ourselves, our workplace, and the planet is to communicate honestly about our vulnerability in carefully chosen moments and also at times of spontaneous improvisation. We can all be interpersonal risk takers, formulators of powerful questions, and creators of safe

---

67 Edmondson, 199.

68 Edmondson, 199.

69 Edmondson, 200.

zones. By giving voice to our vulnerability, we are, indeed, exercising our strength and exhibiting leadership from the ground up. We do this for our library users every day. We just need to channel the same type of energy toward advocacy for the full inclusion and accommodation for ourselves and our disabled peers.

In/dependence

Kim Nielsen's *A Disability History of the United States* exposes our cultural history, the American mythology in which "the idealized notion holds that we are a nation of Horatio Algers, perpetual train engines chugging up the hill, insisting that we can do it ourselves."[70] Nielsen points out the ableist foundations of this mythology, in which our country was supposedly built by independent, strong men unsullied by weakness or need for other humans. Thinking back to the disability models discussed in chapter 1, human relationships in the Horatio Alger mythology were viewed in moral terms, in which independence was good and dependence was bad. Aside from not being a very accurate view, it fostered a societal devaluation of interdependence and mutually supportive relationships with each other. We can see the threads of this cultural mythology incorporated into neoliberalism, in which the "individualized neoliberal subject is said to be empowered through market choices yet the corollary is that inequalities and other miscarriages of justice are defined away."[71]

In "Jerusalem" (1810), the poet Blake mourns the loss of Edenic agrarian communities, their interdependent craft guilds replaced by the Satanic mills of the Industrial Revolution. Anthropologist Mircea Eliade notes the many multi-cultural examples of creation myths with the theme of an idyllic work-free paradise preceding a fall into a realm where humankind is sentenced to hard labor for life.[72] Where work is concerned, the human experience seems, in this viewpoint, to universally involve suffering. A question we want you to consider is: Do these mythologies and rhetorical strategies that embed suffering as part of the nature of work help you?

---

70   Kim E. Nielsen, *A Disability History of the United States* (Boston: Beacon Press, 2013), iii.

71   Nathaniel F. Enright, "The Violence of Information Literacy: Neoliberalism and the Human as Capital," *Information Literacy and Social Justice: Radical Professional Praxis* (Sacramento: Library Juice Press, 2013), 21.

72   Mircea Eliade, *The Myth of the Eternal Return* (Princeton: Princeton University Press, 1954).

Or do they benefit those in power? As Maura Seale notes in her critique of current models of information production, power operates by elevating certain types of discourse over others.[73]

We resist this elevation of dehumanizing discourse when we ask questions. By asking questions, we are creating space for someone else to speak. Although we are currently entrenched in capitalism and our organizations are becoming corporatized in this neoliberal era, we ask you to make space for your voice. In the midst of this rapid change, what disappoints you? For what do you mourn? What are your demands? We advise you to expand upon that small safe zone these questions have created: don't agonize, organize! In the next few chapters we will examine organizing in multiple ways: coming out as self-advocates or allies and reaching outside the organization to build a social movement. There is hope for the future.

---

73   Maura Seale, "The Neoliberal Library," *Information Literacy and Social Justice: Radical Professional Praxis*, ed. Lua Gregory and Shana Higgins (Sacramento: Library Juice Press, 2013), 51.

Chapter 5

Accommodations, Advocacy, and Doing What Works

To Accommodate: The Dynamism of Adaptation, Compromise, and Creative Space

To accommodate is a transitive verb. *To accommodate* is one body adjusting itself to provide something to another body. It is someone with resources or power providing something to another person without those resources or that power. Accommodations are an authorized and bureaucratic way of changing a normative process to "accommodate" people who can't follow the norm for whatever reason—in this context, due to a disability. In U.S. workplaces, accommodations are provided in accordance with the Americans with Disabilities Act (ADA or the Act)[1] or other federal laws, such as section 504 of the Rehabilitation Act,[2] or state-level civil rights laws.

Another meaning of *to accommodate* is to make a settlement or compromise. Ironically, ADA's genesis encompasses a series of political compromises, and the subsequent implementation of the Act falls short of the ideals of its progenitors. Also, the ADA recommends an interactive process in which desired accommodations may be negotiated between employee and employer, and a mutually satisfactory compromise might be reached.

---

1   Americans with Disabilities Act of 1990, Public Law 101–336, 101st Congress (July 26, 1990); Americans with Disabilities Act Amendments Act of 2008, Public Law 110–325, 110th Congress (September 25, 2008), https://www.eeoc.gov/laws/statutes/adaaa.cfm.

2   Section 504 of the Rehabilitation Act of 1973, 29 U.S.C. § 701 *et seq.* (1973) (amended 1998).

Finally, a third meaning of *to accommodate* is to provide space for habitation. In this context, we are concerned with the provision of adequate space for one's working life to unfold. Ideally, the worker's full potential will be realized in terms of productivity and creativity. This chapter will explore all three meanings of accommodations, aspiring to help the reader find nurturing, spacious accommodations in and by which to realize their full potential.

The Legislative History of the Americans with Disabilities Act

Congress passed the ADA in 1990, almost thirty years ago. It was hailed as bipartisan civil rights legislation and endorsed by disability rights activists, President George H. W. Bush, and Democratic and Republican representatives and senators.[3] The ADA targeted discrimination that excluded and marginalized people with disabilities. It was intended to increase the participation of people with disabilities in the workplace and public life. But many scholars feel the implementation of the Act failed to achieve these goals. They base this judgment on the decline and stagnation of employment rates for people with disabilities since 1990; some go further and suggest that the Act caused the decline. Other scholars claim that judicial decisions have constrained the protective potential of the ADA. Still others blame selective enforcement and organizational avoidance.[4]

The ADA was the culmination of a century of lobbying and legislation for civil rights and the creation of a social safety net for people with disabilities. In 1920, following the example of rehabilitation provided for World War I veterans, the Smith-Fess Act (also known as the Civilian Vocational Rehabilitation Act) established rehabilitative services for civilians. Subsequently, the Social Security Act passed in 1935, and the Fair Labor Standards Act set the minimum wage in 1938. Mid-century, in 1954, Vocational Rehabilitation Amendments passed and expanded services, and Social Security Disability followed in 1956. The concept of "accommodations" did not appear in the law until 1978, in section 504 of the

3   Lennard J. Davis, *Enabling Acts: The Hidden Story of How the Americans with Disabilities Act Gave the Largest U.S. Minority Its Rights* (Boston: Beacon Press, 2015).

4   Paul R. Durlak, "Disability at Work: Understanding the Impact of the ADA on the Workplace," *Sociology Compass* 11, no. 5 (2017), https://doi.org/10.1111/soc4.12475.

amendments to the Rehabilitation Act[5]. In 1983, the Job Accommodation Network (JAN) came into being.[6] JAN's utility will be discussed later in this chapter.

Less Government, More Litigation

A look at the history of the drafting and passage of the ADA provides the political and social context to explain the imperfections of policy development and implementation. Part of the success of its passage is due to the cooperative efforts of a broad base of organizations representing people with many types of disabilities. It is also due to the formation of "cross-disability" groups or coalitions.[7] The passage of the Act was the result of a decades-long accretion of events, but it began to solidify with the drafting of the report *Toward Independence* by the National Council on the Handicapped in 1986. This report contained an outline of the proposed ADA legislation.[8] In January of 1988, the Council published its follow-up to *Toward Independence*, titled *On the Threshold of Independence*. The follow-up report included the first full version of the Act. The proposed ADA legislation was introduced to Congress in the Spring of 1988 by sympathetic members who were key disability advocates, including Senator Lowell Weicker and Representative Tony Coelho.[9]

Political scientist Jennifer Erkulwater describes the central compromise that emerged during the politicking for the ADA in the 1980s, an era that reflected the cost-cutting, conservative stances of the Reagan and George H. W. Bush presidential administrations. Social services and entitlement programs were under great scrutiny and constant attack. As a result, disability advocates modified their demands in order to get bipartisan

---

5   Mark C. Weber, "Disability Discrimination by State and Local Government: The Relationship Between Section 504 of the Rehabilitation Act and Title II of the Americans with Disabilities Act," *William & Mary Law Review* 36, no. 3 (1995): 1095, https://scholarship.law.wm.edu/wmlr/vol36/iss3/4/.

6   U.S. Department of Labor, "ADA Timeline Alternative," https://www.dol.gov/featured/ada/timeline/alternative.

7   Laura Rothstein, "Would the ADA Pass Today?: Disability Rights in an Age of Partisan Polarization," *Saint Louis University Journal of Health Law & Policy* 12, no. 2 (2019): 274.

8   Thomas F. Burke, *Lawyers, Lawsuits, and Legal Rights: The Battle over Litigation in American Society* (University of California Press, 2002), 76.

9   Burke, *Lawyers, Lawsuits, and Legal*, 77–78.

support: "Disability rights advocates largely jettisoned the call for a comprehensive social safety net that could facilitate community integration for people who would otherwise become institutionalized."[10] To woo conservatives, advocates repeated the rhetoric that "the ADA would lead to self-reliance and reduce welfare dependency."[11] They emphasized the cost to comply with the law would not fall upon the federal government, but would be passed down to state and local governments and would also fall upon the private sector.[12] In fact, legal scholar Thomas Burke goes so far to say that "for the Reagan and Bush officials the ADA was a kind of welfare reform."[13]

Scholars look back in hindsight and find irony in the adoption of the pro-litigious ADA. The Act appealed "even to politicians who campaign against litigiousness" because not only did it push costs away from the federal level, "in a nation highly distrustful of government" and leaning toward libertarianism, it provided "a mechanism for addressing social problems without seeming to expand the state."[14] In hindsight, the rhetoric that touted the Act as a panacea that would pay for itself was inflated and much too good to be true.

Pick Your Process: Interactive or Adversarial

The ADA was amended in 2008 to expand the definition of "disability," as several court decisions had narrowed the definition.[15] The Act's reliance upon litigation has a downside: "long delays before reaching resolution of cases, high costs associated with resolving a dispute, unpredictable penalties, and distrust and defensiveness on the part of employers."[16] Legal scholar Amy Knapp explains that the intent of the originators of ADA was

---

10   Jennifer L. Erkulwater, *Disability Rights and the American Social Safety Net* (Ithaca, NY: Cornell University Press, 2006), 167.

11   Erkuwater, *Disability Rights*, 170.

12   Erkulwater, 170.

13   Burke, *Lawyers*, 95.

14   Burke, 98.

15   Durlak, "Disability at Work," 3–4.

16   Erkulwater, *Disability Rights*, 232.

to fight paternalism and support the social model of disability.[17] She believes the ADA needs further amendments that would emphasize the interactive process. The type of amendments for which Knapp advocates go beyond merely recommending an interactive process, instead making it a requirement. The process she suggests is focused on both reasonable accommodations and essential job functions.

Knapp contends that this adjustment would remove the current emphasis upon the "real or perceived shortcomings of an individual with a disability, place the focus back onto society, and serve to better integrate individuals with disabilities into the workplace."[18] As it stands now, it is up to the employee to trigger the interactive accommodative process. Knapp feels this should change: "If an employer knows or should know that an employee has a disability, the interactive process should take place regardless of whether the employee has requested a reasonable accommodation. It would be in both parties' best interest to discuss the essential functions of the job and what reasonable accommodations might be available."[19]

Knapp's proposition is an interesting one. As it stands now, the employee is the initiator of the process. This role gives the employee some power, but also can be a negative if the employee procrastinates, perhaps out of fear or a lack of understanding of the process. Putting the onus upon employers makes provision of accommodations a proactive obligation. However, the danger of this proposal is that it might grant employers more surveillance and sanctioning power, and also give them the right to label employees as disabled when the employee in question might not consent to that label. The interactive process will be discussed in more detail throughout this chapter.

Top Down Challenges: President Trump and the EEOC

Change is a constant with regard to the ADA, as court decisions provide interpretations that morph and mold the implementation of the Act. Additionally, lobbyists and legislators can propose changes to the law. Chief executives also exert influence. The current President of the United States

---

17   Amy Knapp, "The Danger of the 'Essential Functions:' Requirement of the ADA: Why the Interactive Process Should Be Mandated," *Denver University Law Review* 90, no. 3 (2012): 718.

18   Knapp, "The Danger of the 'Essential Functions' Requirement of the ADA," 737.

19   Knapp, 736.

is openly hostile toward people with disabilities. Scholars document the record of President Donald Trump's interactions with people with disabilities in the time period just prior to his presidency:

> The main engagement of the Trump campaign with disability has been confrontational and insulting through direct statements from the candidate. His blatant mocking of the physical disability of *New York Times* reporter Serge Kovaleski in November 2015 gained a great amount of attention and condemnation. Trump imitated Kovaleski's body language in a 'jerky fashion'...claiming that he 'felt sorry for the guy,' though he denied this despicable behavior in spite of recorded evidence.[20]

We mention elsewhere that employer attitudes about disability impact the successful implementation of accommodations. Because the United States President is in charge of the executive branch of government, the person in that role indirectly supervises thousands of employees. That person also influences the actions of other legislators and employers. Unfortunately, the current Chief Executive's hostility to the rights of people with disabilities is well documented: "President Trump... is at the forefront of encouraging his administration to dismantle the regulatory underpinnings that make disability policy as effective as it is."[21]

Activists for the rights of people with disabilities need the broad-based political support and positive actions of members of both parties, local and state-level politicians, and all three branches of federal government, especially the Chief Executive, who leads the country and sets the tone. The Equal Employment Opportunity Commission (EEOC), part of the executive branch, is charged with ensuring employment equity and has the power to enforce the Act.[22]

---

20 Stephanie Cork, Paul T. Jaeger, Shannon Jette, and Stefanie Ebrahimoff, "The Politics of (Dis)Information: Crippled America, the 25th Anniversary of the Americans with Disabilities Act (ADA), and the 2016 U.S. Presidential Campaign," *The International Journal of Information, Diversity, and Inclusion* 1, no. 1 (2016): 1–15, https://doi.org/10.33137/ijidi.v1i1.32186.

21 Rothstein, "Would the ADA Pass Today?" 290.

22 U.S. Equal Employment Opportunity Commission, "Laws Enforced by EEOC," https://www.eeoc.gov/laws/statutes/index.cfm.

Legal scholar Samuel Bagenstos surmises that since the signing of the ADA in 1990, two decades hence, people with disabilities have not made great gains. He blames this on inadequate enforcement of the ADA and on the inability of antidiscrimination laws to effect deep social change. He recommends that the EEOC deploy testers to ferret out employers who discriminate during the hiring stage. He also recommends that activists go beyond antidiscrimination law and lobby for social welfare interventions that are "tailored to promote employment, integration, and community participation, and to avoid unnecessary paternalism and dependence."[23]

Thomas Burke, another legal scholar, explains that the EEOC, the chief enforcer of the ADA, is inadequately funded and only investigates a small portion of submitted claims. It bureaucratically processes complaints instead of taking a proactive stance to defend people with disabilities and order positive changes. Like Erkulwater, Burke highlights the shadow side of the Act's litigious consequences: "Because unsatisfied EEOC complainants can easily move on to the federal courts if they wish, courts have taken center stage in ADA enforcement. The Supreme Court has been particularly active, in one crucial case overriding the EEOC's own interpretation of the law. Overall the record of ADA plaintiffs in court has been dismal, a fact that has surprised and saddened disability advocates."[24]

Clearly, the ADA, in current form and practice, is not a panacea. What can we do on an individual level to influence the implementation of federal laws? What can we do to improve the laws? We can get involved with and be active in cross-disability coalitions and lobby our senators and representatives. But how do we cope with the situation here and now? In the next section, we will explore the lived experience of a library worker who attempted the accommodations process.

Accommodations in the Library Work Environment

In libraries, the accommodations you receive are typically negotiated with your human resources department, or your accommodations specialist if your workplace has one, or with your supervisor. There is not much written about how the accommodations process works from the perspective of the recipient, including only one article from the perspective of a library

---

23 Samuel R. Bagenstos, *Law and the Contradictions of the Disability Rights Movement* (Yale University Press, 2009), 136.

24 Burke, *Lawyers*, 100.

worker.[25] In that article, J.J. Pionke shares how at first he tried to accommodate himself to his work environment. Unfortunately, he was not able to do that. He gathered the necessary documentation and tried to work with his human resources department and his supervisor to receive the accommodations he needed in order to be successful. That process took nine months, during which he worked without the accommodations he needed. He also had to hire a lawyer to protect his rights against contentious pushback. When he finally received the requested accommodations, his supervisor shared J.J.'s disability with his peers without consent.

Neither Wendy nor Jessica have initiated or pursued formal accommodations. We have each taken advantage of the more flexible work arrangements allowed to librarians at our respective workplaces to adjust our working conditions as needed. Because we both have chronic health conditions, we both find that flexing our worktime around our bodies' needs is the primary adjustment we need to make. J.J. Pionke's story is a cautionary tale instructing us that while the process of getting accommodations is legally protected in theory, in practice one needs to be very aware of how power works. In the best-case scenario, the interactive process is a civil and collaborative event that leads to timely and helpful accommodations (with the caveat that they must fit within the typically frugal institutional budget). Possible challenges to endure could be bureaucratic barriers and interpersonal microaggressions. The worst-case scenario is a situation that becomes adversarial. The practical aspects of that adversarial eventuality are described in chapter 6.

Belaboring the Point: Here, Again, Is What Works

In a systematic review of the literature, rehabilitation scholars discovered several key facilitators and barriers to employment for people with disabilities:

1. Self-advocacy on the part of disabled persons;
2. Support of the employer and community (specifically, co-workers' and employers' attitudes, understanding, and knowledge of the disability);
3. Amount of training and counseling disabled persons receive; and
4. Flexibility with respect to work schedules and work organization.[26]

---

25   Pionke, "On the Impact of Disbelief," 423–35.

26   Nevala, Pehkonen, Koskela, Ruusuvuori, and Anttila, "Workplace Accommodation," 432–48.

We learned in chapter 1 that Accommodations Theory originates from the medical/rehabilitation view of disability and that cost-benefit analysis drives accommodation-related decision-making. Yet ironically, legal scholars tell us that it was the social model driving the proponents of the legislation.[27] It was the necessity for political compromise that eliminated the other cause on the agenda, namely, advocacy for those who need social welfare solutions. The anti-bureaucratic sentiment that continues to pervade our politics also hampers the successful implementation of the ADA, because the Act needs the strength of EEOC to enforce its application, which has not been forthcoming.[28]

In chapter 3 we described how people with disabilities may fear rocking the boat of corporate culture. J.J.'s experience was unfortunately adversarial. In chapter 2 we described the stressful juggling of risk management. As people with disabilities contend with these sources of fear and stress, it is not surprising that self-advocacy, support, education, counseling, and flexibility are sorely needed.

Self-Advocacy

With both scholarly writings and the voices of disabled activists to teach us and encourage us, and with a vacuum of goodwill at the helm of our country, it behooves us to enhance our self-esteem by inventorying our strengths. In this atmosphere of hostile, nonexistent, or inadequate top-down leadership, leadership from the grassroots and from the middle are crucial. We must be the change we want to see, reframing this challenging state of affairs in the most positive light. This does not mean that we ignore problems or minimize the pain they inflict. But it does mean that there is no better time than now to become a self-advocate or an ally of people with disabilities. The good news is that we library workers tend to be adept at the very skills necessary to improve the process of accommodations. We will now examine existing research on the topic through this rose-colored, hopeful lens.

As library workers, we have an advantage. We are trained to engage with information acquisition, repackaging, dissemination, and analysis. We can use these skills to approach discussions of accommodations

---

27   Knapp, "The Danger of the Essential Functions," 718.

28   Burke, *Lawyers*, 100.

with our colleagues and employers. And those with subject specialties, such as health sciences librarians, can be particularly helpful in specialized research and in working with other professionals in the health sciences and rehabilitation fields. Remember that you have this repertoire of skills and fellow experts to call upon for help. This will help build your confidence as you engage in the self-advocacy required to successfully navigate an imperfect system.

We have social capital as helping professionals and we know how to perform the affective labor of networking and referral. We are used to doing this for others. The next step is to start doing it for ourselves as self-advocates and as allies for people with disabilities—using these skills ethically, for the greatest good.

Advocacy efforts "help give voice to those viewed as being at a societal disadvantage..."[29] Advocates work with people with disabilities to "increase self-determination by empowering them and ensuring they have the knowledge to properly advocate on their own," and "help identify and/or remove the barriers that impede access."[30] Remember that these advocates may be nondisabled people who work for charitable or medical organizations, as well as disabled activists who have personal experience in the liminal space of recipient and provider of care.[31] As information workers, we can immediately gravitate to this advocacy knowledge work. Our ethics and our daily work in libraries have equipped us with familiarity with the basic premises of advocacy work. We'll pursue this idea a little more in chapter 7.

Employer and Community Support

As mentioned in the previous section, support from the employer and the community is another important facilitator of success. This is specifically related to co-workers' and employers' attitudes, understanding, and knowledge of the disability. When we engage in a dynamic process of mutual education, we simultaneously create community and build

---

29 Koch, Beggs, Bailey, Remondet Wall, "Advocacy in the 21st Century," 248.

30 Koch, Beggs, Bailey, Remondet Wall, 248.

31 For more discussion of the idea that disabled people must always be centered in these efforts, see Mia Mingus, "Medical Industrial Complex Visual," *Leaving Evidence* (blog) February 6, 2015, https://leavingevidence.wordpress.com/2015/02/06/medical-industrial-complex-visual/.

solidarity. As we build social bridges, listening to each other to gain knowledge and understanding, some of our attitudes can change, even if we harbor some resistance to diversity. This resistance may not be out of hatred, but may stem from fear of change or reluctance to cede some of our control or privilege. Social psychologist Dolly Chugh observes that "the more power we have and the more money we have, the less likely we are to see our own privilege in the system."[32] She advises that those with privilege make extra effort to listen fully to people with less privilege. Those in marginalized groups may have silenced themselves out of fear or internalized stigma.

Researchers in the field of management discovered that while accommodation is a key factor in the full employment of people with disabilities, many do not request the accommodations they need. This is for a variety of reasons, ranging from fear of stigma to having witnessed contentious processes like Pionke's mentioned above. Management scholars Baldridge and Swift urge managers and organizations to create an environment in which sharing information to improve performance is valued.[33] By learning about employees' identities and proactively expressing their support for disability accommodations, managers can create conditions where employees feel safe to disclose. Former librarian and current disability advocate Rebecca's positive experience with her supervisor's quarterly reviews and monitoring of goals, described in chapter 3, underscores the benefits of a "free exchange of information to improve performance."[34]

Scholars in the field of occupational rehabilitation also address the importance of information acquisition and dissemination. Social worker Lauren Gates emphasizes the social context and identifies the responsiveness of the work environment and the organization to the needs of disabled employees as key factors. She advises fellow rehabilitation and health care workers that to determine accommodation needs you should consider the specific tasks, work processes, and interpersonal interactions at work. Similar to Baldridge and Swift, she sees information dissemination as critical:

---

32 Chugh, *The Person You Mean to Be*, 99.

33 David C. Baldridge and Michele L. Swift, "Withholding Requests for Disability Accommodation: The Role of Individual Differences and Disability Attributes," *Journal of Management* 39, no. 3 (2013): 757–59.

34 Baldridge and Swift, "Withholding Requests for Disability Accommodations," 759.

"Providers [of rehabilitation and health care] need to be sources of information to the workplace about the disability of the worker."[35]

One caveat of this focus on gathering documentation from health care providers is that they are acting as established gatekeepers between what a disabled person needs and what they receive. Disability scholar Jay Dolmage notes that this process itself acts as a barrier and a disincentive to full inclusion.[36] Ellen Samuels names this process "biocertification."[37] In a workplace context, biocertification means that employers require official documents to validate what disabled people already know, because they don't trust us. We are not trustworthy because our mere word is insufficient proof in a world where the medical model rules, biomedical expertise is revered, and the patient's role is passive. In a world where the social model was predominant, the input of authoritative or therapeutic advice could be welcomed and viewed as helpful if the power differential were eliminated and the person with disabilities was afforded inclusion and respect. The biocertification process is most onerous for those who have multiple marginalizations because they must navigate the intersection of medical racism and sexism, and economic barriers.

Again, we encourage you to use your expertise as an information worker. You are conscious of the gatekeeping role and recognize when it is used for good and when it is used to harm. Likewise, bureaucratic routine can be expected and not often deflected; instead of falling into the impersonal emotional energy trap of the paperwork mill, try making friends with the paralegals and administrative clerks with whom you file documents, if possible. Boost your morale by reframing reality: scholar Ruth O'Brien celebrates the ADA as the first legislation that does not consider identity static. She also lauds the Act for its requirement that employers take into account the individuality of employees, and then use this information to engage in an interactive process; thus, it has potential to infuse the dynamism throughout the workplace.[38] By availing yourself of the ADA, you are asserting your individuality in a remarkable and possibly precedent-setting way.

---

35   Gates, "Workplace," 95.

36   Jay Dolmage, *Academic Ableism*, 80.

37   Ellen Jean Samuels, *Fantasies of Identification: Disability, Gender, Race* (New York: New York University Press, 2014), 121–61.

38   O'Brien, *Bodies in Revolt*, 21.

Helping Us Help Ourselves

As mentioned earlier, the third barrier to successful accommodations is lack of training and counseling for disabled persons. There are no statistics showing the level of involvement of experts in the allied health fields in accommodations-related work and consultations. The federal ADA National Network (ADANN) Fact Sheet advises that documentation of a disability may be required from the appropriate health or rehabilitation professional.[39] Of course, employers and employees with resources can hire such professionals as consultants. The federal Job Accommodation Network provides free expertise for both parties.[40] Both employers and employees need to know their legal rights. They both also need to know what kind of accommodations are useful for what types of disabilities. This sort of information dissemination "improves the likelihood that employees will ask for and receive accommodations."[41]

This "increased knowledge and information sharing" are key to the success of the accommodation process.[42] Ideally, employers value the interactive process in which they work with their employee to identify goals and accommodations.[43] The interactive negotiation of accommodations is a "demanding social process," the success of which depends upon

---

39   ADA National Network (ADANN), "Reasonable Accommodations in the Workplace: Reasonable Accommodation Process," https://adata.org/factsheet/reasonable-accommodations-workplace.

40   "JAN provides free consulting services for all employers, regardless of the size of an employer's workforce. Services include one-on-one consultation about all aspects of job accommodations, including the accommodation process, accommodation ideas, product vendors, referral to other resources, and ADA compliance assistance…JAN provides free consulting services for all employees, regardless of the condition. Services include one-on-one consultation about all aspects of job accommodations, including the accommodation process, accommodation ideas, product vendors, referral to other resources, and ADA compliance assistance." Job Accommodation Network, "For Employers", https://askjan.org/info-by-role.cfm#for-employers; "For Individuals," https://askjan.org/info-by-role.cfm#for-individuals.

41   Gates, "Workplace Accommodation as a Social Process," 85.

42   Naomi Schreuer, William N. Myhill, Tal Aratan-Bergman, Deepti Samant, and Peter Blanck, "Workplace Accommodations: Occupational Therapists as Mediators in the Interactive Process," *Work* 34, no. 2 (2009): 158.

43   Schreuer, Myhill, Aratan-Bergman, Samant, and Blanck, "Workplace Accommodations," 158.

participants' willingness "to engage with each other, tolerance for diversity, and responsiveness."[44] One ideal expressed in these studies is that the employer and employee must be on equal footing during the interactive process: "Open communications that prioritize and demonstrate equal value for the individuals involved further enhance job satisfaction."[45] They set the bar very high. They describe a fair, respectful, value-conscious, and nuanced approach: the occupational therapist defines the problem and validates the issues that impede work participation. They select a theoretical model; assess the person, job functions, and environmental conditions; clarify goals, interests, and gaps between the parties; map the resources missing and available to each party; identify strengths and resources; identify readiness for and rejection of changes; and anticipate and reduce attitude problems.[46] If budget allows and parties mutually consent, this course of action might seem preferable to many employees over going it alone. That said, many employees may also resent needing to acquire bureaucratic proof of what they already know.

Some researchers put the onus of employer education upon the person with disabilities. This starts with disabled people educating themselves about ADA protections and using the knowledge they gain about their rights as a foundation for action. Using that information, employees can share the benefits of providing accommodations with their employers, such as how wheelchair ramps for employees also benefit customers, how deliberately including disabled employees grants the employer access to insights into another potential customer base, and how accommodations reduce employee turnover.[47] For disabled workers with the energy and the communication skills, this type of education in the interest of self-advocacy could be the way to go. We note that the researchers suggesting this approach don't seem attentive to power differences, however, so we suggest taking this advice with caution. Mediated intervention might be preferable. For more discussion of self-advocacy, see chapter 2.

---

44 Schreuer, Myhill, Aratan-Bergman, Samant, and Blanck, 151.

45 Schreuer, Myhill, Aratan-Bergman, Samant, and Blanck, 151.

46 Schreuer, Myhill, Aratan-Bergman, Samant, and Blanck, 154.

47 H. Kristl Davison, Brian J. O'Leary, Jennifer A. Schlosberg, and Mark N. Bing, "Don't Ask and You Shall Not Receive: Why Future American Workers with Disabilities Are Reluctant to Demand Legally Required Accommodations," *Journal of Workplace Rights* 14, no. 1 (2009): 49–73.

Diversity Training and Psychoeducation

Think about your workplace. What education and training are proactively provided to employees related to disability rights? Are these development opportunities aimed at people with disabilities or nondisabled people? Are they aimed at administrators, managers, frontline workers? What content is included in this training?

The need for education and training was made evident in the experience that was shared by one of our interviewees. Vanessa, a white, straight, tenured librarian at an academic library at a public university shared her experience in seeking accommodations:

> I'm at the point where I feel I need accommodations, and I also need to know how much leave is available for me to take. I made an appointment with my HR office but it didn't go so well—it wasn't very helpful. I got the feeling from the HR rep—even from her body language—that she was coming from a defensive place. When I asked her about changing my work schedule, she seemed guarded and just handed me some official leave form and hinted that my tenure status somehow gave me flexibility. There seemed to be no protocol in place; she didn't even cover the basic information sources, like JAN.[48] I found the whole experience confusing and almost inhibiting—instead of helpful, as I had hoped. I really just needed some information. Best-case scenario would have been finding an advocate in HR, but I sure wasn't expecting this negative—it almost felt like an adversarial attitude from the get-go. But maybe I am misinterpreting her attitude, I don't know. It just seemed like she didn't want to give me too much information, that somehow I was going to take advantage. I'm not sure where she was coming from, if I was even reading her correctly, but I just don't know where to turn next.

This experience of our interviewee is consistent with research in this area. Disability legislation alone isn't enough. Human resources employees are charged with protecting the organization from lawsuits, which puts them in a potentially oppositional position with employees. Workplace disability

---

48   Job Accommodation Network, https://askjan.org/.

integration requires targeted resources addressing disablist structures and systems. It requires ongoing education for employees and employers, so they are aware of their respective rights and responsibilities.[49] It also requires more research. Rehabilitation scholars point out that more research has been done to document negative employer attitudes toward employment of disabled workers than has investigated how to change those attitudes.[50]

Counseling and Training to Combat Stereotypes

Continuing to use the framework of the discoveries mentioned above, we return to the idea that counseling and training for the person with disabilities is key to their success, as is a supportive community of co-workers. Many scholars recommend training programs for *all* employees. Labor relations scholars suggest that the content of these training programs for employees include "information about disability to help modify expectations and combat stereotypes and provide skills for dealing with people with disabilities that help decrease discomfort and anxiety."[51]

Social worker Lauren Gates advocates for the use of psychoeducational training as "a vehicle through which information and structure for evaluating accommodation adequacy are provided."[52] Gates sees supervisors as key to the process, and found that their support, communication skills, and attitudes are highly influential for the employee with disabilities and the accommodation outcome. Gewurtz and Kirsh found that existing attitudes and perceptions about disability and other diversity-related issues within an organization's culture need to be brought to light: "Such issues could be addressed through education and training targeted at increasing awareness of the contributions persons with disabilities can make in the workplace..."[53] This training can also include information about accommodations and their importance to workplace success for the person with disabilities.

---

49 Rebecca Gewurtz and Bonnie Kirsh, "Disruption, Disbelief and Resistance: A Meta-synthesis of Disability in the Workplace." *Work* 34, no. 1 (2009): 33–44.

50 Brian N. Phillips, Jon Deiches, Blaise Morrison, Fong Chan, and Jill L. Bezyak, "Disability Diversity Training in the Workplace: Systematic Review and Future Directions," *Journal of Occupational Rehabilitation* 26, no. 3 (2016): 264–75.

51 Schur, Kruse, and Blanck, "Corporate Culture," 16.

52 Gates, "Workplace Accommodation as a Social Process," 96.

53 Gewurtz and Kirsh, "Disruption, Disbelief and Resistance," 43.

Planning for a Transparent Accommodations Process

The current model of accommodation is individualistic. A publicly documented, more open process could be healthier for the organizational culture. It could air out concerns and answer questions about fairness. It could build interpersonal bridges that hasten the creation of supportive community. Jessica's union's disability caucus is trying to make that move. They are working with peers who need accommodations, with legal and peer support from the union. Some of the things they are working on include disseminating information about the accommodations process in meetings and on the union website, working with human resources to document the processes they follow and the training they receive, and acting as union representatives during accommodations meetings to make sure their peers' legal rights are protected. If that approach is more radical than what's available to you, there are also other options.

Well-informed accommodation requesters are the most successful. Access to rehabilitation professionals can help to "prepare individuals to request accommodations by providing information on the ADA and the range of accommodation options, processing decisions about accommodations, and teaching skills in disclosing disability and requesting accommodations."[54] Asking for accommodations is a skill in itself, and with experience and support in making these requests, disabled people can gain confidence and be more successful at their work.

As referenced earlier, many rehabilitation scholars recommend that the accommodation planning process be a formal one of care and attention to detail. They suggest a structured approach to identify gaps between work expectations and performance ability and to determine accommodation recommendations based on those gaps. They also suggest monitoring the effectiveness of proposed accommodations and making appropriate adjustments as needed. We find this approach to be methodical and reasonable, but it lacks reference to values or the affective elements of inclusion. We would suggest a strategy that combines this step-by-step approach with a more value-conscious, feelings-based component.

Setting Free All Employees to Handle the Quotidian

Decentralization has the potential to increase job satisfaction among all employees, and especially among those with disabilities. This decentralization

---

54   MacDonald-Wilson, Fabian, and Dong, "Best Practices," 221–32.

could be a starting point toward accommodating specific needs of individuals. By decentralization, we mean "delegating decision-making power to lower levels" so that employees have more freedom in their daily work routine.[55] This "may improve responsiveness to the needs of all employees and especially to those of certain groups of employees, such as older workers, employees with young children, and, particularly, employees with disabilities."[56] This egalitarian and equitable application of the accommodation of decentralization to all employees helps to dispel any residual resentment or concerns about fairness and special or differential treatment of a class of employees.[57]

Introducing JAN and ADANN—Free Expertise at Your Fingertips

In the meantime, while we await changes in federal-level leadership, study federal court interpretations, and hope for restoration of the staffing levels and enforcement power of federal agencies, advocates and allies can work on intra- and inter-organizational collaboration. As documented above, some of the best practices in the literature proposes a team/community-wide effort among disabled persons, co-workers, supervisors, managers, administrators, and health and rehabilitation professionals. If health and rehabilitation professionals are unavailable to you, don't despair. You have the consultants at the Job Accommodation Network (JAN) and ADANN. They offer free and open publications, training opportunities, and consultations.

An example of JAN's helpful online publications is the Accommodation and Compliance Series. It is customized by disability type as well as by user type.[58] You can get free and confidential expertise on workplace accommodations and disability employment issues from JAN. It is a collaborative effort of the U.S. Department of Labor's Office of Disability Employment Policy (ODEP), West Virginia University, and private industry. It offers consultations and an online information clearinghouse for disabled individuals, employers, rehabilitation and medical professionals,

---

55 Baumgartner, Dwertmann, Boehm, and Bruch, "Job Satisfaction," 337.

56 Baumgartner, Dwertmann, Boehm, and Bruch, 337.

57 Schur, Kruse, Blasi, Blanck, "Is Disability Disabling," 402.

58 Job Accommodation Network, "JAN Publications & Articles," https://askjan.org/publications/index.cfm.

union representatives, and attorneys. The one-on-one consultations cover all aspects of job accommodations, including the accommodation process, accommodation ideas, product vendors, referrals to other resources, and ADA compliance assistance.[59]

The other key agency is the ADA National Network (ADANN).[60] It provides information, guidance, and training on how to implement the ADA. Its funding comes from the National Institute on Disability, Independent Living, and Rehabilitation Research. It is comprised of a network of ten regional ADA Centers across the United States. It offers an impressive slate of training opportunities. You can also find recommendations about workplace culture.[61]

Organizational Flexibility

The fourth barrier to successful accommodations is inflexibility with respect to work schedules and work organization.[62] Many research studies corroborate this idea.[63] The benefits of increasing organizational flexibility are that it can enhance trust and perceptions of fairness, and can "highlight how the provision of reasonable accommodations will help to create an organizational culture embracing diversity and inclusion."[64] We need to move away from "rigid rules and structures, towards a culture that fosters autonomy and supports individualized ways of approaching work duties."[65] Also, more expansive, fluid definitions of disability and wellness that encompass the lived experience of "being somewhere in-between" will be more inclusive of people who question whether they are disabled enough to count—which is a concern raised by one of our interviewees. Many disabilities, particularly those that fall into categories of mental or

---

59   Job Accommodation Network, https://askjan.org.

60   ADA National Network (ADANN), https://adata.org.

61   Gould, Harris, and Caldwell, *ADA Research Brief*, 1–3.

62   Nevala, Pehkonen, Koskela, Ruusuvuori, and Anttila, "Workplace Accommodation," 432–48.

63   Gewurtz and Kirsh, "Disruption, Disbelief and Resistance," 33–44; Schur, Kruse and Blanck, "Corporate Culture," 3–20; Baumgartner, Dwertmann, Boehme, and Bruch, "Job Satisfaction of Employees with Disabilities," 323–43.

64   MacDonald-Wilson, Fabian, and Dong, "Best Practices," 227.

65   Gewurtz and Kirsh, "Disruption, Disbelief and Resistance," 43.

chronic illness, are cyclical and not well represented by existing legislation or accommodations.[66]

Goose & Gander Going Beyond the Individual: Extending Accommodations to All Employees

What is good for the goose is also good for the gander. That is, many workplace strategies and accommodations that help disabled workers also help their nondisabled co-workers. Disability accommodations help workplaces be more inclusive, and also "have positive spillovers on other employees that foster overall workplace productivity."[67]

The creation of a more compassionate, supportive community can be facilitated by ensuring that employees with disabilities have co-worker contact opportunities at work and in informal and recreational settings. These social bridges help to debunk stereotypes and build a network of social support. Increased scheduling flexibility helps people with disabilities and also aids nondisabled employees responsible for child or elder care. These are examples of a universal accommodation process that has the potential to increase organizational responsiveness to the needs of all employees. This universal accommodation process finds parallels in justifications for diversity programs in general. Many of the factors that account for bias toward people with disabilities in the workplace such as stereotyping and low performance expectations apply to other disadvantaged groups, such as religious and gender minorities.[68]

Beyond Accommodations: Dynamism of the Compassionate Community/Workplace

The creation and implementation of the ADA has been a long, circuitous journey and it has no foreseeable end. As the personal is political, we avidly follow and seek to actively influence changes that are favorable to people

---

66 Gewurtz and Kirsh, 43.

67 Lisa Schur, Lisa Nishii, Meera Adya, Douglas Kruse, Susanne M. Bruyere, and Peter Blanck, "Accommodating Employees with and without Disabilities," *Human Resource Management* 53, no. 4 (2014): 616.

68 *Promoting Diversity and Inclusion Through Workplace Accommodations: A Practical Guide* (Geneva: International Labor Office, 2016).

with disabilities, and to all workers. In the meantime, we must make the best of our particular circumstance.

Research shows the effectiveness of self-advocacy, a supportive and knowledgeable community, training and counseling, and flexible structures. Thus, we insist upon speaking for ourselves, giving voice to demands and desires of our body, heart, and mind. We are self-advocates, demanding respect and reasonable accommodations to help us adapt to our working environment. Yet we find ourselves wanting more. We aspire to go beyond individualistic accommodations and seek a supportive community. We value wise counsel and seize opportunities for continual enlightenment. And we require flexibility, the time and space in which to rebuild and recuperate, so that we can continue to contribute, produce, and create. We aspire to work productively, creatively, and humanely in a compassionate workplace. And as two white people with disabilities, in a mostly white, white-collar, middle-class information profession, we want more. We want to be allies and advocates in solidarity with our disabled friends for whom anti-discrimination laws are insufficient, we want to be there for those who need social welfare interventions in order to be included in the community and the workforce.

We are inspired and buoyed by the candor, experience, and bravery of our interviewees. We hope this chapter has inspired the reader and opened up a world of possibilities, showing the many alternatives to the adversarial process. The next chapter deals with that adversarial process head-on. Sometimes we are fortunate enough to be in a workplace in which there is space to build community, where the potential for compassion exists. But sometimes we find ourselves in a situation where we must flee or else stand our ground and fight back. Our engagement in an adversarial process is needed for the sake of saving our livelihood. The next chapter advises how to find support outside of your workplace when your options narrow.

Chapter 6

Getting Help and Transgressing Borders

As Sand C. Chang notes in their essay about being a nonbinary gender therapist, what we call professionalism and work-appropriateness are gendered, heteronormative, and often racist and classist concepts. Standard, normative approaches to care work "are inherently biased toward the dominant culture, and it takes intention and effort to make sure these care systems are truly inclusive."[1] While Chang was writing about working as a health care provider, these same issues impact library workplaces. In Joanne Oud's examination of factors influencing the job satisfaction of disabled librarians, she says "If we are serious about equity and inclusion in our profession, we need a better understanding of the barriers faced by librarians with disabilities and a commitment to minimize them."[2] Because of librarianship's notable lack of diversity,[3] we sometimes need to go outside the library to get the support we need.

In this chapter we'll discuss the contexts in which this external support is needed and explore the kinds of support available. Most challenging employment situations, upon analysis, are an amalgam of structural and personal aspects. These are usually structural in origination

---

1 Sand C. Chang, "Token Act," in *Nonbinary: Memoirs of Gender and Identity*, ed. Micah Rajunov and Scott Duane (New York: Columbia University Press, 2019), 55.

2 Oud, "Disability and Equity," 73.

3 Department for Professional Employees, "Library Professionals: Facts & Figures," AFL-CIO: 2019, https://dpeaflcio.org/programs-publications/issue-fact-sheets/library-workers-facts-figures/.

and personal in manifestation. Coping strategies can be implemented on the internal, personal level. Consciousness-raising can be attempted through communication on a person-to-person level. Individuals can request accommodations. But long-term comprehensive solutions can only be accomplished through the implementation of changes at the broader institutional level, and often even further, at the sociopolitical level. Think back to some of the jobs you've held in your work life and discrimination or barriers you encountered. What did these experiences teach you about your capabilities and limitations, and those of the organization, and the entire system? Who, if anyone, helped you weather these events and navigate the system? When did you realize you were not "the only one," that these obstacles were systemic and experienced by many working people?

Structural Problems Cause Personal Problems at the Pancake House

One of Wendy's early jobs was the late shift at the International House of Pancakes. She was seventeen years old. She worked four days a week on swing shift and one day on graveyard shift. Shiftwork is notoriously difficult on the body. Before the end of the shift, after the bar rush, at about four in the morning, Wendy and her coworkers were expected to industriously clean all the areas of their syrupy mess. Even at seventeen, it was more than her body could take. She lethargically attempted to tidy up. Her fellow waitress industriously cleaned, doing more than her share. Finally, Wendy commented on this to the short-order cook. He let her in on a secret: her hard-working companion waitress took speed and that's from whence came her second wind. Everything fell into place. Naiveté was replaced by astounded comprehension. Work requirements exceeded her body's ability to keep up. Luckily for Wendy, she planned to quit the job at the end of the summer to begin college in Santa Fe. So, she did not acquire a speed habit, but she did take advantage of her co-worker's industrious early morning energy spurt. There is something amiss in job requirements that lend themselves to the taking of speed-enhancing drugs. Or was there something lacking in Wendy's body, her constitution, that she was not energetic at four in the morning? (Jessica is firmly of the opinion this was a structural problem, not a Wendy problem.)

Sometimes you try to do your best, or even go beyond your best, but it's just not possible to meet expectations. Sometimes that's because the expectations are unreasonable. For example, think of lean staffing.[4] In this practice, one person calling out sick for their shift means their coworkers are burdened to work beyond their scheduled hours to make up for one person being gone. Not fully staffing the library is a scheduling decision, and that decision is what puts the burden on the non-sick co-workers. But it is often presented as if it's caused by one person being sick. This is not an accident.

Is It Just Me, or Do We Need a New Social Contract?

Those of us who've been in the U.S. workforce for a few decades may be able to think back and observe changing worker expectations over time. Since the Great Recession of 2009, U.S. worker expectations have decreased. We have come to expect less support from the workplace, fewer benefits, minimal raises, and lean staffing as normal. We have mentally adjusted to this new normal, even though it causes us physical and financial harm.[5] This devolution of expectations is a symptom of a multi-decade decline of job quality indicators and institutional protections in the U.S. employment system.

The rise in employment precarity and polarization coincided with the dismantling of the post-war social contract during the 1980s and 1990s. Job insecurity increased as semi-skilled, well-paying middle-class jobs disappeared. Problems like this, which are both structural and systemic in nature, can't be solved by individuals. Sociologist Arne L. Kalleberg recommends the creation of a new social contract. This project would require "the coordinated efforts of government (at the federal, state, and local levels), business, and labor."[6] He envisions a new social contract with the follow-

---

4 Avery Alder, "You know that thing where your coworker calls you in a panic wondering if you can cover their shift so they can stay home sick, and nobody else can do it? So you cancel your plans to cover them? That has been an intentional part of north-american capitalism since the 1990s," https://twitter.com/lackingceremony/status/1141410304644960258; Gayle Porter, "Workaholic Tendencies and the High Potential for Stress among Co-Workers," *International Journal of Stress Management* vol. 8 (2001): 147–64.

5 Lauren Weber, "As Workers Expect Less, Job Satisfaction Rises; Minimal Raises and Lean Staffing have Redefined what Makes a Position Good," *Wall Street Journal*, September 1, 2017, https://www.wsj.com/articles/americans-are-happier-at-work-but-expect-a-lot-less-1504258201.

6 Arne L. Kalleberg, *Good Jobs, Bad Jobs: The Rise of Polarized and Precarious Employment Systems in the United States, 1970s–2000s* (New York: Russell Sage Foundation, 2011), 185.

ing provisos: economic security that protects workers from the consequences of precarious work; guaranteed rights to collective representation and bargaining power; and retraining to prepare workers for good jobs.[7] He defines "good jobs" as: relatively well-paying, with opportunities for periodic raises; having adequate fringe benefits like health insurance and retirement pay; offering control and autonomy over work activities; and allowing some control over scheduling, terms, and termination of employment.[8]

Oh, You Can't Scare Me, I'm Sticking to the Union

Kalleberg sees guaranteed rights to collective representation and bargaining power as crucial elements of this new social contract. We agree and are proponents of the need to organize through unions or other advocacy groups to address root causes and identify legislative solutions. Even for those who can't belong to a labor union for whatever reason, union activism provides spillover benefits because employers need to be more competitive to keep workers.[9]

One drawback of union activism has historically been that union leaders have not always viewed people of color, disabled people, and immigrants as potential worker-allies. Instead, union leaders often viewed these already-marginalized workers as the kind of competition that would decrease opportunities of dominant groups.[10] This is one reason Jessica was so eager to participate in the disability caucus of their union, to have a group of peers with whom to work to identify problems and possible solutions, and counteract the ignorance of their nondisabled union peers. Because the caucus functions within the union, they can bring up issues within that structure. Then, when negotiating with administrative units, they have access to the institutional power of the union to advocate for changes. As mentioned in other chapters, the ADA is designed with the idea that employers will either voluntarily comply or comply after a burdensome lawsuit, so it can be beneficial for disabled workers to have access to other avenues in pursuit of accommodations.

---

7   Kalleberg, 187.

8   Kalleberg, 9.

9   Yates, *Why Unions Matter*, 41.

10   George Lipsitz, *The Possessive Investment in Whiteness: How White People Profit from Identity Politics*, rev. and exp. ed. (Philadelphia: Temple University Press, 2006), 55–77.

Even with this caucus structure in place, Jessica's union has been talking about asking for an ombudsperson to act as a designated external mediator between the union and administration. Ombuds professionals work with individuals and organizations to identify systemic concerns and help resolve conflicts.[11] *The Ombudsman Handbook* states that the need for ombudspersons arises out of the push of external pressures upon organizations and corporations. These pressures include increased litigation, economic concerns related to governmental cutbacks, the trend toward democratization and participatory management, the pace of technological development, credentialism, increasing work/family conflicts, and an aging workforce. Organizations and corporations are also pulled by internal pressures such as the desire for more organizational learning and participative management, less employee litigation, better customer relations, dispute resolution methods that improve the quality of working life, open communication, reduced turnover, greater justice and equity, more humane organizations, and a more democratic corporate culture.[12] In sum, the role of the ombudsperson is to create and maintain a corporate/organizational culture of openness and fairness.[13]

Healthy Communication and Autonomy = Healthy Workplace

The attributes of a healthy workplace for nondisabled workers make for a healthy workplace for disabled workers, and vice versa. When we say this, we're not talking about pushing so-called wellness programs based on eugenic[14] ideologies that do nothing more than offload all the responsibility

---

11 Tessa Tompkins Byer, "Yea, Nay, and Everything in Between: Disparities Within the Academic Ombuds Field," *Negotiation Journal* 33, no. 3 (2017): 213–38.

12 James T. Ziegenfuss, Jr. and Patricia O'Rourke, *The Ombudsman Handbook: Designing and Managing an Effective Problem Solving Program* (Jefferson, NC: McFarland, 2011), 7–15.

13 Ziegenfuss and O'Rourke, 165.

14 The aim of eugenics is to standardize the gene pool. Dominant groups classify other groups as unworthy for various reasons: ethnicity, religion, sexual orientation, etc. In North America, rich, white, Christian, nondisabled people form the dominant group and rhetorically demean other groups, classing them into sub-human categories. Eugenic practices can take the form of sterilization, forced or restricted abortion access, lynching, mass incarceration, immigration restrictions, and various other forms of mass exclusion and rhetorical violence. One example of this that is common in workplace wellness programs is fat-shaming, with fatness equated to ill-health in a scientifically questionable but absolute way.

onto individuals without making necessary systemic changes.[15] For example, providing therapy dogs to employees once a year doesn't solve workplace problems. Further, having that be the primary or only official acknowledgment of mental health care needs implies that those whose psychiatric disabilities aren't solved by these programs don't belong in the workplace.

A healthy workplace distributes responsibility to many. An autocratic workplace is dependent upon the disposition of the authority figures alone and likely has few options to change the organization. Ideally, we would like to see the implementation of Kalleberg's new social contract that allows for more worker autonomy. And we would like to see more work environments conducive to honest communication about individual limits; open communication about accommodations needed from the organization; frank feedback about performance expectations; and negotiations about any gaps between individual/organizational aspirations and reality.

Advocates for Adversarial Processes

Unfortunately, these communications can break down and the relationship between ourselves and our employer can become adversarial. At that point, we need to go outside the organization and seek legal support about the workplace discrimination we are experiencing or about a disputed accommodation request. How does one start this process? Each state in the U.S. has an agency known as a Protection & Advocacy System or Center.[16] We will use Wendy's knowledge of how this works in Colorado to provide a general process overview.

In Colorado, that agency is called Disability Law Colorado (DLC). But before we file a complaint with a field office of the Equal Employment Opportunity Commission (EEOC) or a state agency (such as the Colorado Civil Rights Division), the DLC Resource Guide[17] suggests the follow-

---

15 Dolmage, *Academic Ableism*, 56–57.

16 Find your state services at Administration for Community Living, "State Protection and Advocacy Systems," https://acl.gov/programs/aging-and-disability-networks/state-protection-advocacy-systems# or through the National Disability Rights Network, "Member Agencies," https://www.ndrn.org/about/ndrn-member-agencies/.

17 Disability Law Colorado, "Resource Guide: Disability Discrimination in Employment," 2018, https://disabilitylawco.org/sites/default/files/uploads/DLC%20Employment%20Packet%202018%20FINAL_.pdf.

ing resources, if available, be accessed first: 1) Ask our union to advocate on our behalf; 2) Open the lines of communication with our employer's ADA Coordinator (contact our Human Resources Department); 3) File an internal grievance if that procedure is in place; and/or 4) Negotiate or mediate with our employer. We would add to this list consulting an ombudsperson, if available within your organization. Timing is critical, so be vigilant about deadlines. An EEOC claim must be filed within 300 days from the date the discrimination occurred. Your state agency may have another deadline. Colorado's Civil Rights Division deadline is only 180 days, much tighter than the EEOC's 300.

Disability Law Colorado explains that if we qualify under the law as an individual with a disability, we have a right not to be discriminated against in all employment practices, such as benefits, hiring, job assignments, lay off, leave, pay, promotion, recruitment, retention, training, and all other employment-related activities. The federal laws providing this protection are Titles I and II of the Americans with Disabilities Act and Section 504 of the Rehabilitation Act. State laws may provide additional protection. For example, in Colorado, the Colorado Anti-Discrimination Act offers additional protections. The National Conference of State Legislatures compiles a comprehensive list of employment discrimination laws in all fifty states of the U.S.[18]

A Piecemeal, Sometimes Interactive Process and Incremental Change

We must decide whether our discrimination-related situation rises to the level that makes the instigation of an adversarial process worth our while. Our legal consultant will make the determination whether we have a viable case and the EEOC must issue a right-to-sue letter before a private suit is filed. While it is personally significant whether we win or lose, disability studies scholars critique the accommodations and lawsuit approaches because of their piecemeal nature. We started this chapter with this premise: structural problems cause personal problems, and these structural conundrums can't be solved solely by individuals. Yet ironically, ADA accommodations are very individualized.

The accommodations process is initiated by the employee requesting the accommodation, whether verbally or in writing. As soon as "an employee

---

18 National Conference of State Legislatures, "State Employment-Related Discrimination Statutes," 2015, http://www.ncsl.org/documents/employ/Discrimination-Chart-2015.pdf.

requests a reasonable accommodation, the employer and employee should engage in a productive and interactive exchange to determine the accommodations that are appropriate to the needs of the employee...creating reasonable accommodations is an individualized process and will vary from person to person based on functional limitations."[19] Some scholars contend the ad hoc and decentralized nature of the accommodations process is unhelpful in that it is non-documented and leaves no institutional memory; thus, it effects no overarching change.[20] It could be argued, however, that successful negotiations can create positive interpersonal changes, but those changes are incremental and not systemic in nature. Another scholar sees the ADA law as positive, in that it makes employers "take into account the individuality of their employees" and by so doing, interjects a "dynamic concept of need into the workplace" and introduces the ethic of care.[21]

Education and Intersectionality: The Other Pieces of the Discrimination Pie

Dependent upon random acts of interpersonal kindness and built on a piecemeal basis, this inclusive, needs-conscious, and caring workplace is, for many of us, an aspiration and not a reality. And consider the educational system that prepares workers for the workplace, and the discrimination that many disabled students experience within that system. Almost a third of nondisabled U.S. citizens over the age of twenty-five have a bachelor's degree or higher. In contrast, only 13% of their disabled peers have equivalent education. It takes students with disabilities "at least 25 percent longer to complete the same degree requirements as non-disabled students" and they "are likely to have up to 60 percent more student debt by the time they graduate."[22] For extra fun, factor in race. Racial minority students "exert more effort and are more engaged than white peers" but get lower grades because their ability to focus on learning is diluted by trying to survive racism.[23] These structural barriers don't disappear after graduation.

---

19   Disability Law Colorado, 7.

20   Sharon-Dale Stone, Valorie A. Crooks, and Michelle Owen, "Going through the Back Door: Chronically Ill Academics' Experiences as 'Unexpected Workers,'" *Social Theory & Health* 11, no. 2 (2013): 167.

21   O'Brien, *Bodies in Revolt*, 4.

22   Dolmage, *Academic Ableism*, 21.

23   Dolmage, 137–38.

Any disabled library worker you meet has overcome incredible odds to get where they are and to persist in this field. Disabled library workers who experience other forms of discrimination or marginalization have succeeded against overwhelming odds. All of the disabled librarians of color we interviewed for this project acknowledge that when they make employment decisions, they have to decide whether they'd rather deal with racism or ableism, because a workplace might be supportive in one area but not another. Elspeth, an autistic white librarian with chronic illnesses, shared that she has to decide whether to be open about being a queer trans woman or a person with disabilities, because supervisors and peers are only willing to be supportive so far. The further you transgress beyond normative boundaries, the less support you receive, and yet the likelihood of your need for that support increases.

It's Not Just Structural, It's Also Personal

Wendy's illness is making her move more slowly. It is also interrupting her workflow. When her medication has what is known as an "off" time, she must stop working and allow the intense tremors their full amplitude. Her "off" time is of such intensity that she cannot type anymore, speech is difficult, and sometimes she needs to lie down on her back for an interval (it can be between five and forty-five minutes long). Lately, this is likely to happen a handful of times a week. When this is in its milder phase, she simply tells the student she's helping that they "can drive" (navigate the library's website) while Wendy interacts, makes suggestions, and helps them with research strategies. When her symptoms are too intense, it may look to an outside observer like she stops working. But if we consider Wendy's internal experience, even though she stops using her computer, stops writing, stops reading, etc., she does not stop thinking. She can use this time for productive planning and cogitation. That is, unless she is overwhelmed with anxiety about how this stoppage might be perceived by those with whom she works and those whom she serves.

Wendy welcomes walk-in traffic. Her office is glass-enclosed on the north side, and she is visible through this wide window-wall. How many times has a student approached her office, but turned around upon seeing a tremoring figure? She is not aware of this happening, but surely it has. After teaching a course a couple years ago, Wendy received the following anonymous student comment on her course evaluation: "Her trembling made me very anxious which made it hard to concentrate when it was really bad but I know she can't control it".

In interactions with students, Wendy finds herself apologizing for any distraction or discomfort her Parkinson's symptomology may cause. She does not mean this in a self-deprecating manner. Instead, she is acknowledging that some people are disturbed by the symptomology. She finds this is understandable, as for some the tremor can be a distraction. That said, her disability holds endless didactic possibilities and opportunities. But how do we convince co-workers and library users of this? To what types of support can Wendy turn? This is not an overtly adversarial situation. Earlier in this chapter, we covered adversarial support provided by the EEOC, state-level employment rights agencies, private attorneys, and the Protection and Advocacy Systems/Centers, but what are the other creative alternatives available to support her in dealing with the quotidian day-to-day reality of working as a person with disabilities?

Joining with Your Peeps and Fighting for Your Cause

What truly helps? What mitigates the misunderstanding, bias, or ignorance that precipitates negative reactions to one's disability? What can soothe the anxiety people with disabilities feel about the inadequacy of the social safety net? What can improve communication skills and co-worker relationships? Support, education, and sustenance are needed on all fronts: the physical, psychological/emotional, social, political, and spiritual. We recommend a multi-pronged, pro-active approach and find truth in the following truisms: Don't agonize, organize! Be the change you want to see. Think globally, act locally. And never underestimate the power of small acts of kindness. Simultaneously work on making changes within yourself, join with others with whom you have affinity, and create coalitions to change the system, right the structural wrongs, and thereby effect the change you yearn to see in the world.

Find a stress-reduction technique that works for you. Wendy finds that the mindfulness practice of qi gong is helpful for her. Jessica's mindfulness efforts got derailed by a major bout of depression, but since then they have found working with a cognitive behavioral therapist tremendously helpful in identifying more reasonable expectations for themself. Take advantage of any Employee Assistance Programs at your workplace that offer free sessions of psychological counseling. Finding the right modality and therapist can be a transformative process, turning pain into wisdom and hastening the healing of emotional wounds.

Even as we are saying this, we recognize that people in rural areas, people of color, queer and trans people, and many others have a hard time locating culturally competent therapists. In this case, it may be helpful to seek an affinity group or start one of your own. This could be a group of people with a shared hobby, disability, or cause. It could run the gamut from silly and inane to something profound. Wendy once belonged to a group of sci-fi nerds that bonded watching old episodes of "Battlestar Galactica." An environmental group she co-founded resists the siting of oil & gas fracking operations near vulnerable populations. She belongs to a group of people with Parkinson's disease who explore complementary medical therapies. She also belongs to a writing group. Jessica finds a lot of peer support through social media, both casually and via scheduled chats such as #dsma (diabetes social media advocacy) and #LISMentalHealth (Library & Information Science Mental Health). They have also been engaged with diversity and antiracism efforts within their community for several years. The possibilities are endless.

Here are some suggestions for groups and resources directly related to disability issues. State-level vocational rehabilitation offices offer occupational therapy and job counseling services.[24] Grassroots groups like Colorado Cross Disability Association (CCDA) have issues campaigns for which they lobby. CCDA's current employment-related platform includes these initiatives: we need to fight systems that keep us impoverished, especially poorly designed and hard-to-use "work incentive" programs; we need to expand and publicize the Medicaid Buy In Program for Working Adults with Disabilities; we need to change the Social Security Administration definition of disability; and we need employers to reach out and make affirmative efforts to hire more people with significant disabilities.[25]

There are many disability organizations working on different types of advocacy. Some groups focus on broad legislative or awareness projects on behalf of the whole community. Others are targeted to the specific needs of distinct populations within the disability community, which we'll mention a bit later. Organizations focused on the needs of broader disability populations include INCIGHT, ADAPT, and the Disability Visibility Project. INCIGHT of Portland, Oregon, was started by disabled activists Scott Hadley and Vail Horton.[26] ADAPT is a group of disabled grassroots

24   Employer Assistance and Resource Network on Disability Inclusion, "State Vocational Rehabilitation Agencies," https://www.askearn.org/state-vocational-rehabilitation-agencies/.

25   Colorado Cross Disability Coalition, http://www.ccdconline.org/employment/.

26   INCIGHT, "About," https://www.incight.org/about.

activists who plan civil disobedience actions.[27] Alice Wong's Disability Visibility Project amplifies disabled peoples' perspectives on media and culture through podcasts and other venues.[28]

Perhaps you'd like to get involved with a foundation or a think tank. Many of these organizations create, gather, and disseminate information—what a perfect fit for the skills and interests of library workers. They also may lobby for legislative changes, such as DREDF's 2013 lawsuit on behalf of school inclusion for children with diabetes and other medical conditions[29] and the Disability Rights Advocates and Public Interest Law Project's lawsuit on behalf of disabled renters excluded from rent stabilization programs.[30] The Kessler Foundation provides invaluable data on employment of people with disabilities.[31]

For library workers, we may want to look to professional societies and organizations. Our flagship professional organization, the American Library Association, has one division with a charge related to providing resources to library users with disabilities. This division is the Association of Specialized Government and Cooperative Library Agencies (ASGCLA). One service this division provides is a tip sheet for incorporating library staff with disabilities into the workplace.[32] While this is better than nothing, it's not enough. We would love to see a disability caucus modeled on the ethnic caucuses[33] or a round table modeled on the Rainbow round

---

27 ADAPT, https://adapt.org/.

28 Disability Visibility Project, https://disabilityvisibilityproject.com/about/.

29 Disability Rights Education & Defense Fund, "Diabetes Care," 2013, https://dredf.org/special-education/diabetes-care/.

30 "People with Disabilities Charge that Oakland's Rent Stabilization Program Excludes Them and Must Be Fixed Notwithstanding Costa-Hawkins," *Disability Rights Advocates*, https://dralegal.org/press/people-with-disabilities-charge-that-oaklands-rent-stabilization-program-excludes-them-and-must-be-fixed-notwithstanding-costa-hawkins/.

31 Center for Employment and Disability Research, Kessler Foundation, https://kesslerfoundation.org/research/center-employment-and-disability-research.

32 American Library Association, Association of Specialized Government and Cooperative Library Agencies, "Library Staff with Disabilities: What You Need to Know," http://www.ala.org/asgcla/resources/tipsheets/staff.

33 American Indian Library Association (AILA), Asian/Pacific American Library Association (APALA), Black Caucus of the American Library Association (BCALA), Chinese American Librarians Association (CALA), Joint Council of Librarians of Color, National Association to Promote Library & Information Services to Latinos and the Spanish Speaking (REFORMA).

table,[34] resulting in a recognized professional association whose primary goal is to amplify the voices of marginalized members of the profession.

You can't effect structural and systemic change in the world on your own. If you want to engage in this work, we recommend joining (or forming!) a community group, ad hoc group, or affinity group. For example, if, in reading the list of alternatives to try to avoid the adversarial accommodations process, you noticed a lack of resources in your workplace, you may want to start an ad hoc group to discuss the need for an ombudsperson at your workplace.[35]

Most health conditions have advocacy groups. Therein lies potential for information, political power, and fellowship. For example, Wendy's disability, Parkinson's disease, has the Michael J. Fox Foundation, the National Parkinson's Foundation, the regional Parkinson Association of the Rockies, the Parkinson's Disease Foundation, the Davis Phinney Foundation, and a Young Onset group.

However, not all advocacy groups provide the same supports. Jessica has observed that some advocacy groups have reputations for being less concerned with supporting the daily needs of people living with those conditions than they are with building ties to the pharmaceutical industry.[36] As savvy information experts, library workers know that they need to be skeptically cautious and investigate any group they are considering joining.[37]

Broad-Based Coalitions

We live in an imperfect world. Thus, we compensate for the gaps in the social safety net, common misunderstandings, the shortcomings of the ADA act, and the often-incremental nature of social change. For the activists among our readers, we pass on the advice of sociologist Arne Kalleberg. He lauds the effectiveness of non-union social movements. Worker advocacy

---

34 Rainbow Round Table, http://www.ala.org/rt/glbtrt.

35 Kalleberg, *Good Jobs*, 210.

36 Emily Kopp, "Is Big Pharma Getting 'Patient Advocates' to Do Its Lobbying Work?" *The Daily Beast*, April 6, 2018, https://www.thedailybeast.com/is-big-pharma-getting-patient-advocates-to-do-its-lobbying-work.

37 Wendy must interject that just as library-related vendors sponsor library conferences and distribute their logo-embossed swag while they chat up librarian customers, so do pharmaceutical companies sponsor Parkinson's conferences where their logo-embossed swag and sales pitches proliferate.

groups are often built around the needs of people with specific experiences of marginalization, so immigrant groups, women's groups, racial and ethnic movements, and movements to provide more support for working families have internal solidarity and can provide necessary peer support during the advocacy process.[38] He also recommends broad-based coalitions, such as the Industrial Areas Foundation (founded by organizer Saul Alinsky).[39]

Another coalition, led by Disability:IN and the American Association of People with Disabilities (AAPD), has resulted in the creation of the Disability Equality Index. This index is a benchmarking tool built in cooperation with business leaders and policy experts. This tool numerically scores participating companies according to a standardized set of criteria, with the goal of motivating companies to improve their disability inclusion practices.[40]

Beware the Harmful Hierarchy

Content warning References to racialized police violence.

But a challenge to engaging in workplace advocacy is that ableism has rhetorically and physically created an environment in which the person with a disability is "invisible, disposable, less than human" in contrast to the ideal, normative, hyper-able person around whom library workplaces are organized.[41] Add to that what scholar Jay Dolmage has labeled "disability drift," in which physical and mental disabilities are treated as equivalent.[42] For example, when a cognitively abled wheelchair user is treated as if they were intellectually disabled, that is because the person they're interacting with can't distinguish between disability types. This, unfortunately, has led the disability community to create its own hierarchy, in which physical disability is presented as more desirable than cognitive or psychiatric disabilities.

We can see this in terms of who is chosen as a positive representation of disability versus a negative one. For example, compare depictions

---

38   Kalleberg, *Good Jobs*, 203.

39   Industrial Areas Foundation, http://www.industrialareasfoundation.org/.

40   Disability Equality Index https://disabilityin.org/what-we-do/disability-equality-index/.

41   Dolmage, *Academic Ableism*, 7.

42   Jay Timothy Dolmage, *Disability Rhetoric* (Syracuse: Syracuse University Press, 2014), 46.

of Stephen Hawking versus the seemingly endless list of mentally ill Black men killed by police who are called to help them (a partial, recent list includes Laquan McDonald, Philip Coleman, Quintonio Legrier, and Stephon Watts).[43] Added to the above is a hierarchy of vocations that classifies worthiness based on the types of work a person can be assigned. Those who can engage in privileged types of work are ranked higher than those who are classed as only able to do so-called unskilled work.[44] When we're advocating for the rights of disabled library workers, we need to be intentional in advocating for the rights of people with all types of disabilities engaged in all types of library work.

Self-Advocates Need Support Too

Don't ask how bad my symptoms are, and I won't tell you how much I am suffering.

Wendy's tremors and other symptoms function as a fairly reliable barometer of her stress level. The things that cause the most stress are meetings and public speaking. Like the old Snoopy cartoon showing a weekend bell curve peak with a plummet on Monday, this is a typical pattern for a five-day week:

Monday	difficulty getting going, revving up
Tuesday	improvement, still some difficulty
Wednesday	more improvement, adrenaline has kicked in; sometimes optimal
Thursday	sometimes optimal, usually can push through, though may experience afternoon off times
Friday	quite fatigued, performance declines markedly in the afternoon
Saturday and Sunday	flattened, gradually recover energy, depending upon quality of sleep

---

43   David Perry, "Police Killings: The Price of Being Disabled and Black in America," *The Guardian*, June 22, 2017, https://www.theguardian.com/us-news/2017/jun/22/police-killings-disabled-black-people-mental-illness.

44   Dolmage, *Academic Ableism*, 64.

If you are new to being disabled in the workplace and have not been an assertive person in the past, you will need to change. It has been Wendy's experience that necessity is the mother of invention. Of necessity, she must listen to her body's limits; honestly perform a self-assessment; determine how, as an individual, she can most effectively perform her job duties; and communicate her situation to her supervisor. Then there is negotiation. In a healthy and tenable situation, this involves constructive communication—creative ideas that take into account the greatest good for the organization, the immediate co-workers, the person with disabilities, the tasks at hand, the mission of the organization, the immediate needs of patrons/clients. So, obviously, it can be a complex transaction fraught with points where problems and conflicts can arise.

Increased Assertiveness and Self-Esteem

Advocacy for yourself is going to require a redirection of your energy toward yourself. You will be doing all you can to create the best outcome for yourself. As you practice advocacy for yourself, you will become a better advocate for others through that process. Never fear, self-advocacy does not mean you will lose your altruistic nature. You have the right to be treated in a way that respects your humanity, and that includes the right to work and education.[45] We challenge any suggestion that self-advocacy is a professional or ethical violation. And there is nothing wrong with asking for help.

Developing a support network can make a huge difference in terms of improving self-understanding and self-acceptance. In talking about how to succeed despite pressures put on them as women of color, community college librarians Alyssa Jocson Porter, Sharon Spence-Wilcox, and Kimberly Tate-Malone point to role models and peer support as being extremely important.[46] Robin Brown and Scott Sheidlower found similar results when talking with disabled librarians: role models and peer networks make

---

45 United Nations, "Human Rights," https://www.un.org/en/sections/issues-depth/human-rights/.

46 Alyssa Jocson Porter, Sharon Spence-Wilcox, and Kimberly Tate-Malone, "I, Too: Unmasking Emotional Labor of Women of Color Community College Librarians," in *Pushing the Margins: Women of Color and Intersectionality in LIS*, ed. Rose L. Chou and Annie Pho (Sacramento: Library Juice Press, 2018), 273–300.

a huge difference.[47] Having a community of people facing similar challenges helps with self-acceptance and self-understanding, both in terms of knowing our experiences don't match normative expectations and in helping us know how and whether it's safe to ask for what we need.

Like a New Age mantra or a social media meme, when your self-esteem flags, you must repeat to yourself, "I am worth it." You are weaving a self-esteem safety net that will help you to add to a greater social safety net. It may first appear to be only individual, but if enough contribute, they will connect to a greater structure. As LaVerne Gray shared in her discussion of being a Black woman in librarianship, learning to use your voice is an act of resistance against oppressive silencing, and it "is a cognitive practice whereby women come to knowledge through silence and speaking."[48]

Be kind to your yourself. Academic and activist Susan Wendell cautions that stamina is required for commitment to a cause and, for some of us, our fluctuating "abilities and limitations" can make us "seem like unreliable activists."[49] If we look at this in a different way, though, we can see that temporarily prioritizing our self-care means we are more likely to be able to remain engaged over the long term. Remain cognizant of your limits and practice self-compassion. This is where the importance of having a community of peers and allies is clear, so we can pick up the baton when someone else needs to put it down for a bit.

Self-Reflective Analysis

If you want to be an ally to your disabled peers, we suggest you start with a little self-analysis. Do you push yourself too hard and resent others when you get worn down? Do you think some disabilities are more real than others, or some people are more prone to faking their disability than others? Do you think of yourself as a possible savior? It's ok if your answers to these questions aren't what you'd want to admit to others. We all have to start

---

47   Robin Brown and Scott Sheidlower, "Claiming Our Space: A Quantitative and Qualitative Picture of Disabled Librarians," *Library Trends* 67, no. 3 (2019): 471–86. https://academicworks.cuny.edu/bm_pubs/115/.

48   LaVerne Gray, "The Voice of a Black Woman in Libraryland: A Theoretical Narrative," in *Pushing the Margins: Women of Color and Intersectionality in LIS*, ed. Rose L. Chou and Annie Pho (Sacramento: Library Juice Press, 2018), 147–62.

49   Wendell, Susan, "Unhealthy Disabled: Treating Chronic Illnesses as Disabilities," *Hypatia* 16, no. 4 (2001): 25.

somewhere, and honesty is more helpful than magical thinking. As April Hathcock acknowledges in her excellent blog post aimed at white allies trying to engage in antiracism work, ally work is an ongoing process.[50] You will need to allow yourself to be vulnerable, and to listen to those you're trying to help to be an effective peer advocate. We need you. We need you to speak up when you witness active discrimination or when you notice accessibility barriers. We need you to help us create change.[51]

As Jessica mentioned in an earlier writing, we can improve organizational health for everyone by expanding our conceptions of who belongs in the workplace and how we engage in work.[52] Part of how we do that is by caring for ourselves and each other. In the next chapter, we'll talk more about how to build a caring workplace.

50 April Hathcock, "You're Gonna Screw Up," *At The Intersections* (blog), April 13, 2016, https://aprilhathcock.wordpress.com/2016/04/13/youre-gonna-screw-up/.

51 Julie F. Smart and David W. Smart, "Models of Disability: Implications for the Counseling Profession," *Journal of Counseling & Development* 84, no. 1 (2006): 38.

52 Jessica Schomberg, "Disability at Work: Libraries, Built to Exclude," in *The Politics and Theory of Critical Librarianship*, ed. Karen P. Nicholson and Maura Seale (Sacramento: Library Juice Press, 2018), 126.

Chapter 7

Building a Caring Workplace

Care Is a Community Effort

Content warning death.

When Jessica was fourteen and back at diabetes camp, they learned that their friend Katherine had died. They'd met the previous year and Jessica had looked forward to seeing her again that summer. Most of the counselors were young adults with diabetes and each cohort also had their own doctor or nurse. Rumor had it that this camp had much better food than the non-diabetic camps; they needed to make sure kids ate, so they had to make the food taste good and serve it in consistent portion sizes so everyone would know how much insulin to take. This was of course still a bit of guesswork, since the kids were all extra active—so they also provided juice boxes and regular snacks throughout the day.

But Katherine wasn't going to join them again that year. She'd developed what was called "brittle" diabetes.[1] She wasn't able to control her blood sugars so she had been taken to the hospital. Unfortunately, not even the doctors and nurses at the hospital were able to bring her sugars back

---

1 This term is somewhat controversial at this point. See Wil Dubois, "The Bitterness over 'Brittle Diabetes,'" *Healthline*, February 21, 2017, https://www.healthline.com/diabetesmine/bitterness-over-brittle-diabetes#1.

into range. She died from diabetic ketoacidosis; growth hormones make adolescence hard for diabetics.[2]

From a young age, Jessica has known that life was conditional. Despite the many treatment improvements that have been made since the discovery of insulin, type 1 diabetes is still essentially a terminal illness that appears chronic—as long as you have all the resources you need and if you're lucky.

These resources include: insulin, an insulin delivery mechanism such as syringes or an insulin pump, blood testing supplies, and ready access to the right types of food, water, sleep, and care. Care from health care providers. Care from oneself. Care from those around you. Diabetes often feels isolating, but you truly can't succeed with it alone.

Why did we share this story? Because care, care for ourselves and for each other, is also important in supporting successful library work. Library work often involves team collaboration, ongoing communication, and generally working with humans. As feminist legal scholar Martha Fineman notes, human societies are produced and reproduced by aggregate caretaking labor; it's not an individual process.[3] One way in which diabetes camp provided the care Jessica needed was by making it safe to disclose how they were doing on any given day. It promoted self-awareness and disclosing when they were able to do something and when they needed help. It also provided verbal and material rewards for doing so (often in the form of juice boxes). These rewards required some mechanistic action, in the form of frequent blood sugar checks, but the overall structure was fluid enough to recognize that our capacities change on an ongoing, regular basis.

Theories of Care and Exclusion: The Shadow Side of Libraries

> In the face of grand missions of literacy and freedom, advocating for your full lunch break feels petty. And tasked with the responsibility of sustaining democracy and intellectual freedom, taking a mental health day feels shameful.[4]

---

2   "Teens and Diabetes Mellitus," University of Rochester Medical Center *Health Encyclopedia*, https://www.urmc.rochester.edu/encyclopedia/content. aspx?contenttypeid=90&contentid=P01597.

3   Martha Albertson Fineman, "Cracking the Foundational Myths: Independence, Autonomy, and Self-Sufficiency," *The American University Journal of Gender, Social Policy & the Law* 8, no. 1 (2000): 19, https://digitalcommons.wcl.american.edu/jgspl/vol8/iss1/2/.

4   Fobazi Ettarh, "Vocational Awe and Librarianship: The Lies We Tell Ourselves," *In the Library with the Lead Pipe*, January 10, 2018, http://www.inthelibrarywiththeleadpipe. org/2018/vocational-awe/.

Vocational awe is a theory of library work coined by librarian Fobazi Ettarh. It is a critical model of the idea that libraries are inherently good and sacred, and that the work of library workers is a moral duty. According to this ideal, sacrificing oneself to the work is valorized. Prioritizing one's own physical, emotional, psychological, financial, or social needs is a dereliction of our moral duty as library workers. Failing to meet professional ideals is a failure for us as individuals, not for the institution.[5]

The vocational awe model critiques this mindset. It acknowledges that our organizational structures—how we organize information as well as ourselves—prioritize maintaining an inequitable status quo. While holding library work in such high esteem may be well-intentioned, it has the negative effect of placing library workers upon a pedestal from which we are bound to fall. Profaning the idea (and ideal) that libraries are sacred allows us to come up with new ideas for substantive change. We are referencing this model in the hope of recreating libraries in a way that plans for, deliberately includes, and cares for disabled people.

But the rhetoric of care can also be used to exclude, demean, infantilize, and control people receiving that care. Care, when the needs and application of such is determined in a moral sense, without consultation or consent from the recipient, has the actual effect of marginalizing the receiver.[6] Rhetoric about civilizing, standardizing, assimilating, or normalizing people is a good warning sign that this is happening.[7] Unsolicited, nonconsensual caregiving can also be called saviorism. Saviors in this sense "fundamentally believe that they are better than the people they are rescuing" and thus refuse to relinquish control and refuse to listen to those they are supposedly helping.[8] In a disability context, this has the effect of disempowering and pushing disabled people out of disability justice movements, as well as limiting the potential for substantive change.

Vocational awe and the savior mentality work to maintain cultural imperialism. This can be tied to concepts of perfectionism and efficiency.

---

5 Ettarh, "Vocational Awe."

6 Schomberg, "Disability at Work," 120–21.

7 Gina Schlesselman-Tarango, "The Legacy of Lady Bountiful: White Women in the Library," *Library Trends* 64, no. 4 (2016): 667–86.

8 Jordan Flaherty, "'Saviors' Believe That They Are Better Than the People They Are 'Saving,'" *Truthout*, January 5, 2017, https://truthout.org/articles/saviors-believe-that-they-are-better-than-the-people-they-are-saving/.

As mentioned in the moral model section of chapter 1, these ideas are entwined with the idea that disabled people have irregular bodies and minds. This is also tied to the use of disgust, in both a moral and visceral sense. Disgust has historically been used as a weapon to exclude groups or individuals. Moral, non-disgusting bodies comply with middle-class ideals of refinement and containment. "Unruly corporealities," on the other hand, don't exhibit that same control.[9] They are "leaky, porous" and irregular, and as such violate the corporeal norms of nondisabled performance. They are also potentially dangerous contaminators.

Rhetorical and physical boundaries are therefore created to contain those uncontained corporealities, acting to label, distance, and exclude them. Historically, this was used to justify "ugly laws" which prohibited visibly sick and disabled people from appearing in public.[10] Currently, in a workplace setting, this sense of disgust may lead to targeted behavioral modification strategies, excessive monitoring, and sanctions. It may also include using descriptors such as "lazy" to indicate that someone is undeserving of respect or care. The disproportionate veneration inherent in vocational awe paves the way for the projection of fear, dread, and disgust upon nonconforming disabled bodies and minds.

Accommodations as Care: Valuing Humanity over Hierarchy

How often have you heard people say "this is how we've always done it" as a reason for why something is done in a certain way? Maybe with the added justification that a director who retired twenty years before preferred doing things that way? Sometimes our normal workplace routines are determined cooperatively rather than mandated by a supervisor, but even in those situations it's good to occasionally question whether they're still serving their purpose and if the purpose they're serving is one you want to continue supporting. Using the theoretical lens of vocational awe or disability studies can help when engaging with those questions, because it brings into sharp focus the power relationships that occur in any work decision or process. These "seemingly ordinary arrangements that structure our work days and work lives are not the inevitable form of organizations, but rather are deeply rooted in historical divisions of labor between classes, genders,

---

9   Soldatic and Meekosha, "The Place of Disgust," 144.

10   Susan M. Schweik, *The Ugly Laws: Disability in Public* (New York: NYU Press, 2009).

racial groups, and people with and without disabilities."[11] Normative ideas of workplace organization are often developed in a way that maintains the interests of dominant groups.

We can counter the dominant narrative by thinking of accommodations as a form of care, rather than as compliance with bureaucratic requirements. In this way, we can approach accommodations in a way that recognizes our shared humanity. Challenging ableist assumptions about body normativity allows us to care for each other and for ourselves.

In neoliberal terms, a caring community constitutes a cost-effective workplace accommodation strategy. Having the support of employers and community members (and the safety to engage in self-advocacy) results in the most benefit and costs the least to maintain. What is notable here is that despite ableist rhetoric to the contrary, research shows that caring for oneself and for each other is a good return on investment.[12] This care can be demonstrated in empathic ways, but it can also be demonstrated through the development of systems responsive to diverse needs.[13]

In more revolutionary terms, caring also allows for what disability activist Mia Mingus calls "access intimacy". Access intimacy occurs when disabled people can express their needs to others in a way that is affirmed and understood. It is a transformative practice that prioritizes interdependence and disabled peoples' humanity. It rejects silence, isolation, and shame. As in the neoliberal model of care, it also impacts how systems operate.[14]

When the leaders of a workplace care about their workers, whether out of a sense of reciprocity or because they're contractually bound via union pressure or for some other reason, they show it. They show it by providing workplace accommodations that workers need. They show it by advertising the accessibility of their workplaces. The result of this for people with disabilities is that our work performance improves, we're more satisfied at work, and we work longer. Leaders also show that they care about

---

11   Harlan and Robert, "The Social Construction of Disability," 400.

12   Konrad, "Reimagining Work," 123–41.

13   Nicole K. Dalmer and D. G. Campbell, "Communicating with Library Patrons and People with Dementia: Tracing an Ethic of Care in Professional Communication Guidelines," *Dementia* (2018), doi:10.1177/1471301218790852.

14   Mia Mingus, "Access Intimacy, Interdependence, and Disability Justice," presented at the Paul K. Longmore Lecture on Disability Studies (San Francisco State University, April 11, 2017), https://leavingevidence.wordpress.com/2017/04/12/access-intimacy-interdependence-and-disability-justice/.

workers by listening to workers' ideas about what we need, which has the result of reducing litigation.[15]

Fear and Fatigue as Barriers to Care

As Audre Lorde notes in her cancer journals, silence about our experiences won't protect us.[16] Even when our words are misinterpreted, there is value in sharing them. We still need to take space to acknowledge the costs of that. Jessica talks about how good intentions on the part of peers aren't enough on their own to overcome the fatigue caused by ableist microaggressions:

> Sometimes when I tell people about the stigmatizing bias and aversion people have exhibited upon learning that I have diabetes, they express shock and disbelief. Sometimes when I tell people about how a librarian warned me never to disclose that I've had cancer if I want to get hired, they express anger. I can understand why they want to distance themselves from this sort of demeaning treatment, but those shocked and angry reactions don't actually help me. Instead, they make me feel like they're distancing themselves from the reality I've experienced. For most of them, I know that's not the intent. But it makes me feel like they can't see me. It makes me feel like they're emphasizing how their lived experience is different from mine. It feels othering,[17] their attempts at offering comfort reminding me that I'm not part of the non-disabled norm.[18] And from what I've seen, they're not accompanied by action to make workplaces better for sick people. Overcoming ableism takes courage. It also takes physical and emotional resources, and deliberately expending energy in a

---

15 Gold, Oire, Fabian, and Wewiorski, "Negotiating Reasonable Workplace Accommodations," 25.

16 Audre Lorde, *The Cancer Journals*, 2nd ed. (Aunt Lute Books, 1992), 18–23.

17 Oppressive othering is the process of creating inequitable groups marked as inferior as some way. For more on this, see Donnalyn Pompper, *Practical and Theoretical Implications of Successfully Doing Difference in Organizations* (Bingley, UK: Emerald Group Publishing 2014), 12–16.

18 Several library-twitter friends helped Jessica think through how to express this better, and we would like to thank them for that.

strategic manner. These interactions don't acknowledge that, and often I feel like I need to prioritize helping them process their emotional reactions to my experiences when I'd rather use that energy to improve processes and policies.

Ableist assumptions about work performance disadvantage anyone who doesn't fit pre-determined norms. Think about how you learned what's acceptable in the workplace: how work should be accomplished, how work should be scheduled, how workers look, and how work is evaluated. If your workplaces were like ours, it is unlikely those ideas were presented to you as negotiable. When these normative work expectations are combined with neoliberal assumptions of performance without accommodation, it creates an impossible situation for disabled workers.[19] We are forced to over-prepare[20] to compensate for others' unwillingness to provide accessible resources and must also deal with stigma against using assistive technologies.[21]

We must also find a way through expectations that reward so-called rational behaviors, behaviors that minimize costs and maximize efficiency, even when those expectations aren't in our best interests as humans.[22] Sometimes those expectations lead us to talk about each other as commodities, human capital that can be standardized and controlled in the same way we would talk about buying and selling bales of cotton.[23] Consider Marx's theory of alienation, which "describes how human beings are deprived of control over their lives and how this leads to a sense of powerlessness."[24] This alienation encourages us to view each other through a competitive lens, with artificial rankings of better and worse, more than and less, superior and inferior.

This alienation from the workplace can also accompany alienation from oneself. Research ranging from Arlie Hochschild's work on emotional

19   Konrad, "Reimagining Work," 125.

20   Brown and Sheidlower, "Claiming Our Space," 477.

21   Konrad, "Reimagining Work," 123–41.

22   Nirmala Erevelles, "(Im)material Citizens: Cognitive Disability, Race, and the Politics of Citizenship," *Disability, Culture and Education* 1, no. 1 (2002): 13, http://blogs.ubc. ca/ssed317/files/2008/08/immaterial-citizens.pdf.

23   Rosenthal, *Accounting for Slavery*, 149–52.

24   Slorach, *A Very Capitalist Condition*, 78.

labor[25] to Fobazi Ettarh's work on vocational awe have observed that workers "often feel an incongruity between the emotions they have to show and what they really feel."[26] Think back to the stigmatizing reactions Jessica mentioned earlier, in response to diabetes and cancer. Consider the pressures of vocational awe to demonstrate positivity, passion, and unrelenting commitment to the organization. In this type of work culture, would you feel safe sharing your disability status and advocating to receive accommodations? Would you feel safe taking care of your body's needs? Would you feel valued for showing care for coworkers? Would you feel valued for receiving care from coworkers?

Acknowledging the Costs of Affective Labor

Library work is predominantly done by women.[27] Gendered expectations about the value of work, and the types of work that have value, impact who does which types of library work and how those work types are remunerated. In Roma Harris's anthropological analysis of library work, she observed that reference and cataloging work were stereotyped as being feminine, and were lower in prestige and less funded than work stereotyped as masculine, such as administration and technology.[28] Nearly three decades later, ARL statistics continue to bear out this pattern in terms of salary and staffing inequities between library work areas.[29] The reason this matters in discussions of affective labor is because affective labor is also viewed as feminine and as such is "not recognized or valued as labor."[30] At the same time, because it is expected that library workers engage in affective labor, especially those in positions such as reference services, those workers are at risk of having their own interior experiences distorted in service to the

---

25   Arlie Russell Hochschild, *The Managed Heart: Commercialization of Human Feeling* (Berkeley: University of California Press, 1983).

26   Ettarh. "Vocational Awe."

27   Department for Professional Employees, AFL-CIO Research Department, "Library Professionals: Facts & Figures, Women and Library Professions," 2019, https://dpeaflcio.org/programs-publications/issue-fact-sheets/library-workers-facts-figures/.

28   Harris, *Librarianship*, 121–43.

29   Morris, "ARL Annual Salary Survey, 2015–2016."

30   Lisa Sloniowski, "Affective Labor, Resistance, and the Academic Library," *Library Trends* 64 no. 4 (2016): 656.

institution. As noted by Lisa Sloniowski in discussing Hochschild's research, "the use of emotional labor in capitalist economies correlates to an estranging, sexist, colonization of life by work."[31]

Hochschild defines emotional labor as requiring workers "to induce or suppress feeling in order to sustain the outward countenance that produces the proper state of mind in others...This kind of labor calls for a coordination of mind and feeling, and it sometimes draws on a source of self that we honor as deep and integral to our individuality."[32] In libraries, this can be seen in the expectation that reference librarians perform an interest in patrons' research questions to reduce their anxiety while simultaneously helping them find the information they need, no matter what the librarian themself is experiencing at the moment.[33] Hochschild describes this emotional labor, "the trained management of feeling," as behaving like a commodity with demand for it fluctuating depending on industry competition.[34] If you're struggling to think of how this fits with your lived experience, think of all the times you've heard librarians described as human versions of Google.[35] This is what is happening there: the selves we bring to work are being rhetorically commodified.

Affective labor has the potential to produce stronger social networks and stronger communities.[36] Unfortunately, as mentioned in the discussion about vocational awe, many library workplaces interpret this with the expectation that employees display unrelenting positivity. This is especially problematic because the actual work environment often causes fear and anxiety. We are expected to always be ready for or preparing ourselves for work, always in control of ourselves and our emotions, always presenting ourselves in a way that may belie our internal experiences.[37] Add to these

---

31   Sloniowski, "Affective Labor," 656.

32   Hochschild, *The Managed Heart*, 20.

33   Gina Schlesselman-Tarango, "Reproductive Failure and Information Work: An Autoethnography," *Library Trends* 67, no. 3 (2019): 446.

34   Hochschild, *The Managed Heart*, 24.

35   Laura Bliss, "The Public Librarians Who Serve as Human Google," *CityLab*, October 18, 2016, https://www.citylab.com/life/2016/10/the-public-librarians-who-still-serve-as-human-google/504506/.

36   Sloniowski, "Affective Labor," 645–66.

37   Sloniowski, 645–66.

behavioral expectations the instability of library budgets, fluctuating or contingent work schedules, fears for personal safety while at or getting to work, and stresses caused by inaccessible health care or unavailable child- or eldercare.[38] The disconnect between institutional expectations and support in itself causes stress, as does the cognitive dissonance.

"Must be able to lift 50 pounds."

Workplace nondiscrimination policy is developed with the idea that organizations are neutral and equality will result if everyone has to follow the same rules.[39] Unfortunately, the reality is that organizations are not neutral. In terms of hiring, job postings often include language requiring that applicants have full mobility, dexterity, the ability to lift things, be sighted, and be fully hearing, despite the positions themselves not requiring this type of labor.[40] It is not clear whether those in charge of writing such job descriptions are unaware of their discriminatory nature or are indifferent, but their intent doesn't change the effect: disabled people don't apply and therefore don't get hired, even when they might be excellent in the role.[41]

Library organizations are not neutral. Libraries were developed and are maintained by those in dominant positions in service to the state, a state which has a long history of denying citizenship and humanity to many of the people living within its boundaries.[42] We can't achieve equity without challenging the status quo. This means changing how we make decisions, how we interact with each other, how we engage in work tasks, and what behaviors we reward and how.

---

38 Schomberg, "Disability at Work," 122–23.

39 Harlan and Robert, "The Social Construction of Disability," 400.

40 David M. Perry, "Disabled People Need Not Apply," *AlJazeera America Opinion* (February 5, 2016), http://america.aljazeera.com/opinions/2016/2/disabled-people-need-not-apply.html.

41 Samantha Cook and Kristina Clement, "Navigating the Hidden Void: The Unique Challenges of Accommodating Library Employees with Invisible Disabilities," *The Journal of Academic Librarianship*, published ahead of print March 8, 2019, https://doi.org/10.1016/j.acalib.2019.02.010.

42 nina de jesus, "Locating the Library in Institutional Oppression," *In the Library with the Lead Pipe*, September 24, 2014, http://www.inthelibrarywiththeleadpipe.org/2014/locating-the-library-in-institutional-oppression/.

When examining research on what disabled people say helps them, we find a variety of options that library workplaces could explore. These range from engaging in more flexible conceptions of work time and physical presence to depersonalizing errors in promotion of a teamwork approach to problem solving.[43] One of the biggest challenges to positive change is attitudinal barriers among employers.[44] Poor infrastructure, such as unavailable transportation options in rural areas or difficult-to-schedule transportation options in urban areas, provide another challenge.[45]

Sam, a nonbinary librarian of color with chronic illness, shares their experiences with the hiring process:

> In libraries, the hiring process isn't very accommodating for people who don't process information quickly or who aren't skilled at verbalizing information under pressure. This happens even when those skills aren't needed for the job being hired. The interview process is an unnatural environment that doesn't replicate the actual work environment. For my own interview, I had to plan around my limitations [including the energy toll of taking public transportation], to make sure I wasn't tired and had a good thinking day. There aren't often do-overs for interviews.

More flexible work environments allow options including telecommuting or self-directed scheduling. Telework allows disabled workers to prioritize their faculties on engaging in work instead of getting to work. For many, it also provides more control over their work environment, so they can ensure they have necessary equipment every day. Telework can also provide more flexibility in terms of when employees engage in work, so they can flex their schedules around bodily needs if necessary. For workers with some communication disabilities, telework can also help them develop better communicative rapport with coworkers. Supervisors still need to provide regular feedback, ensure that technological support is provided, and make sure the teleworking employee(s) are engaged with workplace social networks, but those challenges are all manageable.[46]

---

43 Konrad, "Reimagining Work," 123–41.

44 McNaughton, Rackensperger, Dorn and Wilson, "'Home is at Work," 117–26.

45 McNaughton, Rackensperger, Dorn and Wilson, 118.

46 McNaughton, Rackensperger, Dorn, and Wilson, "'Home is at Work," 117–26.

Barbara, a Black queer librarian with multiple chronic illnesses shares her experience:

> I'm on intermittent FMLA [Family Medical Leave Act], be-
> cause of my migraines, and that's been in place for years.
> [My employers] were very helpful with that. They helped me
> when I had to have surgery, and had no sick time, basical-
> ly. They created where I could work from home, to use that
> time. And then I had FMLA, so I could keep my position.

Other options for useful work changes include adaptive strategies for accomplishing work tasks. In one example, a low-vision teacher who could
not see her students raise their hands taught them how to take turns in
conversation. Her supervisors at one school viewed that as a loss of control, while supervisors at another school viewed that as a way of teaching
students a lifelong skill.[47] Letting go of the need to control everything increased her students' self-efficacy instead of increasing their compliance.

Creating a Diverse, Health-Enhancing Workplace

As we mentioned in chapter 1, the model of an ideal worker is built with
the assumption that workers are nondisabled and interchangeable like
parts of a machine. This normative ideal of a worker does not account for
individual needs. In fact, an individual worker expressing their needs is actively discouraged in this mental model.[48] A healthy workplace can only be
built by challenging that ideal.

Sara, a white queer librarian with multiple chronic illnesses, shares
her experience:

> I really like…In terms of my last job even, this job you just
> automatically start out with twenty-five sick days when you
> start working through your first year, and you don't accumu-
> late anymore for your first year, but you start out with that
> stash…It's so nice, it made a world of difference because I
> am chronically ill [and] they have this experience, too, it's
> like, you don't get to control when you get sick, and then
> those doctor's appointments, you have to schedule for when
> they have staff. And so that was just an amazing, I was very

---

47 Konrad, "Reimagining Work," 123–41.

48 O'Brien. Bodies in Revolt, 73–74.

excited about that. And right now, I'm able to telecommute, once a week as needed as an accommodation, and that's so nice. It's not written into the policy, our telecommuting policy is actually pretty strict...But I just have a very wonderful sort of management all the way up from my supervisor to their [supervisor], and they're very understanding, and a very supportive environment.

Our choices can align us with dominant power structures or can allow us to support alternative power structures. We must make a choice; human society is not empty of power relationships. Rhetorical choices that deflect attention from the realities of commodification, exploitation, and historical inequalities support dominant forces. However, by examining where we put our attention, we can be more aware of the power structures under which we operate. We can also build power structures that allow for healing.[49] Even more than that, we can develop processes that take place in a work environment that enhances healing.

As noted in the above interview, Sara was able to get work accommodations because of a generous supervisor. While this is helpful, changing the actual process of how telecommuting rights are distributed may mean that she's not at the mercy of whoever happens to be supervising her at any given time. In fact, a proactively healthy workplace would use the double loop learning style mentioned in chapter 3 to hear Sara's accommodation request as a need that might benefit the collective.[50]

Noticing the rhetoric that influences our thoughts helps us notice where power is held. Noticing where power is held helps us engage in active community building. By changing the focus from the individual to the collective, we can change the focus from commodifying emotional labor to relationship building. In discussing building relationships of reciprocal accountability with students, Jessie Loyer notes that a mindset prioritizing interconnectedness operates through shared activities and responsibilities.[51] This mindset demands and creates awareness of one another's health and well-being. It also helps us identify our roles within relationships. In

---

49   Nicola Andrews, "Reflections on Resistance, Decolonization, and the Historical Trauma of Libraries and Academia," in *The Politics of Theory and the Practice of Critical Librarianship*, ed. Maura Seale & Karen Nicholson (Sacramento, CA: Library Juice Press, 2018), 188–91, doi:10.31229/osf.io/mva35.

50   O'Brien, *Bodies in Revolt*, 135.

51   Loyer, "Indigenous Information Literacy," 150–55.

the sense of community organizing, it aids us in understanding our responsibilities to each other. It also helps us become aware of the skill sets and leadership potential we have within our communities.[52]

We have many options to help us inform how we incorporate care and community-building into our work. Activists and their allies could combine Chugh's growth mindset described in chapter 4 with Loyer's connected mindset. The combination of openness toward learning new patterns, with a strong intention to create a caring community, would give activists a powerful focus. We know where we want to go—we want disabled people to be fully incorporated into caring communities—and there are many paths we can take to get there.

Think back to the story we shared at the beginning of the chapter. Just as the camp teams took time to listen to diabetic campers and customized their treatment, so too can librarians listen and build relationships with diverse users and workers. This doesn't mean demanding our disabled peers prioritize helping us process our emotional reactions to their realities. It does mean acknowledging that it takes work to process those reactions and develop better responses. Meaningful community-building takes substantial work. We can work toward providing the "social and material resources necessary for the achievement of both individual and communitarian plans," de-commodifying labor and enabling workers and community members to engage with and critique power relations that have traditionally objectified and controlled people.[53] This will allow us to reimagine, recreate, and re-produce a non-exploitative workplace that values interdependency. Each of us has the human right to meaningful, gainful participation in public life, one aspect of which is employment. It takes a village full of courageous and energetic workers to create a caring workplace and community.

We must do more than merely reacting emotionally and doing nothing after the feelings subside. We demand more than the mere appearance, the veneer, of care. We can go beyond kneejerk reactions and fully realize that discrimination exists, analyze the dynamic, strategize, and act to change the status quo. Liberation from discrimination requires caring interactions between co-workers, expansion of the imagination, coordinated and sustained political action, and the creation and maintenance of a new reality: a community of care.

---

52 Si Kahn, *Organizing, a Guide for Grassroots Leaders*, Rev. ed. (Silver Spring, Md: National Association of Social Workers, 1991).

53 Erevelles, "(Im)material Citizen," 22.

Chapter 8

Working Well with a Metabolic Disorder

Hello, my lovelies, this is Jessica. Wendy and I have decided to divide the last two chapters between us to share our personal stories. We share a common label, but our experiences and perspectives are in some ways very different. We hope that providing our different perspectives will help you get broader exposure to the possibilities and challenges that come as part of working with disabilities.

In this chapter, I'll be talking about the chronic illnesses I live and work with. I'll share a little background information about what metabolic disorders are and how they impact my daily work-life. I'll also talk about the idea of working well, and what that might mean.

Metabolic Disorders

Content warning References to food, weight, and death.

When we eat food, our digestive system turns that food into energy in the form of carbohydrates and acids. This process is controlled by the endocrine system, which uses hormones to deliver "store energy" and "release energy" messages as needed. When this process is working ideally, our bodies can store and release that energy in a happy balance. For people with metabolic disorders, this process is disrupted. In the case of diabetes, the hormone insulin is either absent or insufficient to deliver those store and release messages in the way the body needs.[1] This can lead to gain-

---

1   Larissa Hirsch, "Metabolism," KidsHealth from Nemours, 2019, https://kidshealth.org/en/parents/metabolism.html.

ing or losing weight in unwanted ways, tiredness, constant thirst, nausea, brain fog, other physical discomforts, and death.[2]

Some people can modify their lifestyle to help their hormones deliver these messages better, and this strategy can delay their need to take medication. But for some of us, we have to start on medication like synthetic insulin immediately, because we don't have the environmental supports needed to make those lifestyle changes or because our bodies just can't produce enough of the hormone for us to stay alive. Most metabolic disorders have genetic or unknown causes, which can be a bit frustrating because we always have to be on the alert for other disorders that might want to tag along. Having adequate access to the medications, tools, and health care providers we need can keep us alive and help us feel better. In exchange, we have to engage in constant self-monitoring and decision-making to try to replicate what our endocrine system can't do on its own.

Being Disordered

While the title of this chapter references diabetes as a metabolic condition, my type 1 diabetes can also be categorized as an autoimmune disease. Autoimmune diseases are caused by the immune system "mistakenly attacking a part of one's own body as if it were a foreign invader...In type 1 diabetes, the immune system destroys the beta cells of the pancreas that produce insulin, leaving its sufferers without the ability to control their blood sugar levels on their own. In Hashimoto's thyroiditis, it's the thyroid gland that's attacked."[3] I don't like referring to myself as a sufferer, because it seems a little dramatic and self-pitying, but the rest of that excerpt provides useful information about autoimmune conditions.

I have both conditions described above—type 1 diabetes and Hashimoto's—along with a few others. For example, since recording the events in the next section, I've realized that eating tree nuts may be the cause of my eczema, for reasons even my doctor doesn't understand. Even trying to eat healthfully can lead to illness and a lot of investigative work to figure out what's going on.

---

2   "Metabolic Disorders," Intermountain Healthcare, Diabetes and Endocrinology, 2018, https://intermountainhealthcare.org/services/diabetes-endocrinology/conditions/metabolic-disorders/.

3   Maya Dusenbery, *Doing Harm: The Truth about How Bad Medicine and Lazy Science Leave Women Dismissed, Misdiagnosed, and Sick* (San Francisco: HarperOne, 2018), 138.

Some people categorize me as someone with metabolic disorder, others as someone with autoimmune disorder; they're both correct. I also have psychiatric disabilities, and intermittent sensory processing issues caused by fluctuating blood sugars. And I'm allergic to nature (for real: grasses, weeds, trees, farm mold—if it grows in the ground it probably makes me sneeze).

I usually just identify as someone with diabetes though, because more people know what that is, and I sometimes need help while dealing with a hypoglycemic episode. Despite how these conditions impact my daily life, most of the time I'll go through the whole day without mentioning any of these concepts to anyone: blood sugar, carbohydrates, medication, medical technology, diabetes, fatigue, muscle tension, dehydration, pain. They're a normal part of my life, but I don't talk about them a lot.

I'm not sure why I don't talk about them much, given that the issues I experience with chronic illness are my normal. It could be that I don't talk about them much because even the annoyances are so prosaic at this point. It might also be that I don't want to be seen as whiny or less-than, or because I've learned over time that discussion of chronic illness is not welcome in a lot of situations. The result is feeling like I'm constantly wearing a mask, or, as Michele Lind Hirsch describes it, scaliola: "I'm painted over to look like something solid. And so people find it hard to believe that underneath I am crumbling plaster."[4]

April 25, 2019, a Good Day

Content warning References to food and blood glucose.

8:00 a.m. Wake up, hot shower to loosen muscles then pile on the lotion to prevent an eczema flare, check blood sugar and give myself a bolus[5] for the bowl of cereal I'm about to eat. Then take my morning pills with a glass of water before running out the door.

9:00 a.m. Walk in to start the first meeting of the morning while my cgm[6] sensor alerts me that my blood sugar is spiking. I real-

---

4   Hirsch, *Invisible*, 102.

5   A bolus is the insulin I take specifically to account for the food that I'm eating, or to correct high blood sugar. People using insulin pumps also have a basal insulin dose that runs throughout the day, to provide the base level of insulin needed.

6   continuous glucose monitor

ize then that I didn't double-check the carbs in the particular cereal I had for breakfast and misjudged the amount of insulin I need. I won't be able to check my blood sugar for at least another hour, which is a long time, so I take a swag[7] bolus before starting the meeting. Thank goodness it's spring, so I have more sunlight to support mental clarity despite experiencing hyperglycemia!

10:00 a.m.   Done with my first meeting and my next meeting is abbreviated because a coworker is absent, so I have time to check my blood sugar using my glucose meter. My cgm sensor says my blood sugar is still rising; my glucose meter provides a more accurate, current number. With this information, I can take a better targeted bolus to hopefully correct this high without overdoing it. Other things to note: this high blood sugar episode, as is often the case, is accompanied by a headache and sweatiness. Oh, and also, the cataloging documentation I'm looking for is not where I was expecting it to be, which is annoying.

11:00 a.m.   My blood sugar is going back toward my goal range, so it's easier to focus on work. Time to catalog some DVDs!

12:00 p.m.   Lunchtime! My blood sugar is still falling in response to the 9 a.m. and 10 a.m. boluses, and it would be reasonable to wait until things stabilize before I eat, but I'm hungry and have meetings this afternoon. So, I'm going to bolus for and eat lunch now anyway and hope for the best, instead of waiting for my sugars to flatten out. My body is basically an ongoing science experiment done in a non-clinical setting, so everything is by guess and by golly. While eating, I have a short conversation with a coworker about her attempts to reduce fines and simplify fee structures, which makes me happy. I also check Twitter to see how my friends are doing.

1:00 p.m.   Email and impromptu work discussions and trying to drink a lot of water to rehydrate after having high blood sugar.[8]

---

7   scientific wild ass guess

8   High blood sugar can cause dehydration. Dehydration can cause high blood sugar. It's a vicious circle.

2:00 p.m.   Another meeting, this time about how to process bestsellers and purchase-on-demand books. We migrated to a new ILS this year, so all our normal routines are a bit up in the air. During the meeting, a coworker handed me some electronic kits that need to be added to the collection for computer science students to check out. Still have the headache from this morning.

3:00 p.m.   See an email inviting me to a 7:30 a.m. campus governance meeting next week and sigh. Move on to the happier work of cleaning up LibGuides. Also answer a coworker's question about an email he needed to send and help another coworker find the right form for what they need to do. Advil and my r&b playlist on Spotify help with the headache. During this hour, my blood sugar drops too far and instead of consuming the recommended dosage of glucose tablets, I choose to eat a homemade brownie that another coworker brought in. #yolo

4: 00 p.m.   Sign a card congratulating a student worker for graduating. Send an email to members of the professional board I'm on with a discussion proposal I want us to consider at the next ALA Annual meeting. Start working on setting up import profiles in Alma for maps and music CDs.

5:00 p.m.   Check blood sugar then gym. I'm trying to maintain this as a habit, because it helps with mobility and keeping the monkeys from taking over my brain. Self-care as someone with chronic illness involves a lot of forcing yourself to do annoying good-for-you things that you'd rather avoid. My evening trips to the gym are often just walking on the treadmill at a steady pace, because that has the least impact on my blood sugar, both immediately and over the next few hours.[9]

6:00 p.m.   Supper. Even routine rides on the blood sugar rollercoaster are draining experiences, so what may seem like a relaxed day to most people ended up wiping me out. But food routines are important, and I know eating supper will help me

---

9   Because I'm an insulin-dependent type 1 diabetic and this is late afternoon, vigorous exercise can cause my blood sugar levels to plummet in dangerous and scary ways. Strength building exercises can cause it to plummet 4–6 hours later. Early morning exercise can actually raise blood sugar levels! It's a complicated game to play.

feel better in the long run. So, do I choose the foods that will make me feel better or do I let fatigue lead me to foods that require no effort and please the id? Why not both!

7:00 p.m.   Watch YouTube makeup videos. Don't judge.

8:00 p.m.   Read. I'm close to finishing Viet Thanh Nguyen's *The Sympathizer*. It's really good but reading it in slow and steady increments is the best approach for me with Serious Books.[10]

9:00 p.m.   More reading, but this time it's fluff: Lily Maxton's *A Lady's Desire*. I'm not usually big on historical romance, but this is short, gay, and delightful.

10:00 p.m.   Check blood sugar, do a quick round of sun salutations to loosen muscles, then evening pills and bedtime. I'd rather stay up later to read, but I need a lot of sleep and my sleep is often interrupted because of diabetes. If I try for nine to ten hours, I may actually get enough sleep to function the next day. Oh, hey, my insulin pump just alarmed to tell me that it's almost out of insulin, so I either swap out equipment now and waste insulin or wake up at 2 a.m. to change it then.[11]

Working Well

What does working well mean? Good question! I don't know, honestly. In the previous section, I provided you with a look into a perfectly normal workday. Or at least, it was perfectly normal for me, and no one I worked with expressed any signs that they found any of my behavior questionable. But to delve a little further into this topic, I'm going to do some research. Despite my skepticism about some of the standards defining professionalism and related concepts, my cataloger brain likes documentation. So, I'm going to start by referring to professional competencies.

---

10   Serious content warning for chapter 21. A lot of bad stuff happens in this book, but months later I still have flashbacks to a scene in this particular chapter.

11   Health care providers often express shock and dismay when I tell them I don't immediately change out my set when I get a low-reservoir warning. I can only assume that's because they don't have to try to get insurance companies to actually pay for insulin. Because that is an exhausting dance in its own right, and one I don't want to have again, I chose to wake up at 2 a.m.

First, I look through "Diversity Standards: Cultural Competency for Academic Libraries."[12] I actively work to enhance my own cultural awareness and help build professional diversity training options, which means that I have a record of performance in this area.

Next, I'll look at guidelines for appointing, promoting, and tenuring academic librarians.[13] I'm an active member in professional associations. I engage in research and disseminate it via professional publications and presentations. I contribute to the educational mission of my institution. Conveniently, these are basically the same standards my employer expects me to meet, which I've successfully done for over a decade as demonstrated by my performance reviews. So, I'd say that I'm meeting these expectations.

I also wear specific hats related to assessment and cataloging. For assessment, the competencies seem to be a mixture of knowledge about higher education assessment and research methods, research and data management ethics, communication skills, and teaching skills.[14] My self-evaluation is that I can either demonstrate my competence in each of these areas or I know who to bring in to balance out my weaknesses. As with my approach to disability advocacy, I have learned that success lies in taking a cooperative and relational approach to my work rather than trying to go it alone.

For cataloging, the competencies include understanding cataloging tools and the conceptual models behind them, how to apply that knowledge, and behavioral expectations.[15] The behavioral competencies seem to be developed with a neurotypical cataloger in mind, which makes me *hmm* to myself. I could articulate how I meet those behavioral competencies, but I also recognize that this part of the competencies is ripe for manipulation by an ableist supervisor or coworker. I'm also concerned that these

12   American Library Association, "Diversity Standards: Cultural Competency for Academic Libraries (2012)," May 4, 2012, http://www.ala.org/acrl/standards/diversity.

13   American Library Association, "A Guideline for the Appointment, Promotion and Tenure of Academic Librarians," September 6, 2006, http://www.ala.org/acrl/standards/promotiontenure.

14   American Library Association, Association of College & Research Libraries, "ACRL Proficiencies for Assessment Librarians and Coordinators," January 23, 2017, http://www.ala.org/acrl/standards/assessment_proficiencies.

15   American Library Association, Association for Library Collections & Technical Services, "Core Competencies for Cataloging and Metadata Professional Librarians," 2017, https://alair.ala.org/handle/11213/7853.

standards might be used to not hire someone raised in a culture with a different set of behavioral expectations. My self-evaluation is side-tracked by the urge to write an article critiquing these competencies.

By reviewing professional competencies and my own workplace's expectations, I feel comfortable saying that I have demonstrated that I can work well according to the standards of my peers. But is that enough? If I had a supervisor who engaged in rampant tone policing, would I be penalized for not presenting myself in a perky, positive way when I'm stuck on a blood sugar roller coaster? If I were to get a supervisor who was successful in mandating that I work on a set schedule that's convenient for them instead of my current more flexible work schedule, would I be able to accomplish everything I accomplish now?[16] If I were assigned to work a service desk for thirty to forty hours a week, would I have enough energy to even function? I strongly suspect the answer to these questions is *no*. I would quickly go from working well to not working at all. As Esmé Weijun Wang shares in discussing her experiences with debilitating mental illness and deliberately not seeking employment in fast food environments: "Place me in a high-stress environment with no ability to control my surroundings or my schedule, and I will rapidly begin to decompensate…I'm a high-functioning person with an unpredictable and low-functioning illness."[17]

But the lessons I've learned from having disabilities also enhance my work. As a person with semi-regular brain fog, I've developed work processes that take advantage of the self I bring to work any given day. I was recently able to share one of those lessons with co-workers who were intimidated by a large project we had taken on. My advice: use low-brain days to do the repetitive parts that require less attention, then you're ready to really engage with the complex aspects on high-brain days. My co-workers found that approach reassuring, and the project less daunting as a result. Disabled or not, we all have daily fluctuations in what we're able to do.

---

16 I work in a union environment, which does provide some protections against unreasonable demands, but I also have spoken with enough people who've had horrible experiences with the formal accommodations process. So, I have a lot of doubts about how successful requesting accommodations would be, given the variety of health conditions I live with. For a first-person experience with a librarian describing the challenges of getting accommodations, see Pionke, "The Impact of Disbelief," 423–35.

17 Esmé Weijun Wang, *The Collected Schizophrenias: Essays* (Minneapolis, MN: Graywolf Press, 2019), 50.

Disability Is Part of Life

I feel lucky that I make enough money to survive with only one job, instead of the multiple jobs I had when I was younger. I feel lucky that my benefits include health coverage that pays most of the cost of my insulin. I feel sad that I probably won't ever be able to pursue my dream of getting a doctoral degree; I don't have the energy to engage in the coursework while working full time, and the lack of universal health care makes it too risky for me to quit my current job in pursuit of more education. I long for daily in-person interactions with people like me, to talk about illness and disability as if it's the normal thing it is. For that last one, I'm working on developing such a network, so I have hope for future connections.

My disabilities impact my work life because they are part of the package that is me. I cannot leave them at the door when I start work. I could try to pass as nondisabled, but that's a safety risk given my diabetes. For me, working well requires acknowledging and respecting the fact that I am an embodied creature with bodily needs.

Chapter 9

Working Well with a Movement Disorder: I Found Meaning When Our Interdependency Increased

Livelihood   A person's means of living; maintenance, sustenance
          Oxford English Dictionary

Loss of Livelihood Looms

It was 2004 and I was supervising the acquisitions and serials department of my university's library. I was chugging steadily down the tenure track like a fully-stoked locomotive, working hard. No wonder I was tired by the end of the workweek. But something was wrong with my body. The sensation I felt was something more serious than quotidian fatigue. I felt tension on my left side, especially in my arm and shoulder. I'd had ulnar compression in the past (nerve entrapment similar to carpal tunnel syndrome), so I self-diagnosed compressed nerves and went to a massage therapist. During the deep massage, after the muscles relaxed and my nerves were calm, I still felt the odd sensation. I realized that this was something serious and new. This odd, very internal twinge threatened me to my very core. (I don't remember if I perceived it as a "tremor," but I knew it was not just the typical muscle tension that I often felt from too many hours at the computer in a day). This differed from the nerve compression I'd experienced before.

A sense of fear enveloped me as I processed my realization, and my primary thought was this: I can't lose my livelihood, my ability to work.

This moment of truth proves to me that work is central to my human identity. I can't speak to the experience of other people who are born with a disability, or have a disability most of their lives. Perhaps my experience is most similar to people who become disabled in middle age. I was forty-four years old, in year two of a thirty-year mortgage, and also in year two of an arduous fifteen-year trek to full professorship. I knew I had to keep working. I chose to proceed as if my self-diagnosis of nerve compression was correct.

The Information Gathering Phase

I was afraid, but repressed my fears. I went to a North American Serials Interest Group (NASIG) conference, and while sightseeing in downtown Milwaukee, Wisconsin, trying to keep up with my colleague and mentor, I turned my ankle quite severely. It swelled up angrily, becoming puffy, red, and painful. After returning to Colorado, I received worker's compensation for treatment of the injured ankle. Near the end of the healing process, the physician's assistant noticed my gait was irregular on just one side; he told me I should get it checked out by a neurologist. Shortly thereafter, I was diagnosed with Parkinson's disease. It is a progressive nervous system disorder affecting one's movement. Typical symptoms include: tremor, slower than normal movement, rigidity, and balance and posture problems. The disease happens because the neurons in the substantia nigra, a dopamine-producing nucleus deep in the midbrain, stop working or die. Dopamine is a chemical that coordinates the body's movement. The causes of Parkinson's are unknown, but scientists think it likely to be a combination of factors, including environmental ones, such as exposure to pesticides.[1]

Initially I was angry, feeling that my body had betrayed me; but I passed through that phase fairly quickly.[2] Subsequently, a take-charge, controlling mode kicked in. As an academic librarian, my research went forward full bore. I scoured the literature, focusing on alternative medicine and trying out many of the most promising alternative treatments.[3] I

---

1   "Parkinson's 101," Michael J. Fox Foundation, https://www.michaeljfox.org/parkinsons-101.

2   Parts of my anger persist because I believe responsibility for my Parkinson's is properly placed upon agribusiness methods and pesticide-producing corporations.

3   Jill Marjama-Lyons, *What Your Doctor May Not Tell You about Parkinson's Disease: A Holistic Program for Optimal Wellness* (New York: Warner Books, 2003); Monique L. Giroux, *Optimal Health with Parkinson's Disease: A Guide to Integrating Lifestyle, Alternative, and Conventional Medicine* (New York: DemosHealth, 2016); Janice Hadlock, "Parkinson's Recovery Project," https://pdrecovery.org/recovery-from-parkinsons/.

wanted to avoid taking drugs as long as possible. After about six years of avoiding synthetic medication (three years unmedicated and three taking the ayurvedic herb mucuna), I started the standard regimen of carbidopa/ levodopa and pramipexole drugs because I was experiencing a non-motor symptom that interfered with my work—I was becoming very indecisive. The drugs were effective and my tremors, rigidity, and indecisiveness eased.

The Return of the Muse

A wonderful side effect of the standard medication was the return of my poetic muse, who had been present in me as a child but had deserted me during most of my adult years. This return of creativity is not unusual; it is documented in the medical literature.[4] Writing poems is very therapeutic for me. They are palliative and convey the power to reconcile and heal.

As an example, I'll share how I was able to decode and interpret a disturbing dream through my writing process. Not long after I was diagnosed, I had a dream that a group of men, all of color, walked away from me in a state of sad resignation. I was devastated. I interpreted this dream to mean that I was disconnected. I returned to my memory of this dream repeatedly. Gradually I discerned that I needed to listen to all aspects of myself—mind, heart and body. To me, the group of men symbolized my brain cells that had stopped functioning—and attention must be paid to them, or they would continue to give up. I felt it was a message from my personal subconscious and the collective unconscious, coming through with clarity. I am a white female and these men were my opposites—the "other"—with whom I needed to create relationship. This powerful dream also held meaning for me on the socio-political level, indicting our society's ongoing oppressive treatment of people of color.

The powerful dream mixed in my subconscious with my awareness that I shared the circumstance of having Parkinson's disease with a well-known man of color, Muhammad Ali. Also, contemporaneously, boxing therapy was being touted as a good activity for people with the disease. In my research about Parkinson's I learned that stress affects symptoms and the flight-fight response is implicated as well. I connected all the above

---

4   Rivka Inzelberg, "The Awakening of Artistic Creativity and Parkinson's Disease," *Behavioral Neuroscience* 127, no. 2 (2013): 256–61; Anette Schrag and Michael Trimble, "Poetic Talent Unmasked by Treatment of Parkinson's Disease," *Movement Disorders* 16, no. 6 (2001): 1175–76.

somewhat disparate factors in my poem below. The words are my way of building a bridge to Ali, someone I considered very different from myself, and to whom I never would have given much thought except that we now had Parkinson's disease in common. I have been a conflict-avoiding, shy, skinny and unathletic white woman, while my image of Ali was of a pugilistic, proud, strong and athletic, African American man. Here is my attempt to relate to him, to ask if I may call him my brother (posthumously, as he passed in 2016). It is entitled "When to Float and When to Sting":

When to Float and When to Sting

"Float like a butterfly, sting like a bee.
The hands can't hit what the eyes can't see."
Muhammad Ali nee Cassius Clay, Jr., 1964

I'm fifty-seven and still can't discern
when to be the butterfly
when to be the bee
Is it better, more right
to stand up and fight or
(in some situations)
is it wiser to bail, turn tail
refuse to give away
precious energy to the fray?
Mr. Ali—may I call you Muhammad,
and may I ask?
How did you decide
when to float and when to sting?

Sometimes, weary from Parkinson's tremor
rigid, unable to move
trapped by a tractor beam
and feeling as if I might fly off the planet
though fettered
pinned like an insect on display
I deliberately dissociate, do the backstroke
in my mind float, gaze up at the blue deep
drink in unconditional love for as long as I can

Mr. Ali—may I call you Muhammad,
and may I ask?
How did you decide
when to float and when to sting?

Sometimes, seeing injustice revived and
rampant I feel hopeless, enraged—
So I dance to distract myself,
my angular limbs jut, and though I am a pacifist
my long arms deliver knock-out KAPOW punch
this wide wingspan startles enemies unseen
I pointedly sing Wonder's accusation:
"You haven't done nothin'"
I throw Who's rock:
"We won't get fooled again"
But here we are defeated stunned trumped stung and stumped looking
for answers
Mr. Ali—may I call you Muhammad?
May I call you friend?
And may I ask—
how did you decide
when to float and when to sting?

We are unlikely allies
You picked your battles wisely
chose when to fight
feinting and punches pulled
Socking it to them
when they drafted you to Vietnam
Muhammad my friend, may I call you Brother?
And may I ask—how did you decide
when to float and when to sting?

Brother, I need you now
like a sister needs a sibling
a familiar partner against whom
she can safely test her strength
arm wrestle, laugh and lose
Can I lean on your legacy
Brother Muhammad, Brother Ali?

We are not so different
We share common foes
disease, stigma, bigotry, injustice
Both of us with Parkinson's
sapping our strength
Precious black beautiful
substantia nigra cells
deep in the center of our brain
Dark dopamine-producing core
makes us behave with purpose
made you move with balletic grace
Your cells diseased dysfunctional
wounded warriors just like mine
They turned tail deserted
went AWOL gave up the fight
Brother Ali, Brother Muhammad
Will you be my trainer?
Prepare me for the next bout?

With torn armor of tin
I am shaky, ghostly, anemic, pale
Mold my muscles out of salt-caked clay
Spoon feed me liver rebuild my body
with bleached broken ribs
My skin is broken and bruised
I need ice, stiches, and athletic tape
wound round my open wounds
Brother Ali, may we follow your example?
Brother Muhammad,
may we borrow your pride?

You have given us your greatest gift—
discernment—knowing whether and
when to float or sting because
we can't move forward until
we all move forward and
everyone does better
when everyone does better
we're down for the count and sometimes
don't know how we'll manage to move

but we know we'll win we'll overcome
we'll rise when black lives matter
reparations will be paid
when black lives truly matter
hearts and minds will be healed
broken bodies and brain cells made whole
Brothers, Sisters, we shall overcome
someday, someday, one day soon
our humanity in common
single substance shared
enough to satiate us all
drink deep filling up
on ocean of plenty sated by
the civil right of unconditional love

Solid as oars our arms ply waves
till shoulder muscles flag
overcome by fatigue
we cease our strokes
lying on our backs like lily-pads
bask and bloom begin to relax
irises effloresce pupils expand
receive vast view of blackest blue
falling fast we surrender certainty
tucked in folds of curtained sleep
baste our dreams to midnight scrim
with silver thread and diamond pins
soft-hued pre-dawn periwinkle light
seeps thru threadbare skein of sky
presaging daytime drama restive
shoulder blades rotate wriggle
hearts flutter unfurling butterfly wings
bodies buoyed borne over rainbow's arc
differences reconciled by justice' prism
untethered free at last we float
not a single soul left behind
Brothers Sisters joined together
fully awake heaven bound
cast away sadness levitate laugh
till our eyes drip so much salt
they sting

Hope in Holism: Living Well with a Chronic Disease

I wish I could wave the proverbial wand and wipe away all distress; absent that, perhaps I could prescribe to you a vacation from your problems, as the psychiatrist (Dr. Leo Marvin) played by Richard Dreyfuss does for the pesky and tenacious client (Bob Wiley) portrayed by Bill Murray in the Frank Oz comedic film, *What About Bob?* But eschewing escapism, and having learned that the only way around a problem is through it, I recommend to you the following lifelong holistic health regimen, and I hope it is transferable to many of you, especially my disabled peers with chronic health disorders. In the holistic approach I find nourishment and sustenance for body, mind, and spirit:

Body/Health Care Basics:

- Alternative medicine practitioners: acupuncture, massage therapy; a neurologist that specializes in movement disorders (I prefer to combine traditional and alternative approaches);

- Food and movement as medicine: healthy gluten-free diet, megadoses of COQ10 and thiamin; exercise using the "Think Big" therapy; counter-balance computer time with exercise and outside time as much as possible.

Joining Mind and Body and Spirit:

- Mindfulness practice that integrates body and mind: I prefer chi gong,[5] other practices such as yoga and tai chi are helpful; dance is available for people with Parkinson's;[6]

- Creative outlet (mine is poetry).

Psychological:

- Ability to express and be heard, to be reciprocal and listen: humor, honest opinions, gratitude, "negative" feelings such as anxiety and fear.[7]

---

5   I practice Wisdom Healing Qigong as taught by Master Mingtong Gu, https://www.chicenter.com/chi/home.

6   Dance for Parkinson's, https://danceforparkinsons.org/.

7   Opinions about euthanasia vary widely; I find that imagining that I may have even a small chance of control of my end-of-life experience (no matter how illusory) helps me feel better when I am at my lowest; I found this documentary about assisted suicide helpful: John Zaritsky, "Suicide Tourist," distributed by PBS, 2010, https://www.pbs.org/wgbh/frontline/film/suicidetourist/.

Social and Political:

- Work: both individual projects (autonomous) and teamwork (collaborative, consensual);
- Relationships with friends and family;
- Building communities, forming coalitions;
- Working toward social justice, reparations, reconciliation.

Spiritual:

- Nature, political activism;[8]
- Openness to paradox and synchronicity in one's life.

Your activities and emphases may be very different from the above. We are each unique. Whatever your journey, I hope it will be healthy and I suggest that you adapt the foregoing to make it fit you.

Peripatetic Career Path of a Librarian: Making Connections and Finding Out What Makes You Unique

My path has been all about finding meaning. It has evolved to be all about seeking and making connections. This was externally affirmed by the results of the Clifton StrengthsFinder assessment that we took at my workplace over a year ago. The test measures the presence of "talent themes," a person's naturally recurring pattern of thought/feeling/behavior. These talent themes can be productively applied to performance in the workplace.[9] My talent themes were:

Input crave to know more; often like to collect and archive all kinds of information (this one seems very librarian-like, and was one several of my colleagues and I seemed to hold in common).

---

8 I recommend the Earth Activist Training based on permaculture, regenerative land management, and Earth-based spirituality, as taught by Starhawk, https://earthactivisttraining.org.

9 Gallup Organization, "Clifton StrengthsFinder," https://www.gallup.com/cliftonstrengths/en/254033/strengthsfinder.aspx.

Connectedness have faith in the links between all things; believe there are few coincidences and that almost every event has a reason.

Strategic create alternative ways to proceed; faced with any given scenario, can quickly spot the relevant patterns and issues (thank goodness that I have this skill, so I can help library users locate, navigate, and sift through all the information with which they are overloaded).

Ideation fascinated by ideas; able to find connections between seemingly disparate phenomena (maybe this reflects my propensity to be a generalist).

Empathy can sense the feelings of other people by imagining themselves in others' lives or others' situations (this talent helps me be an effective reference librarian and research consultant).[10]

I feel that my experience with the disabling aspects of my illness has made me a better librarian. I am more patient, more empathetic, and less perfectionistic. I have slowed down in some ways that can be annoying, but on the other hand, because I am slower, I am a better listener. What do I advise you, dear reader? To loll in your talent themes as I have done above. It will be a good ego boost. You are talented, my friend and colleague, and you deserve to be included in the library workplace. I would not label you as disabled; instead, I say you are extraordinarily experienced! Another way to use the StrengthsFinder, in addition to looking at your own strengths, is to learn about your colleagues' strengths, and then to use that knowledge to compensate for and complement one another's talents.

The Creed of the Conscientized Librarian

Finding meaning used to mean everything to me. I facilitate access to knowledge. Though it is not always easy, I strive to be open to change. I endorse empiricism and the scientific method, yet know that intuitive,

---

10 This quality has helped me as a member of my university's Institutional Research Board: I can put myself in the prospective research participants' shoes, thus facilitating their fully-informed consent and their ethical treatment.

shamanistic approaches can also have validity. I have much to learn about co-existence and listening to points of view that are the polar opposite of mine. I am learning to lose my self-consciousness and gain conscientization.[11] I am working toward the goal of creatively worrying about the right things. I believe much failure is a result of a failure of the imagination. Daily I struggle and sometimes I engage in wishful thinking, but it is unrealistic to expect an easy ride. My goal is to reduce self-criticism and self-sabotaging behavior, to increase compassion toward myself, and to engender self-advocacy skills. Since I value self-reliance, I want to do my share and I hesitate to ask for help—but I have ceased hating to ask and I will ask if need be. Fear is my biggest job performance barrier. Silence is the most common symptom of my fear. Invisibility is the maladaptation I sometimes use to attempt to cope with the fear-filled feelings. Anything that reduces my fear increases the efficacy of my performance. If I give voice to my vulnerability, I make myself visible. What kind of reaction will I get from my workplace, my co-workers, my supervisors? I can't control others, but…if my ultimate goal is to be open hearted and to learn to connect, I must learn to be interdependent.

We Can't Control Others, but We Can Learn to Work Better Together in Groups

We are all familiar with the stereotypes of librarians that continue to live on, reanimated like zombies: Librarians are no-nonsense, responsible people; they wear sensible shoes and bind their hair in buns: according to personality assessments, they are respectful, serious, focused, apprehensive, vigilant (in their enforcement of quietude) and cautious. But they are also tender-hearted, flexible, imaginative, and open-minded.[12] I try to wrap my head around this description and imagine that I can control my co-workers, but I cannot. Really, all I can begin to comprehend is my own personality profile. I learned a lot during the sabbatical I took to write this book. Not surprisingly,

---

11 This is the consciousness of reality and engagement in the struggle to transform it. Danilo R. Streck, Euclides Redin, and Jaime Jose Zitkoski, eds. *Paulo Freire Encyclopedia* (Lanham, MD: Rowman & Littlefield, 2012).

12 Jeanine M. Williamson and John W. Lounsbury, "Distinctive 16 PF Personality Traits of Librarians," *Journal of Library Administration* 56 (2016): 124–43. This article finds that a "distinctive personality profile emerges for librarians—respectful, serious, focused, cautious, vigilant, open-minded, imaginative, flexible, self-reliant, tender-minded, and apprehensive."

I learned about the limits of my self-discipline. Most importantly, I learned that I am interconnected and reliant on my co-workers for a large part of my motivation and for a significant amount of the energy that makes me get up in the morning and experience a balanced, healthfully productive day.

I haven't yet formally requested any accommodations, but I feel I am getting closer to that juncture. I have told a few friends and colleagues (supposedly jokingly) that I would ask to be excused from attending meetings. But in my humor, there is some seriousness. Last summer I returned to work after a ten-day mindfulness retreat. My relaxed state was evident to all. I felt the familiar tension entering my body during meetings. Why are meetings so stressful? How can I change myself so that meetings do not cause me so much stress? The word "accommodations" literally means "made fitting" and I can certainly attest that one size does not fit all. Is the biggest barrier that prevents me from performing my job the tense undertone and the egocentric posturing that goes on in some academic meetings? I need a psychologically safe environment of mutual respect and egalitarian concern in order to perform my job optimally. That said, I must confess that I am sometimes guilty of the obnoxious habit of needing to be the smartest kid in the room, showing off my knowledge. Richard Moniz and his co-authors surveyed librarians and found that workload was the greatest stressor, second only to interacting with library co-workers.[13] While it is comforting to know that I am not the only one, it is regrettably notable that this stressor is so common. The article recommended workshops on time management, instruction techniques, mindfulness, emotional intelligence, and team building to mitigate these stressors.[14] At the end of my sabbatical, I made a wonderful discovery: I like people and I am motivated by the collegiality of my fellow library workers. In the twenty-six years I have worked in libraries, I have encountered a few colleagues who aspired to rule in an authoritarian manner or descended into the muck of picayune critiques, but most are compassionate, egalitarian, constructively honest, and kind. I found meaning in the solitude of my sabbatical when my conscious awareness of our interdependency increased. I have more to learn about meetings, about holding my own, taming my social anxiety, and honing my advocacy skills and my listening skills.

---

13   Richard Moniz, Jo Henry, Joe Eschleman, Lisa Moniz, and Howard Slutzky, "Stressors and Librarians: How Mindfulness Can Help," *College & Research Libraries News* 77, no. 11 (2016): 535.

14   Moniz, Henry, Eschleman, Moniz and Slutzky, 535.

It has been my experience that we librarians excel at being collaborative. We need just a little more coaching and we can become expert at the process of coming to consensus. We can transform our meetings to make them more purposeful and less frivolous, more civil and less contentious. We need to focus on this, work on it a little more. Librarians are good at this and can be even better. When we are all valued fairly and practiced at interdependence, our group interactions become grounded, integral, organic, and productive.[15]

The Continuum of Possibilities Created by the Imaginative Idea-Filled Mind

Are you an idea-oriented, intuitive person like me? People like us can imagine an entire continuum from the worst-case scenario to the best; harness that talent to help yourself instead of tripping yourself up. Start with imagining, then express to the pages of your journal or to a trusted friend, the range of outcomes for a difficult situation, spanning from the worst-case scenario to the better and best outcomes as well. I'm afraid of deep brain stimulation surgery. My worst-case scenario is that I go to the hospital and I am given a lobotomy by mistake. My imagination is so gruesome it makes me laugh. The next worst case is that an infection develops, or I lose some important functioning, such as access to my vocabulary, which would be a tragedy for a poet. The neutral outcome would be no change at all, just continuing to be over-medicated and continuing dyskinesia. The better result is that the tremor goes away and my dosage needs are dramatically cut. The best outcome is that a cure is discovered the day before my trepanning is scheduled, and thus I cancel my surgery and I am cured. This game makes me laugh at my mind. The truth lies somewhere in the middle, with more unrealistic outcomes on either side. I've been mired in survivor's guilt and crucified with savior's complex, secretly expecting miracles and furious when there were none. It is daily practice, "showing up," working in solidarity together in social movements that effects change. Again, I reiterate, I have found no way out except through; unfortunately, that sometimes involves suffering.

---

15 Starhawk provides exercises for leadership of meetings: introductions, grounding, anchoring, gratitude, cultural sharing, evaluation, closing, and potlucks! See Starhawk, *The Empowerment Manual: A Guide for Collaborative Groups* (Gabriola Island, BC: New Society Publishers, 2011), 8–13.

Living and working well is being mindfully present in a space and time somewhere in the middle, between the worst- and best-case scenarios. The worst case is living in fear and anguish knowing that a loved one is in pain; this expresses itself self-destructively and you are not able to help. I lived through that for many years as a sibling of a sister with severe bipolar mental illness. As someone who suffered from survivor's guilt for way too long, I advise counseling if you are in similar straits. I found EMDR techniques particularly helpful. The passage of time and therapeutic poetry writing helped too. Once my wounds healed, I could begin to help others. Getting to that point was a journey of many decades. Everyone is on a different timetable, so I stopped judging myself for that. The benefit of having a growth mindset when helping others (as contrasted with the either/or mindset of a morally superior savior) is that I cannot harbor unrealistic expectations about my ability to make a difference. I am one person, doing what I can. But if enough of us step up, our power increases exponentially: suffering eases and happiness proliferates. The best-case scenario, my idea of heaven, is health and well-being flourishing for all. The middle ground is working toward that goal, making "good" mistakes along the way, living and working in the moment.

Conscientization: Consciousness of Reality and Engagement in the Struggle to Transform It

In an editorial in *JAMA* in 2018, neurologists E. Ray Dorsey and Bastiaan R. Bloem sounded the alarm: a noninfectious pandemic of Parkinson's disease is immanent. They say that neurological disorders are now the leading cause of disability in the world, and among them, the fastest growing is Parkinson's disease. From 1990 to 2015 the prevalence of Parkinson's disease more than doubled, and thus, so did disability and deaths due to Parkinson's disease. An estimated 6.2 million persons in the world currently (as of January 2018) have Parkinson's disease. Projections indicate that the number of people with the disease will more than double by 2040, reaching somewhere between 12.9 to 14.2 million persons. The neurologists liken the trajectory of Parkinson's disease to that of HIV, citing similar issues: environmental influences upon causality, and the needs to increase access to care and funding for research.[16]

---

16   E. Ray Dorsey and Bastiaan R. Bloem, "The Parkinson Pandemic: A Call to Action," JAMA Neurology 75, no. 1 (2018): 9–10, https://jamanetwork.com/journals/jamaneurology/fullarticle/2661302.

Later, at the end of 2018, Dorsey and Bloem renewed their call for activism in another journal's opinion pages, and they were joined by two more neurologists. They are affiliated with renowned institutions: University of Rochester Medical Center; Michael J. Fox Foundation for Parkinson's Research; University of Florida, Gainesville; and Radboud University Medical Center, Netherlands. I quote directly from their op-ed's compelling call to action:

> Those with and at risk for Parkinson['s] disease can form a "PACT" to prevent, advocate for, care, and treat the disease. Where feasible, we should prevent Parkinson['s] disease by reducing and in some cases eliminating the use of chemicals known to increase the risk of Parkinson['s] disease. We have the means to prevent potentially millions from ever experiencing the debilitating effects of Parkinson['s] disease...The Parkinson pandemic is preventable, not inevitable.[17]

Why are people not up in arms, linking arms to fight this? These Parkinson's experts are calling the pandemic preventable, not inevitable. Being the change I want to see, I write poems to express my sadness and my hope. Last fall I wrote an epic poem, "A Poet's Dialogue (and Hokey Pokey Dance) with Death." The following excerpt is called "Footing the Bill" and describes our interconnectedness. I grew up in southeastern Arizona, in the town of Safford, on land formerly belonging to the Apache tribe, thus the references to desert ecology and Apache culture in the images.

Footing the Bill

Prescriptive potion possesses
serendipitous side effects
Elixir awakens muse two decades dormant
Dopamine agonist quickens creative pulse
Parkinsonian poet calls out
cause of idiopathic illness
Cotton farms' pesticide-laced desert dust settles

---

17 Dorsey, E. Ray, Todd Sherer, Michael S. Okun, and Bastiaan R. Bloem, "The Emerging Evidence of the Parkinson Pandemic," Journal of Parkinson's Disease 8, no. 1 (2018): S3–S8.

coats crops creeps up my aquiline underage nose
kisses capillaries breaches blood brain barrier
Conjecture unprovable but just suppose
collateral damage inflicted
neurochemical compromise reached
patience purchases a pound of flesh
in exchange for every simile
grace granted at bard's bargain basement rate
"were nothing but to waste night day and time"
each substantia nigra cell's demise
protracted death pact quid pro quo
Metered foot the payment pledged
an anapest underneath each moribund inkling
Dark diamonds drop stealthily suicidal
silently scream "Geronimo" as they jump
Apache tears shed by third eye
percolate from brain to brow
evaporate evanescent sweat
Neither see spondee make a splash
nor hear it say sayonara unless
untimely I stir dredging up dactyls
from deep in REM sleep
Fingers folded under cheek face death
while I dream in daylight self effacing

Living well is finding meaning mindfully everyday, gratefully listening open-heartedly to my body! We need diversity, to listen to all species. All of us need to learn to collaborate in groups. It has been a privilege to write for you, to commune with you, dear reader, whether you be a disabled library worker, an ally to same, or a curious outsider. Working well is finding solidarity in advocating for yourself and others. Heal yourself and heal the planet. Just as pesticides are bad for everyone (especially someone with a genetic or environmentally-induced tendency toward Parkinson's disease), so too is the healthfully interdependent world and workplace good for everyone. Our purpose is to cease projecting upon others, to welcome them back into the fold of library workers, welcome their whole selves, their bodies, hearts, and minds. Welcome to the library workplace, my new interesting friend who differs markedly from me. Thank goodness, I was beginning to be bored with all the sameness and conformity; let's collaborate together for a socially just cause in an interdependent manner, let's break a few norms!

Bibliography

ADA National Network (ADANN). https://adata.org.

ADA National Network (ADANN). "Reasonable Accommodations in the Workplace: Reasonable Accommodation Process." https://adata.org/factsheet/reasonable-accommodations-workplace.

ADAPT. https://adapt.org/.

Adgate, John L., Bernard D. Goldstein, and Lisa M. McKenzie. "Potential Public Health Hazards, Exposures, and Health Effects from Unconventional Gas Development." *Environmental Science & Technology* 48, no. 15 (2014): 8307–20.

Administration for Community Living. "State Protection & Advocacy Systems." https://acl.gov/programs/aging-and-disability-networks/state-protection-advocacy-systems#

Alder, Avery. "You know that thing where your coworker calls you in a panic wondering if you can cover their shift so they can stay home sick, and nobody else can do it? So you cancel your plans to cover them? That has been an intentional part of north-american capitalism since the 1990s." Twitter, June 19, 2019, 1:19 p.m. https://twitter.com/lackingceremony/status/1141410304644960258.

Alvesson, Mats, and Hugh Willmott. "Identity Regulation as Organizational Control: Producing the Appropriate Individual." *Journal of Management Studies* 39, no. 5 (2002): 619–44.

American Association of University Professors. "Report: Accommodating Faculty Members Who Have Disabilities." January 2012.

———. "Issues: Contingent Faculty Positions." https://www.aaup.org/issues/contingency.

American Library Association. "Core Competences of Librarianship." http://www.ala.org/educationcareers/sites/ala.org.educationcareers/files/content/careers/corecomp/corecompetences/finalcorecompstat09.pdf.

———. "Diversity Standards: Cultural Competency for Academic Libraries (2012)." May 4, 2012. http://www.ala.org/acrl/standards/diversity.

———. "A Guideline for the Appointment, Promotion and Tenure of Academic Librarians." September 6, 2006. http://www.ala.org/acrl/standards/promotiontenure.

American Library Association, Association for Library Collections & Technical Services. "Core Competencies for Cataloging and Metadata Professional Librarians." January 2017. https://alair.ala.org/handle/11213/7853.

American Library Association, Association of College & Research Libraries. "ACRL Proficiencies for Assessment Librarians and Coordinators." January 23, 2017. http://www.ala.org/acrl/standards/assessment_proficiencies.

American Library Association, Association of Specialized, Government, and Cooperative Library Agencies. "Library Staff with Disabilities: What You Need to Know." http://www.ala.org/asgcla/resources/tipsheets/staff.

Americans with Disabilities Act of 1990. Public Law 101–336. 101st Congress, 2nd session (July 26, 1990).

Americans with Disabilities Act Amendments Act of 2008. Public Law 110–325. 110th Congress (September 25, 2008). https://www.eeoc.gov/laws/statutes/adaaa.cfm.

Andrews, Nicola. "Reflections on Resistance, Decolonization, and the Historical Trauma of Libraries and Academia." In *The Politics of Theory and the Practice of Critical Librarianship*, edited by Maura Seale and Karen Nicholson, 181–94. Sacramento, CA: Library Juice Press, 2018. doi:10.31229/osf.io/mva35.

Annamma, Subini A., David J. Connor, and Beth Ferri. "Introduction: A Truncated Genealogy of DisCrit." In *DisCrit : Disability Studies and Critical Race Theory in Education*, edited by David J. Connor, Beth A. Ferri, and Subini A. Annamma, 1–8. New York: Teachers College Press, 2016.

Aquino, Karl, and Americus Reed, II. "The Self-Importance of Moral Identity." *Journal of Personality and Social Psychology* 83, no. 6 (2002): 1423–40.

Aronson, Joshua, Diana Burgess, Sean M. Phelan, and Lindsay Juarez. "Unhealthy Interactions: The Role of Stereotype Threat in Health Disparities." *American Journal of Public Health* 103, no. 1 (2013): 50–56. https://www.ncbi.nlm.nih.gov/pmc/articles/PMC3518353/.

Asato, Noriko. "Librarians' Free Speech: The Challenge of Librarians' Own Intellectual Freedom to the American Library Association, 1946–2007." *Library Trends* 63, no. 1 (2014): 75–105.

Backman, Maurie. "Here's How Many Hours the Average American Worked Per Year." *The Motley Fool* (December 17, 2017). https://www.fool.com/careers/2017/12/17/heres-how-many-hours-the-average-american-works-pe.aspx.

Bagenstos, Samuel R. *Law and the Contradictions of the Disability Rights Movement*. New Haven, CT: Yale University Press, 2009.

Baildon, Michelle, Dana Hamlin, Czeslaw Jankowski, Rhonda Kauffman, Julia Lanigan, Michelle Miller, Jessica Venlet, and Ann Marie Willer. "Creating a Social Justice Mindset: Diversity, Inclusion and Social Justice in the Collections Directorate of the MIT Libraries." Massachusetts Institute of Technology, 2017. https://dspace.mit.edu/handle/1721.1/108771.

Bailey, Alison. "On Anger, Silence, and Epistemic Injustice." *Royal Institute of Philosophy Supplement* 84 (2018): 93–115.

Baldridge, David C., and Michele L. Swift. "Withholding Requests for Disability Accommodation: The Role of Individual Differences and Disability Attributes." *Journal of Management* 39, no. 3 (2013): 743–62.

Barbarin, Imani. "On Being Black and 'Disabled but not Really.'" *Rewire. News* (July 26, 2019). https://rewire.news/article/2019/07/26/on-being-black -and-disabled-but-not-really/.

Batavia, Andrew I., and Richard L. Beaulaurier. "The Financial Vulnerability of People with Disabilities: Assessing Poverty Risks." *Journal of Sociology & Social Welfare* 28, no. 1 (2001): 139–62.

Baumgartner, Miriam K., David J. G. Dwertmann, Stephan A. Boehm, and Heike Bruch. "Job Satisfaction of Employees with Disabilities: The Role of Perceived Structural Flexibility." *Human Resource Management* 54, no. 2 (2015): 323–43.

Beckett, Angharad E. *Citizenship and Vulnerability: Disability and Issues of Social and Political Engagement.* Basingstoke, UK: Palgrave Macmillan, 2006.

Belben, Cathy. "YES, Indeed! Improv and the Art of Library Science." *Library Media Connection* 29, no. 2 (2010): 16–17.

Bichell, Rae Ellen. "Scientists Start to Tease out the Subtler Ways Racism Hurts Health." *NPR Health Shots*, November 11, 2017. https://www.npr.org /sections/health-shots/2017/11/11/562623815/scientists-start-to-tease -out-the-subtler-ways-racism-hurts-health.

Bishop-Root, Dana, Dustin Gibson, and Bekezela Mguni. "Collecting [a] Home for Disability Justice in the Library." *Disability Visibility Project* (blog). February 24, 2019. https://disabilityvisibilityproject.com/2019/02/24 /collecting-a-home-for-disability-justice-in-the-library/.

Bliss, Laura. "The Public Librarians Who Serve as Human Google." *CityLab.* October 18, 2016. https://www.citylab.com/life/2016/10 /the-public-librarians-who-still-serve-as-human-google/504506/.

"Blood Sugar & Other Hormones." *Diabetes Education Online.* Diabetes Teaching Center at the University of California-San Francisco, 2019, https://dtc. ucsf.edu/types-of-diabetes/type1/understanding-type-1-diabetes/ how-the-body-processes-sugar/blood-sugar-other-hormones/.

Borthwick, Chris. "Racism, IQ and Down's Syndrome." *Disability & Society* 11, no. 3 (1996): 403–10.

Bowker, Geoffrey C., and Susan Leigh Star. *Sorting Things Out: Classification and Its Consequences.* Cambridge, MA: MIT Press, 1999.

Bowman, James S., and Jonathan P. West. "Lord Acton and Employment Doctrines: Absolute Power and the Spread of At-Will Employment." *Journal of Business Ethics* 74, no. 2 (2007): 119–30.

Brown, Robin, and Scott Sheidlower. "Claiming Our Space: A Quantitative and Qualitative Picture of Disabled Librarians." *Library Trends* 67, no. 3 (2019): 471–86.

Bureau of Labor Statistics, United States Department of Labor. "American Time Use Survey, 2018." June 19, 2019. https://www.bls.gov/news.release/pdf /atus.pdf.

———. "Librarians." June 19, 2019. *Occupational Outlook Handbook.* https://www.bls.gov/ooh/education-training-and-library/librarians.htm.

———. "Library Technicians and Assistants." June 19, 2019. *Occupational Outlook Handbook.* https://www.bls.gov/ooh/education-training-and-library /library-technicians-and-assistants.htm.

———. "Persons with a Disability 2018, Current Population Survey (CPS)." Presented at ODEP, March 17, 2019. https://www.dol.gov/odep/pdf/DOL _ODEP_2018_Briefing_with_notes_ODEP.pdf.

Burke, Thomas F. *Lawyers, Lawsuits, and Legal Rights: The Battle over Litigation in American Society.* Berkeley, CA: University of California Press, 2002.

Burns, Erin, and Kristin E. C. Green. "Academic Librarians' Experiences and Perceptions on Mental Illness Stigma and the Workplace." *College & Research Libraries* 80, no. 5 (2019): 638–57.

Carney, Stephen Michael. "Democratic Communication and the Library as Workplace." *Journal of Information Ethics* 12, no. 2 (2003): 43–59, 96.

Centers for Disease Control. "Sickle Cell Data Collection Program Report: Data to Action. Knowledge Gaps." September 7, 2018. https://www.cdc.gov /ncbddd/hemoglobinopathies/data-reports/2018-summer/knowledge -gaps.html.

Center for Employment and Disability Research. Kessler Foundation. https://kesslerfoundation.org/research/center-employment-and-disability-research.

Chang, Sand C. "Token Act." In *Nonbinary: Memoirs of Gender and Identity,* edited by Micah Rajunov and Scott Duane, 48–57. New York: Columbia University Press, 2019.

Choudhury, Shakil. *Deep Diversity: Overcoming Us vs. Them.* Toronto: Between the Lines, 2015.

Chugh, Dolly. "Use Your Everyday Privilege to Help Others." *Harvard Business Review.* September 18, 2018. https://hbr.org/2018/09/ use-your-everyday-privilege-to-help-others.

———. *The Person You Mean to Be: How Good People Fight Bias.* New York: Harper Collins, 2016.

Chugh, Dolly, and Mary C. Kern. "A Dynamic and Cyclical Model of Bounded Ethicality." *Research in Organizational Behavior* 36 (2106): 85–100.

Colella, Adrienne J., and Susanne M. Bruyere. "Disability and Employment: New Directions for Industrial and Organizational Psychology." In *APA Handbook of Industrial and Organizational Psychology*, edited by Sheldon Zedeck, 473–503. Washington, DC: American Psychological Association, 2011.

Collins, Patricia Hill. "The Social Construction of Black Feminist Thought." *Signs* 14, no. 4 (1989): 745–73.

Colorado Cross Disability Coalition. http://www.ccdconline.org/employment/.

Consumer Protection Financial Division of the U.S. Government. "Your Money, Your Goals: Focus on People with Disabilities: A Companion Guide to Empower the Disability Community." March 2019. https://files.consumerfinance.gov/f/documents/cfpb_ymyg_focus-on-people-with-disabilities.pdf.

Cook, Samantha, and Kristina Clement. "Navigating the Hidden Void: The Unique Challenges of Accommodating Library Employees with Invisible Disabilities." *The Journal of Academic Librarianship*. Published ahead of print March 8, 2019. https://doi.org/10.1016/j.acalib.2019.02.010.

Cork, Stephanie, Paul T. Jaeger, Shannon Jette, and Stefanie Ebrahimoff, "The Politics of (Dis)Information: Crippled America, the 25th Anniversary of the Americans with Disabilities Act (ADA), and the 2016 U.S. Presidential Campaign." *The International Journal of Information, Diversity, and Inclusion* 1, no. 1 (2016): 1–15. https://doi.org/10.33137/ijidi.v1i1.32186.

Czopp, Alexander M., Margo J. Monteith, and Aimee Y. Mark. "Standing Up for a Change: Reducing Bias through Interpersonal Confrontation." *Journal of Personality and Social Psychology* 90, no. 5 (2006): 784–803.

Dalmer, Nicole K., and D. G. Campbell. "Communicating with Library Patrons and People with Dementia: Tracing an Ethic of Care in Professional Communication Guidelines." *Dementia* no. unassigned (2018). https://doi.org/10.1177/1471301218790852.

Danforth, Scot. "Liberation Theology of Disability and the Option for the Poor." *Disability Studies Quarterly* 25, no. 3 (2005).

Davis, Lennard J. *Enabling Acts: The Hidden Story of How the Americans with Disabilities Act Gave the Largest U.S. Minority Its Rights.* Boston: Beacon Press, 2015.

Davison, H. Kristl, Brian J. O'Leary, Jennifer A. Schlosberg, and Mark N. Bing. "Don't Ask and You Shall Not Receive: Why Future American Workers with Disabilities Are Reluctant to Demand Legally Required Accommodations." *Journal of Workplace Rights* 14, no. 1 (2009): 49–73.

de jesus, nina. "Locating the Library in Institutional Oppression." *In the Library with the Lead Pipe.* September 24, 2014. http://www.inthelibrarywiththeleadpipe.org/2014/locating-the-library-in-institutional-oppression/.

Department for Professional Employees, AFL-CIO Research Department. "Library Professionals: Facts & Figures, Women and Library Professions." 2019. https://dpeaflcio.org/programs-publications/issue-fact-sheets/library-workers-facts-figures/.

Devlin, Richard, and Dianne Pothier. "Introduction." In *Critical Disability Theory: Essays in Philosophy, Politics, Policy, and Law*, edited by Dianne Pothier and Richard Devlin, 1–24. Vancouver: UBC Press, 2006.

DiAngelo, Robin. "ALA President's Program." ALA Midwinter Conference. January 27, 2019. https://www.eventscribe.com/2019/ALA-Midwinter/fsPopup .asp?Mode=presInfo&PresentationID=479061.

Disability Equality Index. https://disabilityin.org/what-we-do/disability -equality-index/.

Disability Law Colorado. "Resource Guide: Disability Discrimination in Employment." 2018. https://disabilitylawco.org/sites/default/files /uploads/DLC%20Employment%20Packet%202018%20FINAL_.pdf.

Disability Rights Education & Defense Fund. "Diabetes Care." 2013. https://dredf.org/special-education/diabetes-care/.

Disability Visibility Project. https://disabilityvisibilityproject.com.

Dohe, Kate, and Erin Pappas. "The Many Flavors of 'Yes': Libraries, Collaboration, and Improv." *College & Research Libraries News* 78, no. 8 (2017). https://crln.acrl.org/index.php/crlnews/article/view/16750.

Dolhun, Rachel, and Marti Fischer. "Sharing Your Parkinson's Diagnosis at Work: A Practical Guide." Michael J. Fox Foundation for Parkinson's Research (2017, May). https://files.michaeljfox.org/100915_MJFF_WORKPLACE.pdf.

———. "Talking about Parkinson's at Work: A Practical Guide, Part 2: Managing Long-Term Professional Relationships." Michael J. Fox Foundation for Parkinson's Research (2017). https://files.michaeljfox.org/052617_MJFF _WORKPLACE_PT2.pdf.

Dolmage, Jay Timothy. *Academic Ableism: Disability and Higher Education*. Ann Arbor, MI: University of Michigan Press, 2017. https://quod.lib.umich .edu/u/ump/mpub9708722.

———. *Disability Rhetoric*. Syracuse, NY: Syracuse University Press, 2014.

Dorsey, E. Ray, and Bastiaan R. Bloem. "The Parkinson Pandemic: A Call to Action." *JAMA Neurology* 75, no. 1 (2018): 9–10. https://content.iospress.com /articles/journal-of-parkinsons-disease/jpd181474.

Dorsey, E. Ray, Todd Sherer, Michael S. Okun, and Bastiaan R. Bloem. "The Emerging Evidence of the Parkinson Pandemic." *Journal of Parkinson's Disease* 8, no. 1 (2018): S3–S8.

Dubois, Wil. "The Bitterness over 'Brittle Diabetes.'" *Healthline*. February 21, 2017. https://www.healthline.com/diabetesmine/bitterness-over-brittle-diabetes#1.

Dunn, Dana S., and Erin E. Andrews. "Person-First and Identity-First Language: Developing Psychologists' Cultural Competence Using Disability Language." *American Psychologist* 70, no. 3 (2015): 255–64.

Durlak, Paul R. "Disability at Work: Understanding the Impact of the ADA on the Workplace." *Sociology Compass* 11, no. 5 (2017): e12475. https://doi.org /10.1111/soc4.12475.

Dusenbery, Maya. *Doing Harm: The Truth About How Bad Medicine and Lazy Science Leave Women Dismissed, Misdiagnosed, and Sick*. San Francisco: HarperOne, 2018.

Eb. "#EbMetaThread On Ableist Slurs." Twitter. October 6, 2017. https://twitter .com/i/moments/915075910746898432.

Edmondson, Amy. *The Fearless Organization: Creating Psychological Safety in the Workplace for Learning, Innovation, and Growth*. Hoboken, NJ: Wiley, 2019.

———. "Psychological Safety and Learning Behavior in Work Teams." *Administrative Science Quarterly* 44, no. 2 (1999): 350–83.

Eliade, Mircea. *The Myth of the Eternal Return*. Princeton, NJ: Princeton University Press, 1954.

Elmborg, James K. "Libraries as the Spaces Between Us: Recognizing and Valuing the Third Space." *Reference & User Services Quarterly* 50, no. 4 (2011): 338–50.

Employer Assistance and Resource Network on Disability Inclusion. "State Vocational Rehabilitation Agencies." https://www.askearn.org /state-vocational-rehabilitation-agencies/.

Enright, Nathaniel F. "The Violence of Information Literacy: Neoliberalism and the Human as Capital." In *Information Literacy and Social Justice: Radical Professional Praxis*, edited by Lua Gregory and Shana Higgins, 13–38. Sacramento, CA: Library Juice Press, 2013.

Erevelles, Nirmala. "(Im)material Citizens: Cognitive Disability, Race, and the Politics of Citizenship." *Disability, Culture and Education* 1, no. 1 (2002): 5–25. http://blogs.ubc.ca/ssed317/files/2008/08/immaterial-citizens.pdf.

Erkulwater, Jennifer L. *Disability Rights and the American Social Safety Net*. Ithaca, NY: Cornell University Press, 2006.

Ettarh, Fobazi. "Vocational Awe and Librarianship: The Lies We Tell Ourselves." *In the Library with the Lead Pipe*. January 10, 2018. http://www .inthelibrarywiththeleadpipe.org/2018/vocational-awe/.

Fairclough, Norman. *Language and Power*. London: Longman, 1989.

Feudtner, John Christopher. *Bittersweet: Diabetes, Insulin, and the Transformation of Illness*. Chapel Hill, NC: University of North Carolina Press, 2003.

Feuerstein, Michael, Amanda K. Gehrke, Brian T. McMahon, and Megan C. McMahon. "Challenges Persist Under Americans with Disabilities Act Amendments Act: How Can Oncology Providers Help?" *Journal of Oncology Practice* 13, no. 6 (2017): e543–e551.

Fineman, Martha Albertson. "Cracking the Foundational Myths: Independence, Autonomy, and Self-Sufficiency." *The American University Journal of Gender, Social Policy & the Law* 8, no. 1 (2000): 13–29. https:/ /digitalcommons.wcl.american.edu/jgspl/vol8/iss1/2/.

Finkelstein, Vic. "Emancipating Disability Studies." In *The Disability Reader: Social Science Perspectives*, edited by Tom Shakespeare, 28–52. New York: Cassell, 1998.

Flaherty, Jordan. "'Saviors' Believe That They Are Better Than the People They Are 'Saving.'" *Truthout*. January 5, 2017. https://truthout.org/articles /saviors-believe-that-they-are-better-than-the-people-they-are-saving/.

Forber-Pratt, Anjali J., Dominique A. Lyew, Carlyn Mueller, and Leah B. Samples. "Disability Identity Development: A Systematic Review of the Literature." *Rehabilitation Psychology* 62, no. 2 (2017): 198–207. https://doi.org/10.1037/ rep0000134.

Fox, Matthew. *The Reinvention of Work: A New Vision of Livelihood for Our Time*. San Francisco, CA: Harper Collins, 1994.

Freire, Paolo. *Pedagogy of the Oppressed*. New York: Bloomsbury, 2000.

Fry, Richard, and Rakesh Kochhar. "Are You in the American Middle Class?" PEW Research Center. https://www.pewresearch.org/fact-tank/2018/09/06 /are-you-in-the-american-middle-class/.

Galer, Dustin. "Disabled Capitalists: Exploring the Intersections of Disability and Identity Formation in the World of Work." *Disability Studies Quarterly* 32, no. 3 (2012). http://dsq-sds.org/article/view/3277/3122.

Gallup Organization. "Clifton StrengthsFinder." https://www.gallup.com /cliftonstrengths/en/254033/strengthsfinder.aspx.

Ganin, Netanel. "Disability in the Library of Congress Classification Scheme, Part 2." *I Never Metadata I Didn't Like* (blog). August 16, 2015. https:/ /inevermetadataididntlike.wordpress.com/2015/08/16/disability -in-the-library-of-congress-classification-scheme-part-2/.

Gates, Lauren B. "Workplace Accommodation as a Social Process." *Journal of Occupational Rehabilitation* 10, no. 1 (2000): 85–98.

Gewurtz, Rebecca, and Bonnie Kirsh, "Disruption, Disbelief and Resistance: A Meta-Synthesis of Disability in the Workplace." *Work* 34, no. 1 (2009): 33–44.

Gianluca, Biggio, and Claudio G. Cortese. "Well-Being in the Workplace through Interaction between Individual Characteristics and Organizational Context." *International Journal of Qualitative Studies on Health and Well-being* 8, no. 1 (2013): 19823.

Giroux, Monique L. *Optimal Health with Parkinson's Disease: A Guide to Integrating Lifestyle, Alternative, and Conventional Medicine*. New York: DemosHealth, 2016.

Gold, Paul B., Spalatin N. Oire, Ellen S. Fabian, and Nancy J. Wewiorski. "Negotiating Reasonable Workplace Accommodations: Perspectives of Employers, Employees with Disabilities, and Rehabilitation Service Providers." *Journal of Vocational Rehabilitation* 37, no. 1 (2012): 25–37.

Goodwin, Stephanie A., and Susanne Morgan. "Chronic Illness and the Academic Career: The Hidden Epidemic in Higher Education." *Academe* (May-June 2012). https://www.aaup.org/article/chronic-illness-and-academic -career#.XWrLkHtOm71.

Gould, Elise, and Jessica Scheider. "Work Sick or Lose Pay? The High Cost of Being Sick When You Don't Get Paid Sick Days." *Economic Policy Institute* (June 28, 2017). https://www.epi.org/files/pdf/130245.pdf.

Gould, Robert, Sarah Parker Harris, Kate Caldwell, Glenn Fujiura, Robin Jones, Patrick Ojok, and Katherine Perez Enriquez. "Beyond the Law: A Review of Knowledge, Attitudes, and Perceptions in ADA Employment Research." *Disability Studies Quarterly* 35, no. 3 (2015). http://dsq-sds.org/article/view/4935/4095.

Gould, Robert. "Turning 25: A Systematic Review on the Social Impact of the Americans with Disabilities Act." PhD diss. University of Illinois at Chicago, 2016.

Gray, LaVerne. "The Voice of a Black Woman in Libraryland: A Theoretical Narrative." In *Pushing the Margins: Women of Color and Intersectionality in LIS*, edited by Rose L. Chou and Annie Pho, 147–62. Sacramento, CA: Library Juice Press, 2018.

Hadlock, Janice. "Parkinson's Recovery Project." https://pdrecovery.org/recovery-from-parkinsons/.

Harlan, Sharon L., and Pamela M. Robert. "The Social Construction of Disability in Organizations: Why Employers Resist Reasonable Accommodation." *Work and Occupations* 25, no. 4 (1998): 397–435.

Harris, Jennifer, and Alan Roulstone. *Disability, Policy and Professional Practice.* London: SAGE Publications Ltd, 2011.

Harris, Roma. *Librarianship: Erosion of a Woman's Profession.* Norwood, NJ: Ablex, 1992.

Hathcock, April. "You're Gonna Screw Up." *At The Intersections* (blog). April 13, 2016. https://aprilhathcock.wordpress.com/2016/04/13/youre-gonna-screw-up/.

Herbermann, Charles George, and Knights of Columbus. *The Catholic Encyclopedia: An International Work of Reference on the Constitution, Doctrine, and History of the Catholic Church.* Special edition under the Auspices of the Knights of Columbus Catholic Truth Committee. New York: Encyclopedia Press, 1913.

Hirsch, Larissa. "Metabolism." KidsHealth from Nemours. 2019. https://kidshealth.org/en/parents/metabolism.html.

Hirsch, Michele Lent. *Invisible: How Young Women with Serious Health Issues Navigate Work, Relationships, and the Pressure to Seem Just Fine.* Boston, MA: Beacon Press, 2018.

Hochschild, Arlie Russell. *The Managed Heart: Commercialization of Human Feeling.* Berkeley, CA: University of California Press, 1983.

Hoff, Wilbur I. "Psycho-Social Considerations of Patient Care in Rehabilitation Programs." *Health Education Journal* 25, no. 1 (1966): 33–41.

hooks, bell. *Teaching to Transgress: Education as the Practice of Freedom.* New York: Routledge, 1994.

INCIGHT. https://www.incight.org/.

Inzelberg, Rivka. "The Awakening of Artistic Creativity and Parkinson's Disease." *Behavioral Neuroscience* 127, no. 2 (2013): 256–61.

Irvall, Birgitta, Gyda Skat Nielsen, and International Federation of Library Associations and Institutions. *Access to Libraries for Persons with Disabilities: Checklist*. IFLA Professional Reports, no. 89. The Hague: IFLA, 2005.

Jaffee, Laura. "Marxism and Disability Studies." In *Encyclopedia of Educational Philosophy and Theory*, edited by M.A. Peters. Singapore: Springer Science, 2016.

Jammaers, Eline, Patrizia Zanoni, and Stefan Hardonk. "Constructing Positive Identities in Ableist Workplaces: Disabled Employees Discursive Practices Engaging with the Discourse of Lower Productivity." *Human Relations* 69, no. 6 (2016): 1365–86. https://doi.org/10.1177/0018726715612901.

Job Accommodation Network. https://askjan.org.

———. "Disability Disclosure." https://askjan.org/topics/Disability-Disclosure.cfm?csSearch=2430572_1.

———. "Employees' Practical Guide to Requesting and Negotiating Reasonable Accommodations under the Americans with Disabilities Act (ADA)." https://askjan.org/publications/individuals/employee-guide.cfm.

———. "Information for Employers." https://askjan.org/info-by-role.cfm#for-employers.

———. "Information for Individuals." https://askjan.org/info-by-role.cfm#for-individuals.

Jocson Porter, Alyssa, Sharon Spence-Wilcox, and Kimberly Tate-Malone. "I, Too: Unmasking Emotional Labor of Women of Color Community College Librarians." In *Pushing the Margins: Women of Color and Intersectionality in LIS*, edited by Rose L. Chou and Annie Pho, 273–300. Sacramento, CA: Library Juice Press, 2018.

Kahn, Si. *Organizing, a Guide for Grassroots Leaders*. Revised edition. Silver Spring, MD: National Association of Social Workers, 1991.

Kalleberg, Arne L. *Good Jobs, Bad Jobs: The Rise of Polarized and Precarious Employment Systems in the United States, 1970s–2000s*. New York: Russell Sage Foundation, 2011.

Kane, Vivian. "Trump Blames Mass Shootings on Mental Illness, 'the Media,' & Video Games." *The Mary Sue*. August 5, 2019. https://www.themarysue.com/trump-blames-mass-shootings-on-everything-but-guns/.

Kerschbaum, Stephanie L. "Faculty Members, Accommodation, and Access in Higher Education." *Modern Language Association* (2013). https://profession.mla.org/faculty-members-accommodation-and-access-in-higher-education/.

Kincheloe, Joe L. *How Do We Tell the Workers? The Socioeconomic Foundations of Work and Vocational Education*. Boulder, CO: Westview Press, 1999.

Knapp, Amy. "The Danger of the 'Essential Functions' Requirement of the ADA: Why the Interactive Process Should Be Mandated." *Denver University Law Review* 90, no. 3 (2012): 715–37.

Knight, Amber. "Disability as Vulnerability: Redistributing Precariousness in Democratic Ways." *Journal of Politics* 76, no. 1 (2014): 15–26.

———. "Feminism, Disability and the Democratic Classroom." In *Negotiating Disability: Disclosure and Higher Education* edited by Stephanie Kerschbaum, 57–74. Ann Arbor, MI: University of Michigan Press, 2017.

Koch, Steven M., Katy Beggs, Joy Bailey, and Jacqueline Remondet Wall. "Advocacy in the 21st Century: An Integrated Model for Self-Advocates, Parents, and Professionals." In *Disabilities: Insights from Across Fields and Around the World* 3, edited by Catherine A. Marshall, 245–66. Westport, CT: Praeger, 2009.

Konrad, Annika. "Reimagining Work: Normative Commonplaces and Their Effects on Accessibility in Workplaces." *Business and Professional Communication Quarterly* 81, no. 1 (2018): 123–41.

Kopp, Emily. "Is Big Pharma Getting 'Patient Advocates' to Do Its Lobbying Work?" *The Daily Beast.* April 6, 2018. https://www.thedailybeast.com/is-big-pharma-getting-patient-advocates-to-do-its-lobbying-work.

Kriebel, David, Joel Tickner, Paul Epstein, John Lemons, Richard Levins, Edward L. Loechler, Margaret Quinn, Ruthann Rudel, Ted Schettler, and Michael Stoto. "The Precautionary Principle in Environmental Science." *Environmental Health Perspectives* 109, no. 9 (2001): 871–76.

Lee, Theresa Man Ling. "Multicultural Citizenship: The Case of the Disabled." In *Critical Disability Theory: Essays in Philosophy, Politics, Policy, and Law,* edited by Dianne Pothier and Richard Devlin, 87–105. Vancouver, BC: UBC Press, 2006.

Lengnick-Hall, Mark L., ed., *Hidden Talent: How Leading Companies Hire, Retain, and Benefit from People with Disabilities.* Westport, CT: Praeger, 2007.

Libraries We Here (blog). https://librarieswehere.wordpress.com/.

Lichtenstein, Art A. "Participatory Management: A Critical Look." *Journal of Library Administration* 31, no. 1 (2000): 29–40.

Lindsay, Sally, Elaine Cagliostro, and Gabriella Carafa. "A Systematic Review of Workplace Disclosure and Accommodation Requests among Youth and Young Adults with Disabilities." *Disability and Rehabilitation* 40, no. 25 (2018): 2971–86.

Lipsitz, George. *The Possessive Investment in Whiteness: How White People Profit from Identity Politics,* Revised and expanded edition. Philadelphia, PA: Temple University Press, 2006.

Liu, William Ming, Theodore Pickett, Jr., and Allen E. Ivey. "White Middle-Class Privilege: Social Class Bias and Implications for Training and Practice." *Journal of Multicultural Counseling and Development* 35, no. 4 (2007): 194–206.

Lorde, Audre. *The Cancer Journals,* 2nd edition. Aunt Lute Books, 1992.

Loyer, Jessie. "Indigenous Information Literacy: nêhiyaw Kinship Enabling Self-Care in Research." In *The Politics of Theory and the Practice of Critical Librarianship*, edited by Maura Seale and Karen Nicholson, 145–58. Sacramento, CA: Library Juice Press, 2018. https://mruir.mtroyal.ca/xmlui /handle/11205/361.

MacDonald-Wilson, Kim L., Ellen S. Fabian, and Shengli Dong. "Best Practices in Developing Reasonable Accommodations in the Workplace: Findings Based on the Research Literature." *The Rehabilitation Professional* 16, no. 4 (2008): 221–32.

Madfis, Eric. "Triple Entitlement and Homicidal Anger: An Exploration of the Intersectional Identities of American Mass Murderers." *Men and Masculinities* 17, no. 1 (2014): 67–86.

Malhotra, Ravi A. "Justice as Fairness." In *Critical Disability Theory: Essays in Philosophy, Politics, Policy, and Law*, edited by Dianne Pothier and Richard Devlin, 70–86. Vancouver, BC: UBC Press, 2006.

Marganski, Alison J. "Making a Murderer: The Importance of Gender and Violence Against Women in Mass Murder Events." *Sociology Compass* 13, no. 9 (2019): e12730.

Marjama-Lyons, Jill. *What Your Doctor May Not Tell You about Parkinson's Disease: A Holistic Program for Optimal Wellness*. New York: Warner Books, 2003.

Markel, Karen S., and Lizbeth A. Barclay. "Addressing the Underemployment of Persons with Disabilities: Recommendations for Expanding Organizational Social Responsibility." *Employee Responsibilities and Rights Journal* 21, no. 4 (2009): 305–18.

McColl, Mary Ann, Alison James, William Boyce, and Sam Shortt. "Disability Policy Making: Evaluating the Evidence Base." In *Critical Disability Theory: Essays in Philosophy, Politics, Policy and Law*, edited by Dianne Pothier and Richard Devlin, 25–46. Vancouver, BC: UBC Press, 2006.

McCook, Katherine de la Peña. "Collective Bargaining is a Human Right: Union Review for 2011." *Progressive Librarian* 38/39 (2011): 69–90.

McCright, Aaron M. "Anti-Reflexivity and Climate Change Skepticism in the US General Public." *Human Ecology Review* 22, no. 2 (2016): 77–108.

McKay, Ramah. "Critical Convergences: Social Science Research as Global Health Technology?" *MAT*, May 14, 2019. http://www.medanthrotheory.org /read/11308/critical-convergences.

McKenzie, Kwame. "Racial Discrimination and Mental Health." *Psychiatry* 5, no. 11 (2006): 383–87.

McMahon, Kate. "Today my new work team put skittles in the first aid box." Twitter, June 11, 2019, 2:01 p.m. https://twitter.com/KateMcMahon__ /status/1138521648963948544.

McNaughton, David, Tracy Rackensperger, Dana Dorn, and Natasha Wilson. "'Home Is at Work and Work Is at Home': Telework and Individuals Who Use Augmentative and Alternative Communication." *Work* 48, no. 1 (2014): 117–26.

Meekosha, Helen and Russell Shuttleworth. "What's So 'Critical' about Critical Disability Studies?" *Australian Journal of Human Rights* 15, no. 1 (2009): 47–75.

"Mental illness and violence." *Harvard Mental Health Letter.* 2011. https://www.health.harvard.edu/newsletter_article/mental-illness-and-violence.

"Metabolic Disorders." Intermountain Healthcare, Diabetes and Endocrinology. 2018. https://intermountainhealthcare.org/services/diabetes-endocrinology/conditions/metabolic-disorders/.

Mingus, Mia. "Access Intimacy, Interdependence, and Disability Justice." Presented at the Paul K. Longmore Lecture on Disability Studies. San Francisco State University. April 11, 2017. https://leavingevidence.wordpress.com/2017/04/12/access-intimacy-interdependence-and-disability-justice/.

———. "Medical Industrial Complex Visual." *Leaving Evidence* (blog). February 6, 2015. https://leavingevidence.wordpress.com/2015/02/06/medical-industrial-complex-visual/.

Mitchell, David, and Sharon Snyder. "The Eugenic Atlantic: Race, Disability, and the Making of an International Eugenic Science, 1800–1945." *Disability & Society* 18, no. 7 (2003): 843–64.

Mladenov, Teodor. "Performativity and the Disability Category: Solving *The Zero Theorem.*" *Critical Sociology* (2018): 1–14.

Moeller, Christine M. "Disability, Identity, and Professionalism: Precarity in Librarianship." *Library Trends* 67, no. 3 (2019): 455–70.

Moniz, Richard, Jo Henry, Joe Eshleman, Lisa Moniz, and Howard Slutzky. "Stressors and Librarians: How Mindfulness Can Help." *College & Research Libraries News* 77, no. 11 (2016): 534–36. https://crln.acrl.org/index.php/crlnews/article/view/9582/10952.

Morgan, Robin. "The Personal is Political is Revolution." *Robin Morgan* (blog). July 3, 2019. http://www.robinmorgan.net/blog/tag/parkinsons-disease/.

Morris, Shaneka. "ARL Annual Salary Survey, 2015–2016." Washington, DC: Association of Research Libraries, 2016.

Morrison, Daven, and Phillip Resnick. "Violence in the Workplace." *American Psychiatric Association Foundation Center for Workplace Mental Health.* 2012. http://www.workplacementalhealth.org/Mental-Health-Topics/Violence-in-the-Workplace.

Mostert, Mark P. "Useless Eaters: Disability as Genocidal Marker in Nazi Germany." *The Journal of Special Education* 36, no. 3 (2002): 157–70.

National Alliance on Mental Illness. https://nami.org/.

National Conference of State Legislatures. "State Employment-Related Discrimination Statutes." 2015. http://www.ncsl.org/documents/employ/Discrimination-Chart-2015.pdf.

National Disability Rights Network, "Member Agencies." https://www.ndrn.org/about/ndrn-member-agencies.

National Partnership for Women and Families. "Paid Sick Days Improve Public Health." February 2019. http://www.nationalpartnership.org/our-work /resources/workplace/paid-sick-days/paid-sick-days-improve-our-public -health.pdf.

Neath, Jeanne. "Social Causes of Impairment, Disability, and Abuse: A Feminist Perspective." *Journal of Disability Policy Studies* 8, no. 1–2 (1997): 195–230.

Nevala, Nina, Irmeli Pehkonen, Inka Koskela, Johanna Ruusuvuori, and Heidi Anttila. "Workplace Accommodation Among Persons with Disabilities: A Systematic Review of Its Effectiveness and Barriers or Facilitators." *Journal of Occupational Rehabilitation* 25, no. 2 (2015): 432–48.

Nicholson, Karen P. "The McDonaldization of Academic Libraries and the Values of Transformational Change." *College & Research Libraries* 76, no. 3 (2015): 328–38. https://ir.lib.uwo.ca/cgi/viewcontent.cgi?article=1035&context=fimspub.

Nielsen, Kim E. *A Disability History of the United States*. Boston, MA: Beacon Press, 2012.

Nittrouer, Christine L., Rachel C.E. Trump, Katharine Ridgway O'Brien, and Michelle Hebl. "Stand Up and Be Counted: In the Long Run, Disclosing Helps All." *Industrial and Organizational Psychology* 7, no. 2 (2014): 235–41.

Nussbaum, Martha Craven. *Frontiers of Justice: Disability, Nationality, Species Membership*. Cambridge, MA: The Belknap Press, 2006.

O'Brien, Ruth. *Bodies in Revolt: Gender, Disability, and a Workplace Ethic of Care*. New York: Routledge, 2005.

Ocampo, Carlota. "Drapetomania." In *Encyclopedia of Multicultural Psychology*, edited by Yolanda Kaye Jackson. Thousand Oaks, CA: SAGE Publications, 2006.

OCLC. *Competency Index for the Library Field: Compiled by Web Junction*. 2009. https://www.webjunction.org/content/dam/WebJunction/Documents /webJunction/Competency%20Index%20for%20Library%20Field.pdf.

Oud, Joanne. "Disability and Equity: Librarians with Disabilities Face Barriers to Accessibility and Inclusion." *American Libraries* 50, no. 1–2 (January 2, 2019): 73. https://americanlibrariesmagazine.org/2019/01/02/disability -and-equity/.

———. "Systemic Workplace Barriers for Academic Librarians with Disabilities." *College & Research Libraries* 80, no. 2 (2019): 169–94.

———.. "Academic Librarians with Disabilities: Job Perceptions and Factors Influencing Positive Workplace Experiences." *Partnership: The Canadian Journal of Library and Information Practice and Research* 13, no. 1 (2018): 1–30.

"Parkinson's 101." Michael J. Fox Foundation. https://www.michaeljfox.org /parkinsons-101.

Parkinson's Disease Foundation. "Parkinson's Disease Foundation Mobilizes Community to Address Unmet Needs of Women with Parkinson's." [Press Release] (September 16, 2015). https://www.parkinson.org/about-us/ Press-Room/Press-Releases/women-with-pd.

Paulson, Amanda. "Why Climate Change Divides Us." *The Christian Science Monitor* (October 12, 2016). https://www.csmonitor.com/USA/Politics/2016/1012/Why-climate-change-divides-us.

Pawley, Christine. "Hegemony's Handmaid? The Library and Information Studies Curriculum from a Class Perspective." *Library Quarterly* 68, no. 2 (1998): 123–44.

"People with Disabilities Charge that Oakland's Rent Stabilization Program Excludes Them and Must Be Fixed Notwithstanding Costa-Hawkins." *Disability Rights Advocates.* https://dralegal.org/press/people-with-disabilities-charge-that-oaklands-rent-stabilization-program-excludes-them-and-must-be-fixed-notwithstanding-costa-hawkins/.

Perry, David M. "Disabled People Need Not Apply." *AlJazeera America Opinion.* February 5, 2016. http://america.aljazeera.com/opinions/2016/2/disabled-people-need-not-apply.html.

———. "Police Killings: The Price of Being Disabled and Black in America." *The Guardian.* June 22, 2017. https://www.theguardian.com/us-news/2017/jun/22/police-killings-disabled-black-people-mental-illness.

Pervez, Noor, and Finn Gardiner. (Self-Advocacy) Interview with Alice Wong. *Disability Visibility Project,* podcast audio. July 14, 2019. https://disabilityvisibilityproject.com/2019/07/14/ep-55-self-advocacy/.

Phillips, Brian N., Jon Deiches, Blaise Morrison, Fong Chan, and Jill L. Bezyak. "Disability Diversity Training in the Workplace: Systematic Review and Future Directions." *Journal of Occupational Rehabilitation* 26, no. 3 (2016): 264–75.

Pilling, Merrick Daniel. "Invisible Identity in the Workplace: Intersectional Madness and Processes of Disclosure at Work." *Disability Studies Quarterly* 33, no. 1 (2013). http://dsq-sds.org/article/view/3424/3204.

Pionke, J.J. "The Impact of Disbelief: On Being a Library Employee with a Disability." *Library Trends* 67, no. 3 (2019): 423–35.

Pompper, Donnalyn. *Practical and Theoretical Implications of Successfully Doing Difference in Organizations.* Bingley, UK: Emerald Group Publishing, 2014.

Porter, Gayle. "Workaholic Tendencies and the High Potential for Stress among Co-Workers." *International Journal of Stress Management* 8, no. 2 (2001): 147–64.

Price, Margaret. "The Bodymind Problem and the Possibilities of Pain." *Hypatia* 30, no. 1 (2015): 268–84.

Professional and Specialized Services of the Occupational Health and Safety Branch, Ontario Ministry of Labour. *Health and Safety Guidelines: Rest Breaks for Video Display Terminal (VDT) Operators.* 1993. https://www.ccohs.ca/oisherhsinfo/alerts/alert81.txt.

Project: Time Off. "The State of American Vacation 2017." https://www.ustravel.org/sites/default/files/media_root/document/2017_May%2023_Research_State%20of%20American%20Vacation%202017.pdf.

Promoting Diversity and Inclusion Through Workplace Accommodations: A Practical Guide. Geneva: International Labor Office, 2016.

Puhl, Rebecca M., Sean M. Phelan, Joseph Nadglowski, and Theodore K. Kyle. "Overcoming Weight Bias in the Management of Patients with Diabetes and Obesity." *Clinical Diabetes* 34, no. 1 (2016): 44–50. https://clinical .diabetesjournals.org/content/34/1/44.

Reaume, Geoffrey. "Understanding Critical Disability Studies." *Canadian Medical Association Journal* 186, no. 16 (2014): 1248–49.

Rioux, Marcia H., and Fraser Valentine. "Does Theory Matter? Exploring the Nexus between Disability, Human Rights, and Public Policy." In *Critical Disability Theory: Essays in Philosophy, Politics, Policy and Law*, edited by Dianne Pothier and Richard Devlin, 47–69. Vancouver, BC: UBC Press, 2006.

Robert, Pamela M., and Sharon L. Harlan. "Mechanisms of Disability Discrimination in Large Bureaucratic Organizations: Ascriptive Inequalities in the Workplace." *The Sociological Quarterly* 47, no. 4 (2006): 599–630.

Rosa, Kathy, and Kelsey Henke. "2017 ALA Demographic Study." *ALA Office for Research and Statistics.* http://www.ala.org/tools/sites/ala.org.tools/files/content/Draft%20of%20Member%20Demographics%20Survey%2001-11-2017.pdf.

Rose, Sarah F. *No Right to Be Idle: The Invention of Disability, 1840s-1930s.* Chapel Hill, NC: University of North Carolina Press, 2017.

Rosenthal, Caitlin. *Accounting for Slavery: Masters and Management.* Cambridge, MA: Harvard University Press, 2018.

Rosenthal, Keith. "Bringing Marxism to Discussions of Disability." *SocialistWorker.Org.* May 9, 2017. https://socialistworker.org/2017/05/09/bringing-marxism-to -discussions-of-disability.

Rothstein, Laura. "Would the ADA Pass Today? Disability Rights in an Age of Partisan Polarization." *Saint Louis University Journal of Health Law & Policy* 12, no. 2 (2019): 271–310.

Samuels, Ellen Jean. *Fantasies of Identification: Disability, Gender, Race.* New York: New York University Press, 2014.

Schlesselman-Tarango, Gina. "The Legacy of Lady Bountiful: White Women in the Library." *Library Trends* 64, no. 4 (2016): 667–86.

———. "Reproductive Failure and Information Work: An Autoethnography." *Library Trends* 67, no. 3 (2019): 436–54.

Schomberg, Jessica. "Disability at Work: Libraries, Built to Exclude." In *The Politics and Theory of Critical Librarianship*, edited by Karen P. Nicholson and Maura Seale, 115–28. Sacramento, CA: Library Juice Press, 2018.

Schomberg, Jessica, and Kirsti Cole. "Hush…: The Dangers of Silence in Academic Libraries." *In the Library with the Lead Pipe.* April 17, 2017. http://www .inthelibrarywiththeleadpipe.org/2017/hush-the-dangers-of-silence-in -academic-libraries/.

Schomberg, Jessica, and Shanna Hollich. "Introduction." *Library Trends* [special issue: Disabled Adults in Libraries] 67, no. 3 (2019): 415–22. https://cornerstone.lib.mnsu.edu/lib_services_fac_pubs/170/.

Schrag, Anette, and Michael Trimble. "Poetic Talent Unmasked by Treatment of Parkinson's Disease." *Movement Disorders* 16, no. 6 (2001): 1175–76.

Schreuer, Naomi, William N. Myhill, Tal Aratan-Bergman, Deepti Samant, and Peter Blanck. "Workplace Accommodations: Occupational Therapists as Mediators in the Interactive Process." *Work* 34, no. 2 (2009): 149–60.

Schultz, P. Wesley, Jessica M. Nolan, Robert B. Cialdini, Noah J. Goldstein, and Vladas Griskevicius. "The Constructive, Destructive, and Reconstructive Power of Social Norms." *Psychological Science* 18, no. 5 (2007): 429–34.

Schur, Lisa, Douglas Kruse, and Peter Blanck. *People with Disabilities: Sidelined or Mainstreamed?* New York: Cambridge University Press, 2013.

———. "Corporate Culture and the Employment of Persons with Disabilities." *Behavioral Sciences & Law* 23, no. 1 (2005): 3–20.

Schur, Lisa, Douglas Kruse, Joseph Blasi, and Peter Blanck. "Is Disability Disabling in All Workplaces? Workplace Disparities and Corporate Culture." *Industrial Relations* 48, no. 3 (2009): 381–410.

Schur, Lisa, Lisa Nishii, Meera Adya, Douglas Kruse, Susanne M. Bruyere, and Peter Blanck. "Accommodating Employees with and without Disabilities." *Human Resource Management* 53, no. 4 (2014): 593–621.

Schweik, Susan M. *The Ugly Laws: Disability in Public.* New York: NYU Press, 2009.

Seale, Maura. "The Neoliberal Library." In *Information Literacy and Social Justice: Radical Professional Praxis*, edited by Lua Gregory and Shana Higgins, 39–61. Sacramento, CA: Library Juice Press, 2013.

Section 504 of the Rehabilitation Act of 1973, 29 U. S. C. § 701 *et seq.* (1973) (amended 1998).

Senge, Peter M. *The Fifth Discipline: The Art & Practice of the Learning Organization.* New York: Doubleday, 1990.

Sills, David L. *International Encyclopedia of the Social Sciences.* New York: Macmillan, 1968.

Sloniowski, Lisa. "Affective Labor, Resistance, and the Academic Library." *Library Trends* 64 no. 4 (2016): 645–66. https://yorkspace.library.yorku.ca/xmlui/handle/10315/31500.

Slorach, Roddy. *A Very Capitalist Condition: A History and Politics of Disability.* London: Bookmarks Publications, 2016.

Smart, Julie F., and David W. Smart. "Models of Disability: Implications for the Counseling Profession." *Journal of Counseling & Development* 84, no. 1 (2006): 29–40.

Smith, Carrie. "Unions 101: What Library Unions Do—And Don't Do—For Library Workers." *American Libraries* (November/December 2018). https://americanlibrariesmagazine.org/2018/11/01/library-unions-101/.

Soldatic, Karen, and Helen Meekosha. "The Place of Disgust: Disability, Class and Gender in Spaces of Workfare." *Societies* 2, no. 3 (2012): 139–56.

Starhawk. *The Empowerment Manual: A Guide for Collaborative Groups.* Gabriola Island, BC: New Society Publishers, 2011.

Stetka, Bret. "Parkinson's Disease and Pesticides: What's the Connection?" *Scientific American.* April 8, 2014. https://www.scientificamerican.com/article/parkinsons-disease-and-pesticides-whats-the-connection.

Stergiou-Kita, Mary, Cheryl Pritlove, and Bonnie Kirsh. "The 'Big C'—Stigma, Cancer, and Workplace Discrimination." *Journal of Cancer Survivorship: Research and Practice* 10, no. 6 (2016): 1035–50.

Stone, Sharon-Dale, Valorie A. Crooks, and Michelle Owen. "Going through the Back Door: Chronically Ill Academics' Experiences as 'Unexpected Workers.'" *Social Theory & Health* 11, no. 2 (2013): 151–74.

Streck, Danilo R., Euclides Redin, and Jaime Jose Zitkoski, eds. *Paulo Freire Encyclopedia.* Lanham, MD: Rowman & Littlefield, 2012.

Stuntzner, Susan, and Michael T. Hartley. "Balancing Self-Compassion with Self-Advocacy: A New Approach for Persons with Disabilities." *Annals of Psychotherapy and Integrative Health* (2015). https://self-compassion.org/wp-content/uploads/2015/08/Stuntzner_Hartley.pdf.

"Teens and Diabetes Mellitus." University of Rochester Medical Center *Health Encyclopedia.* https://www.urmc.rochester.edu/encyclopedia/content.aspx?contenttypeid=90&contentid=P01597.

Tompkins Byer, Tessa. "Yea, Nay, and Everything in Between: Disparities Within the Academic Ombuds Field." *Negotiation Journal* 33, no. 3 (2017): 213–38.

Toth, Kate E., and Carolyn S. Dewa. "Employee Decision-making about Disclosure of a Mental Disorder at Work." *Journal of Occupational Rehabilitation* 24, no. 4 (2014): 732–46.

Tremain, Shelley. "On the Subject of Impairment." In *Disability/Postmodernity: Embodying Disability Theory,* edited by Mairian Corker and Tom Shakespeare, 32–47. New York: Continuum Press, 2002.

Tyjewski, Carolyn. "Ghosts in the Machine: Civil Rights Laws and the Hybrid 'Invisible Other.'" In *Critical Disability Theory: Essays in Philosophy, Politics, Policy, and Law,* edited by Dianne Pothier and Richard Devlin, 106–28. Vancouver, BC: UBC Press, 2006.

United Nations. "Human Rights." https://www.un.org/en/sections/issues-depth/human-rights/.

United Nations Human Rights Office of the High Commissioner. "Convention on the Rights of Persons with Disabilities, Article 27, Work and Employment." 1996–2019. https://www.ohchr.org/EN/HRBodies/CRPD/Pages/ConventionRightsPersonsWithDisabilities.aspx#27.

U.S. Department of Labor. "ADA Timeline Alternative." https://www.dol.gov/featured/ada/timeline/alternative.

U.S. Equal Employment Opportunity Commission. "Laws Enforced by EEOC." https://www.eeoc.gov/laws/statutes/index.cfm.

Vallas, Rebecca, and Shawn Fremstad. "Disability is a Cause and Consequence of Poverty." *Talk Poverty* (September 19, 2014). https://talkpoverty.org /2014/09/19/disability-cause-consequence-poverty/.

Verbrugge, Lois M., and Alan M. Jette. "The Disablement Process." *Social Science & Medicine* 38, no. 1 (1994): 1–14.

von Schrader, Sarah, Valerie Malzer, and Susanne Bruyère. "Perspectives on Disability Disclosure: The Importance of Employer Practices and Workplace Climate." *Employee Responsibilities and Rights Journal* 26, no. 4 (2014): 237–55.

Wade, Cheryl L. "Effective Compliance with Antidiscrimination Law: Corporate Personhood, Purpose, and Social Responsibility." *Washington and Lee Law Review* 74, no. 2 (2017): 1187–238. https://scholarlycommons.law.wlu.edu / wlulr/vol74/iss2/22/.

Wang, Esmé Weijun. *The Collected Schizophrenias: Essays*. Minneapolis,MN: Graywolf Press, 2019.

Wasserman, David, Adrienne Asch, Jeffrey Blustein, and Daniel Putnam. "Disability: Health, Well-Being, and Personal Relationships." In *The Stanford Encyclopedia of Philosophy* (Winter 2016 ed.), edited by Edward N. Zalta, https://plato.stanford.edu/archives/win2016/entries /disability-health.

Weber, Lauren. "As Workers Expect Less, Job Satisfaction Rises; Minimal Raises and Lean Staffing have Redefined what Makes a Position Good." *Wall Street Journal (Online)*, September 1, 2017. https://www.wsj.com/articles /americans-are-happier-at-work-but-expect-a-lot-less-1504258201.

Weber, Mark C. "Disability Discrimination by State and Local Government: The Relationship Between Section 504 of the Rehabilitation Act and Title II of the Americans with Disabilities Act." *William & Mary Law Review* 36, no. 3 (1995): 1089–133. https://scholarship.law.wm.edu/wmlr/vol36/iss3/4/.

Wendell, Susan. "Unhealthy Disabled: Treating Chronic Illnesses as Disabilities." *Hypatia* 16, no. 4 (2001): 17–33.

———. *The Rejected Body: Feminist Philosophical Reflections on Disability*. New York: Routledge, 1996.

Wilde, Melissa J., and Sabrina Danielsen. "Fewer and Better Children: Race, Class, Religion, and Birth Control Reform in America." *American Journal of Sociology* 119, no. 6 (2014): 1710–60.

Williams, Joseph P. "Air Pollution Rates Higher in Historically Redlined Neighborhoods." *US News & World Report* (May 24, 2019). https://www .usnews.com/news/healthiest-communities/articles/2019-05-24/asthma -air-pollution-rates-higher-in-historically-redlined-neighborhoods.

Williamson, Jeanine M., and John W. Lounsbury. "Distinctive 16 PF Personality Traits of Librarians." *Journal of Library Administration* 56, no. 2 (2016): 124–43.

Wooten, Lynn Perry, and Erika Hayes James. "Challenges of Organizational Learning: Perpetuation of Discrimination Against Employees with Disabilities." *Behavioral Sciences & the Law* 23, no. 1 (2005): 123–41.

World Health Organization. *WHO Global Disability Action Plan, 2014–2021: Better Health for All People with Disability.* Geneva, Switzerland: World Health Organization, 2015. http://apps.who.int/iris/bitstream/10665/199544/1/9789241509619_eng.pdf.

World Institute on Disability. "New Earth Disability." September 25, 2018. https://wid.org/2018/09/25/ned/.

Yates, Michael D. *Why Unions Matter,* 2nd ed. New York: Monthly Review Press, 2009.

Zaritsky, John. "Suicide Tourist." PBS, 2010. https://www.pbs.org/wgbh/frontline/film/suicidetourist/.

Ziegenfuss, James T. Jr., and Patricia O'Rourke. *The Ombudsman Handbook: Designing and Managing an Effective Problem Solving Program.* Jefferson, NC: McFarland, 2011.

Index

CPSIA information can be obtained
at www.ICGtesting.com
Printed in the USA
FSHW020423110421
80265FS